The Bible in the American Short Story

November 2017

For Mr. and Mrs. Finard

For your generous support of Jewish Studies at Colgate University.

With gratitude,

NEW DIRECTIONS IN RELIGION AND LITERATURE

This series aims to showcase new work at the forefront of religion and literature through short studies written by leading and rising scholars in the field. Books will pursue a variety of theoretical approaches as they engage with writing from different religious and literary traditions. Collectively, the series will offer a timely critical intervention to the interdisciplinary crossover between religion and literature, speaking to wider contemporary interests and mapping out new directions for the field in the early twenty-first century.

ALSO AVAILABLE FROM BLOOMSBURY

The Bible in the American Short Story, Lesleigh Cushing Stahlberg and Peter S. Hawkins
Blake. Wordsworth. Religion, Jonathan Roberts
Dante and the Sense of Transgression, William Franke
Do the Gods Wear Capes?, Ben Saunders
England's Secular Scripture, Jo Carruthers
Forgiveness in Victorian Literature, Richard Hughes Gibson
The Glyph and the Gramophone, Luke Ferretter
The Gospel According to David Foster Wallace, Adam S. Miller
The Gospel According to the Novelist, Magdalena Mączyńska
Jewish Feeling, Richa Dwor
John Cage and Buddhist Ecopoetics, Peter Jaeger
Late Walter Benjamin, John Schad
The New Atheist Novel, Arthur Bradley and Andrew Tate
Rewriting the Old Testament in Anglo-Saxon Verse, Samantha Zacher
Victorian Parables, Susan E. Colón
Beyond the Willing Suspension of Disbelief, Michael Tomko
Pentecostal Modernism, Stephen Shapiro and Philip Barnard

FORTHCOMING

Faith in Poetry, Michael D. Hurley
Romantic Enchantment, Gavin Hopps
Sufism in Western Literature, Art and Thought, Ziad Elmarsafy
Weird Faith in 19th Century Literature, Mark Knight and Emma Mason

The Bible in the American Short Story

**LESLEIGH CUSHING STAHLBERG
AND
PETER S. HAWKINS**

Bloomsbury Academic
An imprint of Bloomsbury Publishing Plc

B L O O M S B U R Y
LONDON · OXFORD · NEW YORK · NEW DELHI · SYDNEY

Bloomsbury Academic

An imprint of Bloomsbury Publishing Plc

50 Bedford Square	1385 Broadway
London	New York
WC1B 3DP	NY 10018
UK	USA

www.bloomsbury.com

BLOOMSBURY and the Diana logo are trademarks of Bloomsbury Publishing Plc

First published 2018

© Lesleigh Cushing Stahlberg and Peter S. Hawkins, 2018

Lesleigh Cushing Stahlberg and Peter S. Hawkins have asserted their rights under the Copyright, Designs and Patents Act, 1988, to be identified as Authors of this work.

British Library Cataloguing-in-Publication Data
A catalogue record for this book is available from the British Library.

ISBN: HB: 978-1-4742-3716-1
ePDF: 978-1-4742-3718-5
eBook: 978-1-4742-3717-8

Library of Congress Cataloging-in-Publication Data
A catalog record for this book is available from the Library of Congress.

Cover design: Eleanor Rose
Cover photograph shows a detail of Monroe, Ohio 1992 (from the book *Bible Road: Signs of Faith in the American Landscape*, 2007) © Sam Fentress

Series: New Directions in Religion and Literature

Typeset by Deanta Global Publishing Services, Chennai, India

To find out more about our authors and books visit www.bloomsbury.com. Here you will find extracts, author interviews, details of forthcoming events and the option to sign up for our newsletters.

For Noa and Ezra, two short stories that grow longer by the day.

— LCS

For the long story of friendships that have endured into a fifth decade: Carl Charlson, J.D. McClatchy, and Barbara Mowat.

— PSH

Contents

Preface

For a time, it seemed that every two or three years there appeared a new trade book that put the Bible and the American writer into some sort of dialogue. A cursory scan of a library bookshelf gives an indication of how much interest there has been in this approach, from *Congregation: Contemporary Jewish Writers Read the Jewish Bible* (1987) and *Incarnation: Contemporary Writers on the New Testament* (1990) to *Unscrolled: 54 Writers and Artists Wrestle with the Torah* (2013) and *The Good Book: Writers Reflect on Favorite Bible Passages* (2015).

This spate of work suggests that publishers want to prove to the book-buying public that the divide between the Bible and literature is not so wide, indeed to insist that—strange as it may seem—the two actually have something important to do with one another. Certainly they used to. In his introduction to *The Good Book*, Adam Gopnik declares, "The Bible remains an essential part of the education of what used to be called the well-furnished mind."[1] It is as if he is trying to convince his reader of something he knows to be true, but isn't quite certain that his reader will agree. His supporting evidence, moreover, is centuries old: "Most of what we value in our art and architecture, our music and poetry—Bach and Chartres, Shakespeare and Milton, Giotto at the Arena Chapel and Blake's Job among his friends—is entangled with these old books and ancient texts."[2] And yet, despite the fact that Gopnik's case for Scripture's importance looks to the past, *The Good Book* as a whole looks forward by engaging contemporary writers in the conversation. This is also the case with most of the books on this Bible and Literature shelf: they bring together ancient Scripture and contemporary writers.

Perhaps the common impulse here is to correct a cultural assumption that Scripture is sacred territory whereas literature is secular. These anthologies beg to differ. They alert their reader to the fact that brand-new bestselling works—even those by young iconoclastic writers—are often seriously engaged with ancient traditions. Maybe only obliquely, or maybe head-on, but somewhere, somehow, in the background of the book that everyone's reading this season there might just be an echo of *The Holy Bible*.

One might reasonably have assumed otherwise. These days, even in America where so many claim to believe in God and to worship regularly, biblical literacy is at an all-time low. This ebb is especially evident among those who are not part of a religious tradition, who are most likely to turn to what writers think about Scripture. By and large those who read the *New York Times* or the *New Yorker* are not mindful of clerics, theologians, and biblical scholars, who seem to write on "official paper" rather than from the heart or the gut. They'd rather hear from John Updike, or Marilynne Robinson, or Adam Gopnik on the Bible. Whereas biblical "professionals" are invested in the meaning of the text for a select audience—not to mention being burdened by one kind of authority or another—writers speak to all of us. They are not specialists, except in the ways of knowing how to make a powerful image or a compelling narrative. Moreover, they invariably give us something of themselves. In addition to telling us what they have found in Jonah or the Acts of the Apostles, they reveal their own often ambivalent relationship to the Bible. Flashes of the autobiographical run through these reflections.

This present book is concerned with those instances when writers' biblical attachments somehow find their way into their fiction. Instead of looking at manifestations of religion in literature per se—a worthy pursuit, and one taken up in other volumes in Bloomsbury's New Directions in Religion and Literature—we are interested more narrowly in the various ways that the Bible continues to resurface in one particular genre, the American short story, since the mid-twentieth century. We do not look much at the genre's venerable beginnings in Hawthorne, Melville, and Poe, but rather consider it from its flowering since the Second World War. We are equally interested in two breeds of author: those for whom Scripture is sacred—and here, predictably, Flannery O'Connor is our starting point—and those for whom affiliation with the Bible is more tentative, elusive, or unknown. Similarly, we are concerned with all manner of relationship to the Bible, from those that are so overt that the retelling or adaptation is impossible to miss to those that are more difficult to assess, as when a story makes use of a single quotation, an allusion, a story title, a textual trace.

Instead of aiming our study at genres that have already received abundant attention from religion and literature critics in the past— the novel, drama, and poetry—we take up short fiction. This decision indicates more than a desire to sing the unsung or to broaden the genre consideration of Bloomsbury's "Gospel According To" series.[3] Given our predilection for the Bible both *as* literature and *in* literature (described more fully below), we have particular reasons for our choice. Long before Gogol, De Maupassant, Chekhov—long before its early-nineteenth-century flourishing in Britain, France, Russia, and the United States—the short story could already be found, in ancient form, in both Testaments. Scripture contains the very brief books of Ruth, Jonah, and Esther, as well as the even shorter parables of Jesus, who took his place in a narrative tradition already established by Hebrew prophets and rabbis.

But in addition to the presence of discrete short stories within Scripture, there is also the liturgical reading practice of both synagogue and church, whereby the long narrative of Torah or the Gospels is experienced as one bite-sized story after another. In worship, biblical episodes that belong to a long narrative flow, say, in Genesis or the Gospel of Matthew, are encountered as if they were independent units. The worshipper experiences them, in effect, less as episodes and more as discrete stories that have a rudimentary introduction, development, climax, and conclusion.

Finally, we are intrigued by what may be the peculiar ability of the short story to convey religious experience at a time like our own. Many readers now shy away from the grand narratives that once held sway, preferring instead those short takes or momentary glimpses of the divine that T.S. Eliot spoke of as "hints and guesses/Hints followed by guesses."[4]

Or is the spiritual temper of our time not really the point at all? Is there something more fundamental still about the genre that links it to religion in the most basic sense? Theorist Charles May has argued this case, maintaining that the short story remains close to the original source of narrative as it appears in myth, folktale, fable, and fairy tale. Unlike the novel, with its commitment to the realistic rendering of the social context of everyday life, the short story often plunges deep into a particular incident—a moment, idea, crisis, sensation. Because of its intensity, its focus on the particular, the short story can explore those "moments in which we become aware of anxiety, loneliness, dread, concern, and thus find the safe, secure and systematic life we usually lead disrupted and momentarily destroyed."[5] That said, it can also capture moments of wonder, connection, restoration—even redemption.

In this exploration, our hope is that by drawing attention to the presence of the Bible in some contemporary American short fiction— whether seen unmistakably front and center or caught sight of only at the periphery—we may come closer to understanding how the ancient world of Scripture continues to foster a deeper awareness of the world in which we live.

* * *

We come to this present venture from two faith perspectives, both of which have the Bible at heart. Each of us is steeped in a religious tradition and its literary expression: one Christian, the other Jewish. Each of us also has the pleasure of engaging these matters in the classroom—one at a Divinity School, the other at a liberal arts college. In our quite different academic settings, we explore with our students the literary life and afterlife of the Bible—for instance, in "Religious Themes in Contemporary Short Fiction" at Yale, and in "The Literary Afterlife of the Bible" at Colgate.

One of us, Peter Hawkins, has long focused on the pervasive presence of Scripture throughout the Christian literary tradition, specifically in Dante's scriptural imagination, as seen most extensively in *Dante's Testaments* (1999). At the same time, he has also investigated religion in post-Second World War American literature. His four-volume series co-edited with Paula J. Carlson, *Listening for God: Contemporary Literature and the Life of Faith (1994–2003)*, offers a positive assessment of the Christian tradition's ongoing vitality in fiction. Many of the writers included in the series date from what Paul Elie has identified as a twentieth-century "Golden Age" of the Christian writer.

The other, Lesleigh Cushing Stahlberg, has focused on the afterlife of the Hebrew Bible in Jewish literature. A Canadian, she has been fascinated by the prevalence of the Bible in so many aspects of American life since she came to the US twenty years ago. In addition to her work on its presence in Jewish fiction, she has written on the use and abuse of Scripture more generally in the nation's public sphere. Her book *Sustaining Fictions* (2008) looks at the practice of biblical "retelling," offering a lexicon of terms for assessing what she calls "the nearly imperceptible glide of the literary afterlife of the Bible from Scripture to commentary to literature."[6]

Together as colleagues we have followed this "glide" by organizing conferences that later became two collections of jointly edited essays centered on the Hebrew Bible as read by both Jews and Christians: *Scrolls of Love: Ruth and the Song of Songs* (2006) and *From the Margins I: Women of the Bible and their Afterlives* (2009). We have also participated in a three-year study of Religion and Literature at the University of Notre Dame.

This is our latest joint effort, and differs somewhat from the ones that came before. Some of the book was written side by side, some of it separately at long distance. The reader will sense the collaboration, the coherence of how the pieces fit together and build on one another, but will also be able to detect two voices, discern two perspectives. Rather than sand down or smooth over our individual styles to give the impression of a single author, we have each elected to write as we write but influenced and edited by the other.

If the book has two authors, so too does it have (at least) two audiences. The student of the Bible interested in its reception—in the impact of the Bible on literature, and on American literature more specifically—will find in these pages an orientation to the American short story and a look at the many ways the Bible is very much alive in this contemporary genre. The student of American literature, and of the short story in particular, will develop a sense both of the Bible as itself a work of literature and of the influence its literature has had on American civic life and letters. This reader will encounter familiar figures—masters of the contemporary American short story—but see them perhaps in a new perspective, through the lens of the Bible.

Two authors, two religious traditions, two audiences, and yet we hope the patchwork comes together in a coherent whole, in a book that moves from the broader questions of the Bible, America, and the Short Story to the specifics of the Bible's place in the American short story. The book is organized as follows:

In Chapter 1, we begin with a sweeping survey of the peculiar place of the Bible in cultural history, suggesting its impact on politics, education, and literature. From the beginning, the mythology of this country has been constructed by the Bible: America has been conceived as the Promised Land, the Wilderness, a New Eden, a New Canaan, a New Jerusalem. Americans are the Chosen People, the new Israel.

Not quite as distinctive as the role the Bible has played in America is the position of the short story in our literature, the subject of the book's second section. The short story exploded on the European scene in the nineteenth century in Russia, France, and Germany, but for a number of reasons it flourished particularly in the United States, where economic factors contributed to its rise. Thanks to the magazine industry, one could earn money writing short stories in America, prompting even an author like Melville, who disdained the form, to produce them. In Chapter 2, we explore the literary characteristics of the genre, and then trace its history and flourishing in this country.

We next consider the ways the Bible itself can be understood as a collection of short stories. There is, to begin with, the apparent brevity of its original sources. There is also the preservation of discrete stories and brief episodes within the longer narrative arcs of the canon. These are read and experienced in synagogue and church episodically. As we will see, whether at home, school, or in the house of worship, the Bible is known to Americans as if it were a collection of short stories.

In Chapter 3, we look first at some of the distinctive features of Scripture's narrative art. An anthology of books spanning centuries, the Bible contains many voices and genres. One of these, as clearly seen in Ruth, Esther, Jonah, and in the parables of the Old and New Testaments, is the short story. We next offer our own readings of the scriptural short story, attending first to Ruth and then to the parables of Jesus.

We next move on to a selection of writers who have made open use of the Scripture and offer our own close readings of particular stories. We begin with Flannery O'Connor, who is often held up as America's exemplary Christian writer. In "Has Fiction Lost Its Faith?,"[7] a lament about the "post-Christian" state of American letters, Paul Elie sees the years since her death (as well as those of Walker Percy and John Updike) as a wandering in the wilderness. For our part, we see signs that the Christian writer may already have come through the wilderness to inhabit a new place in the biblical Promised Land. To be sure, none of the other writers we treat engages the Bible as frontally as O'Connor did, but engage it they do. Following our discussion of O'Connor and the Bible, we turn to American Jewish writing and specifically Allegra Goodman, a writer whose subjects are not merely Jewish, but deeply scriptural. Goodman's fictions are full of fraught family dinners and religious rituals, all shot through with biblical resonances.

O'Connor and Goodman deploy Scripture in distinct ways. In O'Connor's case, biblical context is provided not only by the Bible Belt environment of the Deep South but also by the prodding of the narrator. Her characters are often functional nonbelievers or merely routine churchgoers. What happens in the course of a story, however, is that their world is shattered and the author's interjected scriptural reference offered as a way for the reader to understand what has happened. In Goodman, on the other hand, characters are all too aware that they are living in a biblical landscape. Theirs is a world of reading the same book every year, of standing again at Sinai, of finding oneself in the biblical story and the biblical story in one's own world.

We then move to John Updike and Jamie Quatro, both Protestants but of different sensibilities and different generations. Church plays a major role in the fictional realities of both. Updike's Pennsylvania farm town and Massachusetts exurb are peopled by mainline ministers who preach sermons and congregants who hear them. Through clergy characters, his novels engage the Bible extensively. References in his short stories are more oblique and allusive, but a biblical current runs through all the work. In contrast to the extraordinary volume of Updike's writing, we have as yet only one collection of Quatro's stories. They are set on Lookout Mountain, on the border between Tennessee and Georgia. This is a churched landscape, but rather than focusing on clergy, Quatro gives us evangelical laywomen who are immersed in Scripture and openly evoke it as they live their complicated lives. The Bible is their default frame of reference.

Our next two writers quite openly retell a biblical story. Steven Millhauser plays with the Bible in various ways, but in "A Voice in the Night" he gives a series of retellings of 1 Samuel 3. Millhauser's narrator preserves the biblical story itself while also providing commentary on it. He then resets it twice in the context of his narrator's life, showing first its imprint on him as a boy and then on him as an older man ("the author"). Kirstin Valdez Quade plunges the reader into the gospel Passion story, but instead of moving between a New Testament event and present-day New Mexico, she shows what happens when Jesus's crucifixion is re-enacted in a small town by a wholly unlikely would-be Jesus. Quade tells "the old, old story"—but, to recall Emily Dickinson, tells it "slant."

Tobias Wolff is not what one might think of as an especially biblical writer, although he is formed by the Catholic tradition and occasionally turns in explicit ways to the Scripture. In Chapter 10, we present three stories with varying degrees of biblical engagement. The first shows how the Bible features in a conflict between a Muslim and a Catholic; the second presents a character who spouts Scripture in a moment of crisis; in the third, the Bible is a pre-text for the narrative, with Wolff re-presenting the welter of sibling rivalry as found in the Hebrew Bible and in the Gospel parable of the Prodigal Son.

The last two stories we consider make no sustained allusion to the Bible. Written by Jewish writers, both works—each in their own way—are concerned with religion. Bernard Malamud's "The Magic Barrel" is about a rabbi in search of a wife; Nathan Englander's "The Gilgul of Park Avenue" describes the turmoil brought on by the sudden conversion of a New York WASP to Judaism. We read these two stories through a biblical lens, using the Book of Hosea to shine light on Malamud's rabbi and the New Testament story of the conversion of Saul to illuminate Englander's *gilgul*. Sometimes bringing a biblical text to bear on a story that contains similar themes but that might not be making deliberate allusion to Scripture can cause the two writings to interact with one another in a mutually enriching way.

As with our discussion of Goodman, in the course of exploring our stories and writers in Part 4, we often bring in others (Hemingway figures in our discussion of Quade, Philip Roth in Englander). All the same, ours is by no means an exhaustive treatment of the American short story nor even a survey of the Bible in the contemporary manifestation of this genre. Given the goals of this Bloomsbury series, we have not attempted to be comprehensive, but rather to identify writers who, apart from being engaged with religious concerns (of whom there are many), have a particular connection with the Bible, not only one that is in passing.

That said, on occasion the "in passing" use of Scripture seems worth noting and exploring. We study a few writers at some length but can merely gesture toward others, who deserve more attention than we can allot here. Among these, Denis Johnson, George Saunders, and Joy Williams come quickly to mind. Their writing is consistently quirky, irreverent, provocative, purposefully off-kilter; their attention to the Bible, however, is only occasional. Of Williams's newest work—the "witty theological fables" of her *Ninety-Nine Stories Of God* (2016)—James Wood says, "She lightly plays with deep questions: God's disappearance or invisibility; how to speak of a deity, or how a deity speaks to us; the problem of suffering. She likes to float a puzzle and let it drift off the page."[8] The same could also be said of Johnson's *Jesus' Son* or Saunders's story "Winky." Although it is hard to know what to make of the deployment of Scripture in these works—so different from what we find in those writers we treat—the fact that the Bible is *there* is impossible to miss.

A note on terms and translations

In order to avoid tedious repetition, we employ the terms "Bible" and "Scripture" interchangeably. We have generally used "Hebrew Bible" when making reference to those books shared by Jews and Christians, but when actually citing others who use the term Old Testament—including Jews like Malamud—we have not changed an author's words or made editorial comment.

As the King James Version has long been "the American Bible," we have generally relied on this translation. We will also sometimes use the New Revised Standard Version, which reflects current archaeological, historical, and philological knowledge, and the Jewish Publication Society translation, which is the standard scholarly English translation for Jews. Increasingly, the New International

Version, preferred by many evangelical churches and now the authorized version of the Southern Baptist Convention, is becoming America's Bible.

A note of thanks

With thanks for institutional support from Colgate University, the Finard Family chair in Jewish Studies, and the Yale Institute of Sacred Music. We are grateful as well to individuals who have contributed insight and skill to our work: Mark Knight and Emma Mason, Rona Johnston Gordon, and Grishma Frederic.

1

America as a Biblical Nation and the Bible as an American Book

In December 1968, NASA launched Apollo 8, the first manned spaceship to orbit the moon. The three astronauts aboard were the first humans to see the Earth as a whole planet, the first to see the far side of the moon, and the first to capture photos of Earth from space. Marking these momentous firsts, the flight was aired as a live television broadcast on Christmas Eve 1968, which was the most-watched television broadcast to date. Astronaut Bill Anders spoke initially: "We are now approaching lunar sunrise, and for all the people back on Earth, the crew of Apollo 8 has a message that we would like to send to you." The message, read by each of the three astronauts in turn, consisted of the opening ten verses of Genesis in the venerable King James Version (KJV). They then ended the reading and the broadcast: "And from the crew of Apollo 8, we close with good night, good luck, a Merry Christmas—and God bless all of you, all of you on the good Earth." The astronauts assumed that a reading from Genesis would be resonant for their American audience, and (as the following survey will illustrate) their assumption was well founded. They were speaking to an America that was not only biblically literate but also had long understood itself to be a biblical nation.

The astronauts' instinct to put a biblical imprint on the Earth echoes the instincts of European explorers and early settlers. In one logbook,

Christopher Columbus wrote, "I was in great need of these high seas because nothing like this had occurred since the time of the Jews when the Egyptians came out against Moses who was leading them out of captivity."[1] As the names of settlements given by those who came to stay indicate, and as we will soon see, Columbus would not be alone in understanding this new land in biblical terms. The map of the northeast of the United States, for instance, is peppered with towns whose names are taken straight from the Bible: Connecticut's Bethel, Canaan, Hebron, and Sharon; New York's Babylon, Jericho, Jerusalem, and Lebanon; Pennsylvania's Emmaus, Ephrata, Nazareth, and Zion. Seven states house a Bethlehem; twenty-eight a Goshen. A quest for American Salems will take a road tripper to thirty-one states.

Even the symbolic geography of the United States is biblical. Many Puritan writers conceived of "America as the literal Promised Land and American experience as a biblically foreshadowed 'text' about God's unfolding plan for human redemption."[2] The metaphor of the Promised Land is but one of four geographic metaphors that mapped America onto the Bible and the Bible onto America. America was understood as the wilderness through which the Israelites wandered on the way to the Promised Land; as an Egypt ruled by a Pharaoh from which the Israelites were delivered through an exodus; and, as a New Eden. These tropes underscore the fact that the United States is a nation "highly conscious of its biblical foundations."[3]

Puritan settlers described their voyage through a "wilderness" and "desert" to their new Canaan.[4] Puritan father William Bradford spoke of encamping in "a hideous and desolate wilderness" near their landing place in Massachusetts. They chose it because the settlers could not, "as it were, go up to the top of Pisgah to view from this wilderness a more goodly country."[5] From the hideous wilderness, it was no doubt difficult to imagine that there could even be such a desirable place on these foreign shores.

For many early Americans, the predominant metaphor for America was not the wilderness wandering before settlement in the Promised Land, but rather Egypt, the site of bondage. Before the Revolutionary War, American writers cast the British as Egyptians led by a Pharaoh who was "endeavoring to oppress, enslave and destroy these American States."[6] The call to fight against England was framed in biblical terms, with scriptural appeal made not to Exodus but to Paul (eg. Rom. 13): Americans turned to Romans to shape their thinking about government and submission to authority. When they entered into war against England, the biblical landscape shifted back from the New Testament to the Old. William Billings' "Lamentation over Boston" used the metaphors of exile in Psalm 137 to describe the colonists being driven out of the city during the Revolutionary War. Benjamin Franklin proposed that an image of Pharaoh and his army drowning in the Red Sea be cast on the nation's great seal along with the motto "Rebellion to tyrants is obedience to God." Thomas Jefferson turned to the same book of Scripture for the seal, but proposed instead the Israelites being guided out of Egypt by a cloud of smoke and a pillar of fire (Exod. 13:21-22). The model ultimately selected depicts an eagle and thus contains an allusion to God's comment to Moses, "I bore you on eagles' wings and brought you to myself" (Exod. 19:4).[7]

The imagery of the Exodus became even more prevalent in the discourse around slavery. The enslaved saw themselves as Israelites in bondage to "the pharaoh of American slaveholders."[8] For their part, abolitionists grounded their denunciation of slavery in their readings of Exodus. Congregationalist Samuel Hopkins, whose church was the first to preach openly against the enslavement of African Americans, described the slaveholders' hearts as having been hardened like Pharaoh's. For White Southerners, the pharaoh was not them but the North, which sought to "deny them their liberty by taking their property and independence," just as the "British pharaoh, George III" had done to Americans before the Revolutionary War.[9]

The symbols of Exodus continued to abound during the Civil War: in the Southern imagination, "Lincoln was Pharaoh; Jefferson Davis, Moses; and Yankees in general, Judas."[10] In the Northern view, "slavery tarnished the brilliance of their model republic in the eyes of the world and, more important, God."[11] Northern Christians feared inciting God's wrath, knowing that God had sent biblical Israel into Babylonian Captivity and could do the same to his United States. There was, in the Northern view, a way to make things right in God's eyes: a reading of Revelation 20 cemented the idea that a victory for the Union might bring about the Kingdom of God on the Earth. Both the North and the South appealed to the Bible to support their views about slavery. Southerners deployed a literalist reading that turned to the passages about slaveholding and the treatment of slaves; Northerners followed a liberalist reading that focused on God's liberation of the slaves in Exodus and on biblical teachings about the oppressed.[12] When Lincoln prevented Southern states from leaving the Union, Presbyterian minister Benjamin Morgan Palmer proclaimed, "the heart of our modern Pharaoh is hardened." Northerners inverted the imagery in songs like "Our Lincoln's Act Immortal," which envisions Lincoln conversely as a modern Moses.[13]

After the biblical Exodus come the forty years of wandering in the wilderness, but in the post–Civil War era (unlike in the Puritan imagination), the focus was less on the journey than on the arrival in the Promised Land. In the Bible, God covenanted himself to his chosen people and assured them a land. In America, Kentucky landowner, mapmaker, and self-styled historian John Filson sought to promote settlement in Kentucky with claims that "it is like the land of promise, flowing with milk and honey."[14] The image of America as Promised Land was articulated especially strongly among those who felt disenfranchised in the United States. Jews, Mormons, blacks have all turned to Scripture to give themselves a sense of place in America.

For almost two millennia, from the destruction of the Temple and the fall of Jerusalem in 70 CE to the modern period, the Jewish condition was particularly marked by displacement, wandering, homelessness. Unable to own land or be citizens in most of Europe, Jews conceived of themselves as living in a state of exile, a state well articulated in the Hebrew Bible. Indeed, this was the state of the Scriptures themselves: the Bible "comes to us . . . not in its original languages; it is uprooted from its original territory. It is a book in exile."[15] So too are the Jews who forsook their original languages and original territories, for the English of America. Well before the creation of the State of Israel in 1948, the United States provided a homeland for many Jews, such that early Jewish American literature "often figured America rather than Israel as the metaphoric Promised Land that would redeem Eastern European immigrants from the danger and disenfranchisement of (metaphoric) Egypt."[16] In her journal, teenager Mary Antin cast her emigration from Belarus to the United States as a journey to the "promised land"; indeed, the phrase became the title of her 1912 memoir of leaving Jewish life in Czarist Russia, her

American public-school education, and her assimilation into American culture. This expression was not merely literary, it was also given a theological cast: the leaders of Reform Judaism in America declared in an 1898 resolution, "America is our Zion."[17]

Mormons, perhaps the only group in the world to describe the Jews as gentiles, work their own confluence of Zion, Promised Land, and America. The Latter-day Saints' assertion that "the Lord prepared a new land to attract the peoples of the world who sought liberty and religious freedom"[18] does not merely echo the view of the republic's founders who regarded America as a Promised Land: it is, for the Church of Latter-day Saints, a scriptural truth. Throughout the Book of Mormon, references to the United States are glossed "promised land" or "land of promise" (1 Nephi 12:1, 13:4, 14:2, etc.).

For African Americans, the potential of America to be a Promised Land—or to house a Promised Land within it—has also been resonant. The flight of black migrant workers and escaped slaves to Kansas in the 1860s[19] and the great migration of African Americans from the rural south to the urban north post-1940 have both been cast as journeys to the Promised Land.[20] A generation later, Martin Luther King Jr. alerted his listeners to the many ways that America had not yet achieved the ideal of the Promised Land. In his "I've Been to the Mountain Top" speech, he declared, "It's all right to talk about 'streets flowing with milk and honey,' but God has commanded us to be concerned about the slums down here, and his children who can't eat three square meals a day." In that speech, King saw himself as having gone to the mountain top. He proclaimed, "I've seen the Promised Land. I may not get there with you. But I want you to know tonight, that we, as a people, will get to the promised land!" Presciently, King cast himself as Moses on Mount Nebo, whom God allowed to see the Promised Land but not to enter it. King was assassinated the following day.

If the metaphor of the Promised Land signaled God's sanctioning of America as a home for his chosen people (whomever they might be), the metaphor of America as the New Eden signaled the country as the home of God himself. This identification was first made by sixteenth-century explorers and was very consciously deployed by the new settlers. Early English arrivals described Virginia as a New Eden, "the paradise of the world," "a land even as God made it."[21] From then on, Americans have translated the dream of a recovered Eden into the American dream itself.[22] In a pamphlet urging independence from England, Thomas Paine declared, "we have it in our power to begin the world over again," to reverse the decline that began after the flood of Noah through the creation of a new, free country.[23] The "conflation of America and Eden laid the foundation for the 19th-century myth of the garden in the west."[24] Nearly two centuries after Paine, Ronald Reagan quoted his words in an address to the Nation Association of Evangelicals, evoking again the sense of America as a place from which to begin anew.[25]

This trope has had great resonance not only politically and literarily but also visually: America as a New Eden is expressed in the work of painters as diverse as Hudson River school's Thomas Cole (1801–48) and "folk artist" Earl Cunningham (1893–1977)—a marine painter working mostly in Maine and Florida from the 1910s to the 1970s. Even in un-Edenic times it was a meaningful theme: Civil War–era painters like Frederic Church and Sanford Gifford "contended with the destruction of the idea that America was a 'New Eden.'"[26] American artists were not interested in "the landscape marked by man's presence but they regarded nature as a virgin territory, a landscape that had not been sullied by human kind, in which the hand of God, its creator, could be seen."[27] The sense that the natural world reflected the divine was compatible with a national identity that understood "Americans as the chosen people, a nation with a moral mission." Woven together, these were the basis for casting America as a "paradisiacal landscape."[28]

As we have just noted, the biblical imprint was made not only on the land but also on its people. The world the Puritans sought to establish—designated as a "covenanted society," "new Israel," "Bible Commonwealth"—was grounded in an understanding of the Bible as central both to personal faith and to social order.[29] They believed that the Bible prescribed civil conduct and that social order was instilled through education and through legislation. Thus the Bible formed the foundation of early American law codes and became a mainstay of the American public school.

Through "a union of biblical typology and American nationalism,"[30] the United States understood itself as a biblical nation from early on. The new settlers were to follow biblical law in the new biblical land.

Old Testament law governed communal life, ownership and property, Sabbath observance, tithing, sexual mores and so forth. Moral and ethical law was drawn from both Testaments. The Connecticut Colony established a legal code premised on the notion that "the Scriptures hold forth a perfect rule for the direction and government of all men in all duties which they are to perform to God and men." Therefore, "in all public offices which concern civil order,—as the choice of magistrates and officers, making and repealing laws, dividing allotments of inheritance, and all things of like nature,—they would be all governed by those rules which the Scripture held forth to them."[31] Conservatives argue that all foundational American law is rooted in the Bible. The fixed moral laws of the Declaration of Independence (framed as unalienable rights) of the Declaration of Independence are articulated throughout the Bible;[32] the principles of the Constitution are outlined in Deuteronomy;[33] the three branches of government are derived from Isa. 33:22.[34] Biblical influence is not limited to early legal codes, however. We continue to find the imprint of the Bible throughout American law— in the appearance of Moses on the frieze above the Supreme Court; in the practice of taking oaths and swearing in presidents on a Bible; in the Blue Laws of many states that restrict the sale of alcohol or the opening of businesses on "the Lord's Day"; in the placement (and inevitable subsequent removal) of Ten Commandments monuments in law courts; in the zeal for capital punishment in the Bible Belt.

If biblical values were upheld in early American law, so too were they inscribed on early Americans' hearts and minds. Puritans taught them in the home. Deacon John Paine described the ideal of the Puritan mother: "A careful mother eke She was / into her children all / in teaching them gods word to read / when they were but Small / in reading of gods holly words / most diligent She was."[35] Here, the mother was in charge of religious education, which began with reading Scripture and devotional texts. The outcome was not merely biblical literacy, but literacy generally. Puritan minister Increase Mather came from a highly educated family, for whom education began at home. "I learned to read of my mother," he wrote.

One survey of the Bible in American education notes that, "Intimately related to the origins and development of American educational institutions, the Bible was taught by both clergy and laity in the churches, homes, and schools of colonial America."[36]

The Massachusetts Bay Colony "called for the establishment of schools to help children develop the 'ability to read and understand the principles of religion and the capital laws of this country' and thereby frustrate 'one chief project of ye olde deluder, Satan, to keep men from the knowledge of ye Scriptures.'"[37] In the Colonial period, both boys and girls were taught to read, but only boys were subsequently taught to write. Girls were, of course, taught to sew, and the later eighteenth century witnessed a new phenomenon: young girls stitching samplers that had biblical or moral teachings on them. The teaching of reading in early America followed the English practice that Francis Bacon called the "ordinary road of Hornbook, Primer, Psalter, Testament, and Bible."[38]

Far from the educated northeast, "children of the hinterland frequently had access to only two books, the Bible and a home medical encyclopedia."[39] The former would have been read regularly in the American household, serving as both religion and literature. At the turn of the twentieth century, even poor children in the South were also likely to have had a copy of the *Child's Bible Reader*, which found its way into thousands of Southern homes courtesy of door-to-door salesmen. Again, Scripture was ingested as stories—although these were not stories for stories' sake but moral lessons that would shape their reader.

From the passage of the "Ye olde deluder Satan Act" through the early 1840s, reading the Bible for moral lessons was a mainstay in the American public education system.[40] Sometimes students encountered the scriptural text itself, excerpted or doled out in bites that conveyed a particular message or taught a particular lesson. These, like liturgical readings, were a way of delivering the Bible as a series of shorts. In many school districts, English primers contained biblical stories. *The New Instructor* (1803) taught students many of the Proverbs of Solomon and a wide selection of biblical narratives from Genesis, Exodus, and Daniel as ways not only to put into practice the grammar and vocabulary being explained but also to provide moral edification.[41] Schoolbook publisher William Holmes McGuffey included this note in early editions of his primers: "From no source has the author drawn more copiously in his selections than from the Sacred Scriptures."[42] From its first printing in 1836 through the 1920s, when sales began to decline, *McGuffey's Eclectic Readers* sold 122 million copies, each of which is certain to have been read by multiple children.[43] Again, in each of these instances, students effectively encountered the Bible—in the King James or in paraphrase—as a collection of short stories.

Things began to change with the arrival of waves of Catholic immigrants from Ireland and Germany, who brought with them an understanding of the role of the Bible that was distinct from earlier Protestant arrivals. This spurred debate about the value of Bible reading in schools. In 1869 the Cincinnati Board of Education ruled against the teaching of religious books—including the Bible—in common school, beginning sustained consideration of the constitutionality of reading the Bible in the public school.[44] Even amid these debates, at beginning of the twentieth century "Bible study was still regarded as an essential component of the education of the young in a good part of the country."[45] Indeed, until *Abington School District v. Schempp* and *Murray v. Curlett*, companion cases brought before the Supreme Court in 1963, the Bible remained a feature of American education from between 1647 and 1963: no publically educated child was left behind. As a result, the United States was not only a biblical nation but one whose citizens were biblically literate.

"The Bible has been the greatest single influence on our literature"[47]

Thus far we have merely glimpsed how the Bible is threaded through American history, government, law, rhetoric, education, and art. Biblical images and the notion of a biblical nation also pervade American letters. Carlos Baker describes the particular impact of the Old Testament on the literature of New England during the early national period, when our prose fiction began: "All children were raised on the Bible from the cradle, and writers could assume, as we can no longer do, that the stories of Moses in the bulrushes, or Lot's wife, or Ruth amid the alien corn, of Abraham's sacrifice, were known to them as our children know the complex lore of missiles and moon-conquest."[48]

From the seventeenth century through the 1960s, the era of moon landings and broadcasts from space, the Bible had remained a constant in America. From a literary perspective, the Bible had become America's book. Indeed, the apocalyptic and millennial thought characteristic of the earliest American literature reveals a sense that "the Bible was proleptically American."[49] Readers understood the Bible as speaking about America, as providing a map for and a model of the nation. Its political landscape reflected America's; its promise—a land flowing with milk and honey, a New Eden—was America's. We see this especially in the pulpit. From the colonial sermons that equated America with Zion, to the development of the American jeremiad (a political sermon) and the fulminations of modern-day televangelists, the Bible has provided a key to interpreting the contemporary world. The Bible is not an ancient book—it is written in the present tense, modern and American.

That the Bible was so central to the construction of American identity meant that it had a corollary centrality in the creation of American literature. As late as 1850, a decade after the early national period, Melville could still declare, "We Americans are the peculiar, chosen people—the Israel of our time; we bear the ark of the liberties of the world."[50] James Fenimore Cooper would make use of biblical analogy to describe the frontier experience. Walt Whitman's poetry is indebted to the prosody, rhythm, and diction of the King James Bible.[51] Robert Alter notes that "in nineteenth-century Protestant America, the Bible, almost always in the King James Version, was a constant companion for most people." It was read to them in church, and they often read it aloud at home. It "gave them ideas about God, the world, history, and human nature that they wrestled with, and a whole set of images, rhythms, and diction that nurtured their own literary style." The language and beauty of the King James "stamped itself on the imagination of many American writers," and nineteenth-century American literature, from *Moby Dick* to Lincoln's speeches, reverberates with Scripture.[52]

A century after Melville, the Bible was still very much alive in the American novel. Steinbeck recalls his Episcopalian mother reading him Bible stories from the age of three: "Literature was in the air around me. The Bible I absorbed through my skin."[53] He revisits the biblicized American myth—the myth of this continent as the New

Eden and the American as the new Adam—throughout his fiction.[54] Faulkner's work is rife with biblical allusion and symbolism; in his fiction, he returns repeatedly to the stories of Abraham, David, and Christ. In his semi-autobiographical novel *Go Tell It on the Mountain,* James Baldwin takes his reader to Old Testament stories of Noah's curse of Ham, Jacob's wrestling with the angel, and Moses's leading Israel out of Egypt. Throughout her work, Toni Morrison takes hers to the Bible as well—to Ruth, Job, the Song of Songs.

By no means all writers who make use of the Bible are themselves believers. Although Nathaniel Hawthorne is highly critical of Puritan piety, his fiction in nonetheless replete with biblical allusions. Even Edgar Allen Poe, who spoke more highly of the Qur'an than of the Bible, was not immune: one critic contends that his writings "are surprisingly rich biblicisms, and one story, 'The Cask of Amontillado' (1846), has been read as a demonic parody of the Passion."[55] Emily Dickinson's poetry "requires extensive verbal familiarity with the Bible if its full import as a rejection of conformity with received traditions is to be fully understood."[56] Mark Twain's 1905 short story "Eve's Diary"—a retelling of the Eden narrative—was banned from libraries in Massachusetts because an illustration of a naked Eve contained within it was held to be a pornographic image. Reflecting on the incident, Twain wrote to a friend: "The truth is, that when a Library expels a book of mine and leaves an unexpurgated Bible lying around where unprotected youth and age can get hold of it, the deep unconscious irony of it delights me and doesn't anger me."[57] In interviews, Faulkner seemed to express ambivalence about Christianity despite his persistent use of its Scripture. In a letter to Fitzgerald describing his quest for a title for his new work, Hemingway complained, "Well, Fitz, I looked all through that bible, it was in very fine print and stumbling on that great book *Ecclesiastics* [sic], read it aloud to all who would listen. Soon I was alone and began cursing the bloody bible because there were no titles in it—although I found the source of practically every good title you ever heard of."[58] Hemingway neglects to mention that some of these good biblical titles are on his own books (*The Sun Also Rises, The Garden of Eden*). Until at least the first half of the twentieth century, even those American authors who were outright skeptical about religion and holy writ seemed to owe the Bible some debt.

He that hath ears to hear, let him hear

At first blush, the contemporary American literary landscape seems markedly different. With the Bible largely having been ousted from the public-school curriculum and attendance at mainstream churches and synagogues at all-time lows, teachers and preachers alike lament that Americans' scriptural literacy can no longer be assumed. To some extent, the cause for concern is not merely anecdotal. In *Religious Literacy: What Every American Needs to Know and Doesn't* (2007), Stephen Prothero documented "the nearly grotesque biblical illiteracy of even religiously observant Protestant, Catholic, and Jewish university students."[59] It would seem we have shifted from a biblical nation to one that "knows not Joseph"—nor catches the allusion of this phrase to Exod. 1:8.

It would be incorrect, however, to argue that Americans have completely abandoned the Good Book. Although church and synagogue attendance has radically diminished in mainstream denominations, the one place an American is certain to encounter the Bible is in a church or synagogue. In these settings, the Bible tends to be experienced as short stories. Certainly, some biblical passages are read in their entirety. In synagogues and churches alike, psalms are recited or sung and recognized as discrete literary units. Six times a year, on particular holidays, Jewish liturgy prescribes the reading of the whole of a short biblical book, either on one's own or corporately as part of the service of worship. During Holy Week, Christians hear the story of the Passion. But in the main, the Bible is portioned out to congregations in liturgical "bites." For the weekly service, Christian lectionaries typically select one passage from the Old Testament or Acts, one from the Psalms, one from the Epistles or Revelation, and one from the three synoptic gospels or John.[60]

Jews similarly dole out the larger narrative in liturgical pieces. Over the course of fifty-four weeks, Jewish congregations read their way from the beginning of Genesis through the end of Deuteronomy. The calendar for weekly Torah readings was set out by the medieval philosopher Maimonides and is followed by Jews around the world. The weekly reading (*parshah*) is accompanied by a fixed reading from the Prophets (called a *haftarah*). These supplemental readings tend to be thematically linked to the weekly *parshah*. The effect of the weekly reading is that the congregant who understands the Hebrew will come away from services having heard a longish short story and a short commentary upon it. Many Americans still prefer to read the Bible themselves than have it read to them. A 2016 survey of scriptural reading habits showed that 48 percent of Americans read the Bible at some point in the past year. Most of those people read it at least monthly; 9 percent reported reading it daily. Almost all read it in translation, the one most preferred being the KJV.[61] This is indeed America's translation, found in every Bible on which a president has been sworn in and in nearly every presidential speech citing Scripture. As the investigators of the study note, "Clearly, then, the King James Bible is far from dead, since more than half of individual respondents and two-fifths of congregations still prefer it."[62]

Not only is the Bible very much present in the lives of many Americans, there is a whole swath of the country that both reads the Bible regularly and orders its cultural life around it. Many of the religiously observant Americans who are faithful Bible readers consume culture specifically created for them. Evangelical books are the most lucrative sector of the publishing market, and Christian presses produce—and sell—hundreds of specialized Bibles. They are made for every reader: moms, dads, children, teachers, lawyers, doctors, nurses, patients, single women. (The divorced and the elderly seem the only untapped markets.) The *Denim Bible* has sixteen pages of color illustrations designed to appeal to today's youth, while the *Teen Life Application Bible* identifies those biblical passages especially useful in navigating adolescence. *Women of the Word* helps women study the Bible with both their hearts and their minds; *5-Minute Bible Workouts for Men* helps men flex their scriptural muscles. *Revolve* presents the complete New Testament in the format of a glossy fashion magazine. The *NIV Boys' Bible* has sidebars alerting young readers to especially gross and gory passages. The *BattleZone* Bible is metal-plated; the *Duraword Bible* is weatherproof.

Beyond actual Bibles, we find an evangelical culture permeated by Scripture. Biblical fiction makes up a whole segment of the Christian publishing industry—romances like *From Heaven Fought the Stars: A Biblical Adventure of Romance and War in the Time of Deborah* and

Jonah: A Sweet Biblical Amish Romance; fictionalized biographies of biblical characters like *Sarai* in Revell Publishing's "Wives of the Patriarchs Series" and *Delilah: Treacherous Beauty*; historical fictions like *The Promise of Canaan* and *The Walls of Arad*. In the direct-to-video television show *Bible Man*, a superhero uses the Bible to fight evil; in *Veggie Tales* (which had mainstream success and a run on NBC) anthropomorphic fruits and vegetables star in retellings of biblical stories. Contemporary Christian musicians like Servant, the Third Day, and Petra use religious and biblical imagery in their lyrics. Amusement parks like Holy Land USA and biblically themed mini-golf courses around the country provide Christians families with recreational biblical experiences whereas the Creation Museum in Petersburg, Kentucky, offers educational ones.

With Christians having their own television and radio stations, publishing houses, and movie studios, the chasm between evangelical and mainstream culture in America is wide. It is not the case, however, that the one is steeped in the Bible while the other has utterly abandoned it. To the contrary, we find biblical traces everywhere in contemporary American culture. Americans encounter the Bible at the football stadium, as players wear scriptural verses in their eyeblack[63] and spectators hold up signs reading "John 3:16." On the radio, Kanye West sings about Jesus and U2 revisits the Psalms. On television, programs ranging from *Jane the Virgin* to *The Simpsons* are sprinkled with biblical allusions, while two recent prime-time offerings, *Kings* and *Of Kings and Prophets*, are retellings of the books of Samuel and Kings. At the movie theater mainstream releases like *Noah*, *The Prince of Egypt*, and *Exodus: Gods and Kings* return audiences to Genesis and Exodus, while *The Nativity Story* and Mel Gibson's *The Passion of the Christ* (the highest-grossing R-rated film in history) revisit the life of Jesus. A remake of *Ben-Hur* hit theaters in the summer of 2016, with promotional material pledging that Jesus would have an even bigger role in this version than in the original. Back when bookstores were plentiful, readers could pick up modern gospels by Gore Vidal (*Live from Golgotha*), José Saramago (*The Gospel according to Jesus Christ*), and Christopher Moore (*Lamb: The Gospel according to Biff, Christ's Childhood Pal*). Sorting fiction selections by date reveals that a host of contemporary Jesus novels—Naomi Alderman's *The Liar's Gospel*, Colm Tóibín's

Testament of Mary, Richard Beard's *Lazarus is Dead*, Philip Pullman's *The Good Man Jesus and the Scoundrel Christ*, and J. M. Coetzee's *Childhood of Jesus*—were all released within twenty-four months of each other. Clearly American culture-makers think there is an American appetite for the Bible even within the secular consuming public.

Similarly, American politicians (or their speechwriters) seem to understand the Bible as a shared American resource. Not only do our presidents continue to be sworn in on it, they almost all make use of it rhetorically. George W. Bush famously cited Psalm 23 in his address to the nation following the attacks on 9/11: "Even though I walk in the valley of the shadow of death" (New American Standard Bible). President Obama used Jn 15:13—"Greater love hath no man than this, that a man lay down his life for his friends"—in a speech about strengthening gun control. Elsewhere, in answering questions about immigration, he paraphrased the Sermon on the Mount: "Make sure we're looking at the log in our eye before we are pointing out the mote in other folks' eyes."[64] He used verses from Ezekiel, John, and Romans in his 2016 tribute to fallen police officers in Dallas.[65] The question, of course, is: Can the non-evangelical American public hear these echoes of Scripture?

It seems the answer might well be no. Despite the persistent influence of the Bible even in "secular" American culture, there are indications that we have become a biblically illiterate nation. According to Prothero's findings, only half of American adults can name even one of the four gospels and most Americans cannot name the first book of the Bible. If this is indeed the case, biblical resonances of movie titles like *A Time to Kill*, *Children of Men*, *A River Runs through It*, and *Chariots of Fire* are certain not to be picked up by the American audience. No more recognizable, then, are the biblical underpinnings of novels like *Gilead*, *Song of Solomon*, or *East of Eden*, despite the biblical titles of each. It appears we are "operating . . . from a position of a massive cultural deficit where knowledge of biblical foundations [is] concerned."[66]

Biblical illiteracy has a profound impact on cultural literacy. Robert Alter sees this clearly: "I look at the erosion of biblical literacy as a literary person, and from this viewpoint, it has dire consequences."[67] The KJV in particular "has permeated many of the masterworks of

English literature since the later seventeenth century, and without familiarity with the Bible, readers are bound to miss an important dimension of many great English novels, poems, as well as expository prose"[68] if they are unfamiliar with Scripture. As we argue here, the reader of contemporary literature may also be missing out. What is lost is not merely awareness of biblical allusions or the recognition of specific biblical passages, but the awareness of "a certain stylistic power drawn from the Bible,"[69] an ear for its language and cadence. As Alter notes, "The compact rhythms and taut diction in the prose of Cormac McCarthy, with its fondness for the use of parallel clauses without syntactic complication, owes a good deal to the King James Version, but a reader may feel the force of the style without actually realizing that it has a biblical source."[70]

We contend that the Bible remains an American book, a source of inspiration and influence for contemporary writers no less than for those with whom we began our discussion. Moreover, as we have signaled, the Bible is often experienced in the American home, school, and place of worship in discrete, digestible units—indeed, almost as short stories. In the chapters to follow we will first look at the genre, then see how it is present in both Testaments of Scripture, and finally consider how it appears in the work of writers who draw upon the "old, old story" in a wide variety of ways.

2

The Short Story as an American Genre

It is of the essence of all short stories to be brief.[1] For Edgar Allen Poe, perhaps its first theorist and an early master of the form, the "short prose-narrative" can be read at one sitting, requiring "from a half-hour to two hours in its perusal." Time is always of the essence for Poe, and so the writer who wants to keep the reader focused must avoid any "undue length." Its essence, therefore, is distillation; its charge, to eliminate the superfluous or redundant, anything that prevents "a certain unique or single effect" that distracts from a sense of achieved "totality."[2] Whereas "works of magnitude" take the reader far and wide, they do not afford the pleasure of what can be taken in "at one view." They do not afford an experience of the work as a whole—"the perfection of its finish . . . the nice adaptation of its constituent parts . . . the unity or totality of interest."[3] To write less, therefore, is to achieve more. To quote Raymond Carver, "Get in, get out. Don't linger. Go on."[4]

But before the writer "gets out," it is important to have an ending that brings down the curtain in a powerful way. Stories that conclude with a twist of surprise—De Maupassant's "The Necklace," O. Henry's "The Gift of the Magi"—do so with a flare. If not done skillfully, or if done too often, this move can seem like a trick. "The good ending," according to John Updike, "dismisses us with a touch of ceremony, and throws a backward light on significance over the story just read. It *makes* it, as they say, or unmakes it—a weak beginning is forgettable, but the end of the story bulks in the reader's mind like the giant foot in a foreshortened photograph."[5]

Attempts to define the nature and effect of short fiction often begin by contrasting it with the novel, with its big canvas, plenitude of characters, richness of descriptive detail, expansion of social context, and sustained performance. Its task, on the other hand, is to seize the moment, to focus plot and character on what is essential. Although no one dreams of writing the Great American Short Story, many argue its merit. For William Faulkner, a novelist with several collections to his credit, the short story is "a crystallized instant" in which "character conflicts with character or environment or with itself."[6] Next to poetry, it is "the hardest form" because it demands "a nearer absolute exactitude": "In the novel you can be careless but in the short story you . . . have less room to be slovenly and careless. There's less room in it for trash."[7] In this vein, Francine Prose claims that the best way to understand a great piece of short fiction is "to take a story apart (line by line, word by word) the way a mechanic takes apart an automobile engine, and ask ourselves how each word, each phrase, and each sentence contributes to the entirety."[8] (For "mechanic" one could substitute the New Critic.)

Or, shifting genre comparisons once more, we could liken the story to a well-crafted play, in which "setting, situation, and character are established through exposition; the plot then introduces complication; and the action rises toward a climax or crisis, after which the action descends toward some kind of resolution."[9] This descent often takes the form of an epiphany or moment of realization—"a distinct shift in consciousness; a deepening of insight"—that may well take place most fully *not* for the character in question but for the reader.[10] At least since James Joyce's short story collection *The Dubliners*, this moment of heightened awareness has come to seem a hallmark of short fiction. Push finally comes to shove in the eleventh hour, before the curtain descends, and the reader is left to make sense of what's been seen. Raymond Carver puts it this way:

> I have a three-by-five card up there [above my desk] with this fragment of a sentence from a story by Chekhov: "and suddenly everything became clear to him." I find these words filled with wonder and possibility. I love their simple clarity, and the hint of

revelation that is implied. There is a bit of mystery, too. What has been unclear before? Why is it just now becoming clear? What's happened? Most of all—what now? There are consequences as a result of such sudden awakenings. I feel a sharp sense of relief—and anticipation.

A good answer to these questions might take the form of one of Carver's own short stories, where a character who did not know what had hit him was nonetheless sure that something had. When "suddenly everything became clear to him," a single moment in the ordinary course of events becomes something new and strange. It is possible in a short story, he said, "to write about commonplace things and objects using commonplace but precise language, and to endow those things—a chair, a window curtain, a fork, a stone, a woman's earrings—with immense, even startling power. It is possible to write a line of seemingly innocuous dialogue and have it send a chill along the reader's spine."[11] Rarely, however, do Carver's characters experience that chill. More often their revelation is, in Günter Leypoldt's term, an "arrested epiphany," a realization "with an often disquieting sense of menace, that there is something out of joint in their world, that at some level they are on the brink of making a tremendous discovery, but that they remain far from grasping what exactly it could be."[12]

******

Literary critics have spilled much ink attempting to define the short story as a genre. According to Francine Prose, who doubles as storyteller and critic, that task is ultimately futile. There are simply too many "sorts and conditions" to pin a story down apart from the arbitrary issues of length and number of words. It seems wiser to proceed by analogy or metaphor, as the writers quoted above know instinctively.[13] A short story is a glance, a firefly's flash, a crystallized instant, or (to go from high to low) a kind of road trip: "If a poem is the single landmark we pull over to admire and the novel is the cross-country trip, the story is the urgent drive to an important event. A mad rush to the hospital."[14]

But perhaps Steven Millhauser put it best when he likened the short story (with a nod to William Blake) to a grain of sand that contains the universe. Millhauser's novel *Martin Dressler* won the Pulitzer Prize for Fiction in 1997; his heart, however, has always been elsewhere, as witnessed in the several collections of his short fiction, most recently *Voices in the Night* (2015), and in his soaring *New York Times* apologia, "The Ambition of the Short Story" (2008).[15] For him, the "modest" story rather than the "brashly pretentious" novel realizes Blake's goal of seeing the universe in a grain of sand. Mastering the minimal, the short story concentrates on some apparently insignificant portion of the world in the belief that the fragment is, in fact, a short cut to the universe. The story lavishes attention not on the massive but on the minute:

> It seeks to know that grain of sand the way a lover seeks to know the face of the beloved. It looks for the moment when the grain of sand reveals its true nature. In that moment of mystic expansion, when the macrocosmic flower bursts from the microcosmic seed, the short story feels its power. It becomes bigger than itself. It becomes bigger than the novel. It becomes as big as the universe.

*****

Some would have it that Americans—writers from the United States[16]—have a particular claim on this grain of sand. Frank O'Connor, author of *The Lonely Voice: A Study of the Short Story* (1963), even declared it to be "a national art form."[17] It would be more accurate to say that it has flourished in the United States in particular ways that have as much to do with the nineteenth- and early-twentieth-century publishing industry as with aspects of the American temperament.

The short story's antecedents, of course, are ancient. Whether rendered in poetry or prose, the brief narrative is as old as writing itself. It is with the early nineteenth century, however, that the modern short story makes its appearance, and more or less at the same time throughout Europe—in Germany (Heinrich von Kleist and E. T. A. Hoffman), France (Prosper Merimée, Alphonse Daudet, de Maupassant), and Russia (Gogol, Turgenev, Dostoevsky, Tolstoy, and at the end of the century—last but certainly not least—the genre's acknowledged master, Chekhov). By contrast, in Britain, from the eighteenth century on, the novel was the genre of choice.

Often, however, novels were published serially, most famously by Dickens, and appeared therefore in short-story-sized installments. Story publishing came later, with short fiction finding its public in newspapers and journals that enjoyed large circulations. Around the time of the First World War, a number of well-regarded writers placed the short story "at the very centre of their creative practice": Rudyard Kipling, D. H. Lawrence, Joseph Conrad, Arnold Bennett and H. G. Wells.[18] In Ireland Joyce's *Dubliners* appeared in 1914, soon followed by collections of stories by Elizabeth Bowen, Frank O'Connor, and Sean O'Faolain, and then, more recently, by those of William Trevor, Edna O'Brien, and Colm Toibin.[19]

Given this backstory in Britain, Ireland, and Europe, where do literary historians place its beginnings in the "new world"? Appearing first as "sketches" and "tales" that owed a debt to German folk models, something like the modern the short story appears in 1820 with Washington Irving's "The Legend of Sleepy Hollow" and "Rip Van Winkle." Following close behind come Hawthorne (*Twice-Told Tales*, 1837), Poe (*Tales of the Grotesque and Arabesque*, 1840), and Melville, who hated writing stories and protested to do so only for the ready money. Nonetheless, according to storyteller and novelist William Boyd, in "Bartleby, the Scrivener" and *Piazza Tales* (1856), Melville made the genre in many ways what it became: "It is Melville who establishes the benchmark for what the short story can attain and allows us to set the standards by which all the other great writers of the form can be measured."[20]

From these nineteenth-century figures onward, the short story took root in America and flourished. The sheer number of brilliant practitioners is dazzling: Bret Harte, Mark Twain, Ambrose Bierce, Stephen Crane, Henry James, Edith Wharton, Sarah Orne Jewett, Willa Cather, O. Henry, Jack London, Ernest Hemingway, F. Scott Fitzgerald, William Faulkner, and Eudora Welty.[21]

What accounts for this extraordinary production of short fiction? Boyd attributes at least some of it to the "blitzkrieg of nineteenth-century magazine publishing" that flourished when books—novels, in particular—did not.[22] When it came to long fiction, the English took the lead. International copyright laws "allowed publishers to pirate British work and print it cheaply," leaving American novelists (like Melville, for instance) at a great disadvantage.[23] For writers who did not require hardcover, however, there were other ways to get work in circulation and, moreover, to earn a living in a proliferation of newspapers, magazines, gift books, and other print media eager for short fiction.

Poe made of necessity a choice, even a patriotic one, when he argued that the magazine rather than the book was the "appropriate expression of American culture": "the whole energetic, busy spirit of the age tended wholly to the Magazine literature—to the curt, the terse, the well-timed and the readily diffused, in preference to the old forms of the verbose, the ponderous and the inaccessible."[24] Poe puts a very positive spin here on an "energetic, busy" national temperament. Writing at the same time, de Tocqueville viewed with suspicion and distaste the same "native" qualities Poe celebrated. For him, Americans in their reading habits were concerned about saving time and making a profit for their labor: "They like books which are easily got and quickly read, requiring no learned research to understand them . . . and above all they like things unexpected and new . . . What they want is vivid, lively emotions, sudden revelations, brilliant truths, or errors able to arouse them and plunge them, almost by violence, into the middle of the subject."[25]

It comes as no surprise that a Frenchman writing *Democracy in America* between 1835 and 1840—observing this raw new country in the "afterglow" of Andrew Jackson's presidency (1829–37)—should find much to disdain. Short attention spans, an appetite for what is quick, lively, sudden, and superficially brilliant: these may all be fool's gold and the sign of a loutish republic. But they are also characteristics of the best short fiction, much of which rose up on this Continent "almost by violence." Conscious of a sustained American "boom" in short fiction not to be found elsewhere, Boyd suspects that there are also zeitgeist reasons that we presently prefer our art in highly concentrated form: "Like a multi-vitamin pill, a good short story can provide a compressed blast of discerning, intellectual pleasure, one no less intense than that delivered by a novel, despite the shorter duration of its consumption." The "potency," he says, "is manifest and emphatic."[26]

The success of the contemporary short story, however, turns our thinking from matters of zeitgeist and national temperament back to the economic sphere. The genre continues to thrive in

America because there are still a number of magazines that publish the "well made" story, whether traditional or experimental, at the standard length of 10,000 words or the much shorter cuts as brief as a sentence or a few paragraphs. To be sure, there are not the many publishing opportunities that once were there for Hemingway, Fitzgerald, or Faulkner. Looking back, Updike recalls that when he was in his twenties, when he and John Cheever were staples at the *New Yorker*, he could support his young family by selling six or seven stories a year. At the *Saturday Evening Post* and other now defunct magazines, short stories were "bread and butter" for their authors, "an avenue for such as now awaits rock stars."[27]

Nonetheless, by one count there are today almost 250 North American publications that produce short fiction, ranging from the establishment *New Yorker* (which currently brings into print British writers like Zadie Smith and Tessa Hadley) to myriad "little magazines" that, whether in print or online, circulate lesser-known authors of new (often experimental and nonconformist) work.[28] Prizes and the anthologies connected to them also support storytellers in a variety of ways. *The Best American Short Stories* has been published continuously since 1915. (The 2016 centenary volume *100 Years of the Best American Short Stories* offers, together with the assembled fiction, a detailed, decade-by-decade picture of the genre's ebb and flow since the series' founding.) The O. Henry Prize was established in 1919 and has continued every year with scarcely an interruption. In partnership now with the PEN/American Center, it produces an annual volume consisting of twenty prize-winning stories. So too, since 1976, does the Pushcart Prize, which makes a special effort to incorporate new presses and authors. (In 2016 it celebrated its fortieth anniversary with *The Pushcart Prize XL: Best of the Small Presses*.)

Apart from this emphasis on print, whether in hard copy or upon a screen, there is also the auditory experience of storytelling thanks to Public Radio International's program "Selected Shorts."[29] To listen to superb actors before a live audience in New York's Symphony Space, or to join in that experience at a later time via podcast, is to experience something of the childhood pleasure of being read to out loud, being told a story to hold on to. This program has featured humorists like David Sedaris ("The Life You Save May Be Your

Own") and Stephen Colbert ("The Enduring Chill") bringing Flannery O'Connor to voice, and actress Jane Kaczmarek doing the same for Tobias Wolff's "In the Garden of the North American Martyrs." However we take in our new stories, whether in books, magazines, or over the radio, there is simply no satisfying the desire for stories: Tell me more.

3

The Greatest Stories
Ever Told

In the American context, the Bible is sometimes spoken of as "the greatest story ever told," a moniker taken from the title of a 1965 film that recounts the story of Jesus, beginning with the nativity and ending with the resurrection. That the phrase has come to refer to the entirety of the Bible—not just the Gospels, but the whole New Testament; not just the New Testament, but the Old Testament too— is an indication of how the Bible is understood by many religious readers: as a single story that begins with the creation of the heavens and the earth in Genesis 1. For Jews, whose canon does not contain the New Testament and whose books appear in a different order than they do in the Christian Bible, the biblical story ends with the promise of the restoration of the Temple (2 Chron. 36:23). For Christians, the story ends with the end of history and a promise of a new heaven, a new earth, and a new Jerusalem, with the imminent return of Jesus (Rev. 22:21). For Jewish readers, the central theme of their expansive story is God's relationship with his people Israel. For Christian readers, it is the promise of salvation from sin and death through Jesus Christ, God's only begotten son. For Jews and Christians alike, all the books and stories of their respective Bibles are understood to advance one overarching theme or the other. Hence a diverse library of books, containing a range of literary genres, written over sixteen centuries by multiple authors in at least three distinct languages—Hebrew, Aramaic, and Greek—becomes what it is evidently not: a single book[1] that can be collectively conceived of as a single story. Indeed, as "the greatest story ever told."

Whereas the religious communities that hold it sacred stress the overarching narrative or flow to the work—it contains multiple accounts of the history of God's relationship with Israel/the church—it seems obvious to the less invested reader that the Hebrew Bible is not a continuous, linear account of anything at all. It is a literary anthology with just about everything in it: myth, epic, fable, parable, apocalypse, aphorisms, legal codes, censuses and genealogies, historical records, love poems, songs of praise and lament, wisdom literature, and prophetic utterances. The Christian New Testament is likewise an anthology. It opens with four biographies of Jesus, proceeds to a travelogue of sorts in the Acts of the Apostles, moves on to a collection of letters, and ends with an apocalypse. These books were all written over a period of roughly a century and in the same vernacular (Koine Greek), which makes them more similar linguistically than the books in the Hebrew Bible are to one another. Generically, however, there is notable variety in this canon as well. The Bible of Jews and of Christians, in other words, is a rich and diverse literary compendium.

The short(er) story in the Bible

In terms of our own interest here, one-third of the Bible is prose narrative—or, more plainly, story. In the Hebrew Bible, the longer narrative is made up of shorter ones: the story of the monarchy, for instance, unfolds across a number of books. In the narrative portions of the New Testament, a single story—the life of Jesus—is told by four distinct authors, each of whom presents slightly different shorter episodes or stories to tell the larger narrative. Furthermore, the reading of these books in a liturgical setting, whether in synagogue or church, breaks them into smaller stories or episodes. As a result, the Bible is typically experienced as at once a very long story and a lot of shorter ones.

Both testaments preserve self-contained narrative units. The Book of Genesis, for example, is often seen as the first chapter of the larger narrative of the Bible, as the prologue that sets up everything that is to follow. And yet, Genesis has its own story line, within which are found varied and distinct shorter stories. There is the overarching story of God, land, and people: God creates land and people, lands and their peoples emerge as nations, and God cleaves to one particular people and to the land he promises them. But then there are more discrete units as well. The closing of Genesis offers us an extended story of the travails and triumphs of one person in particular, Jacob's beloved son Joseph. Spanning thirteen chapters (Gen. 37 and 39–50), the story is often characterized as a novella. The four chapters devoted to Noah and the flood (Gen. 6–9) are frequently presented as a single short story in later literature—particularly in children's literature—despite the fact that close reading reveals fissures in the story that suggest multiple authors and multiple sources. Then there are chapters in Genesis that have a coherence to themselves. Chapter 34, sometimes given the title "The Rape of Dinah," for example, has what many consider to be the key elements of a short story: setting, characters, and plot.

One of the first scholars to pay attention to the literariness of the Bible was Hermann Gunkel (1862–1932). Concerned with identifying the antecedents of the biblical stories and establishing the settings in which they arose, Gunkel was especially alert to forms and patterns in biblical literature. He thought of the Bible as presenting legend cycles—larger literary units that bring together separate, shorter legends in an artfully arranged composition. Turning to Genesis for an example, Gunkel considered the stories about Abraham and Lot to be a legend cycle, within which he identified six "constituent elements" (shorter legends): the kinsmen's migration to Canaan; their separation at Bethel; the appearance of God to Abraham; the destruction of Sodom and Gomorrah; the birth of Ammon and Moab; and the birth of Isaac.[2] It was Gunkel's view that the earliest forms of biblical narrative were all very short—he notes, "many of the stories of Genesis extend over scarcely more than ten verses"[3]—because, in his view, "the earliest story-tellers were not capable of constructing artistic works of any considerable extent; neither could they expect their hearers to follow them with undiminished interest."[4] The longer legend cycles incorporate a number of these shorter pieces, reflecting an increasing narrative sophistication that came when later tellers and hearers had a "more fully developed aesthetic faculty."[5]

Whether or not we agree with Gunkel's quasi-evolutionary account, his observation that the longer narratives of the Bible seem to be consisted of many, much shorter narratives is quite useful to us. The hearer of Genesis is not simply hearing one long story (which is merely the first installment of an even longer story), but many, many short stories as well.

The style of biblical narrative

Stephen Prickett has claimed that, for English and American readers at least, the novel has so influenced our understanding of what literature is that we are surprised to find how little the literature of the Bible actually resembles literature as epitomized by the novel.[6] D. H. Lawrence asserted that "*all* the Bible . . . is one of the supreme old novels"[7] but, as we have just seen, it is *not* one book, *not* one story. It also bears few of the hallmarks of the novel. If the novel is usually concerned with intimate human experience as lived out in realistic and historically identifiable settings over the passage of linear time, and is generally marked by exploration of interior character (often reflected in descriptions of characters' exterior features, mannerisms, actions) and by detailed description of time and place, then the Bible is virtually its antithesis. The narrative of the Bible often describes not individual but national or corporate experience—and often does not report human experience itself but rather the divine perception of human experience. When it does focus on a particular character, however, the biblical narrative seldom gives its reader insight into the character's psychology, perception, motivation, or emotion. Description of social and historical settings is scant; description of characters' physical attributes even rarer.

The Bible's syntax is simple and its vocabulary limited, with prose writers seeming to prefer to repeat a word rather than use a synonym. Biblical conversations tend to be brief and metaphors rare. And yet the narrative effect is very powerful. Robert Alter tells us that "the masters of ancient Hebrew narrative were clearly writers who delighted in an art of indirection, in the possibility of intimating depths through the mere hint of a surface feature, or through a few words of dialogue fraught with implication."[8] Others use words like reticent, laconic, and terse to describe biblical narrative. Little is actually said; much is implied.

In his comparison of Genesis and *The Odyssey*, Erich Auerbach famously described biblical narrative as being "fraught with background." This is particularly true when it comes to characterization. In Homer's epics, virtually nothing is left to the imagination—his audience knows where the characters come from, what they look like, what they want, what they think, whom they adore, and whom they revile. Moreover, the narrator lets us know what to think about all he has described. The Bible, in sharp contrast, is marked not only by a "characteristic refusal of explicit judgment,"[9] but also by a paucity of description—narrative or otherwise. Not only are Biblical characters' physical features are only described if they are salient to the plot, and their personal qualities rarely expressed explicitly.[10] A distinctive feature of biblical narrative is that we develop our understanding of its characters from what they do and say, not from any judgment by or psychological insight from the narrator.

It is to some extent the paucity of detail that generates so much biblical interpretation—and so much biblical fiction. Ancient Jewish and Christian interpreters alike occupied themselves with filling in the gaps in the biblical stories. They fleshed out characters' personalities, supplied missing plot elements, and smoothed out choppy chronologies. We often speak of this creative exegesis as midrash, a term we will encounter again in our consideration of Allegra Goodman and other Jewish American short story writers.

For our purposes, it is the narrative art of the Bible—inflected, as it often seems to be, with poetic qualities—that is of greatest interest as we think about how the biblical style has had an influence on or has strong affinities with the modern short story genre. In *The Art of Biblical Narrative*, Alter characterizes the Hebrew Bible as a type of historiography that he calls historicized prose fiction. Such a characterization, which strips away notions of Scripture and Holy Writ, helps us bring the Bible into closer dialogue with contemporary literature. Alter is attentive to a set of techniques that, in his view, exemplify biblical narration: type scenes and convention, dialogue, repetition, and characterization. Of particular interest for Alter are the moments when the narrative departs from the established norms: What do we make of the omission of an expected element from a type-scene? How does the alteration of key words in a repeated dialogue have an effect on an exchange? How do these contribute to characterization? These are questions that also arise in our readings of contemporary short stories: How does a departure from the anticipated form reveal something about a story's characters or their motivations? We often find ourselves especially interested in what Walter Allen calls the surprise of the short story, the way it gives us what we did not expect.

In the pages ahead, we turn our attention to the narrative art of the biblical short story, in both its longer and its shorter forms. We first explore the Book of Ruth as a short story, reading it in light of contemporary expectations of the genre. We then turn to the parable, an especially compact version of the short story, exploring the literary qualities of the genre generally and the narrative art of the parable of the Prodigal Son in particular.

The short story in the Bible: The Book of Ruth

Many readers have had difficulty knowing what to make of the tiny Book of Ruth. In the Christian Bible, where it is wedged between the stories of the settling of Canaan in Joshua and Judges and the tales of the beginnings of the monarchy in the books of Samuel and Kings, it seems to present itself as a history. In the Jewish Bible, located alongside Esther, Song of Songs, Ecclesiastes, and Lamentations, it is one of the five scrolls read in full as part of the festival calendar. There, in the Jewish liturgical context of the holiday of Shavuot, which celebrates both the barley harvest and the giving of the Ten Commandments, it becomes closely associated with Moses and the law, despite making no overt mention of either.

Set "in the days that the judges ruled" (1:1), Ruth recounts the migration of a family—Elimelech and Naomi and their sons Mahlon and Chilion—from Bethlehem to Moab in order to escape a famine. After a time, Elimelech dies and the two sons take Ruth and Orpah, Moabite women, as wives. When her sons also die, Naomi decides to return to Bethlehem, which is no longer suffering from famine.

Initially both daughters-in-law resolve to follow their mother-in-law, but ultimately, after Naomi attempts to persuade them that she has little to offer the women, Orpah returns to her father's house. Ruth, however, cleaves to her mother-in-law, making a declaration of love and loyalty so powerful it has become a mainstay of wedding ceremonies for both Christians and Jews. "Entreat me not to leave thee, or to return from following after thee," she cried, "for whither thou goest, I will go; and where thou lodgest, I will lodge: thy people shall be my people, and thy God my God: Where thou diest, will I die, and there will I be buried: the Lord do so to me, and more also, if ought but death part thee and me" (1:16-17). Naomi ceases to argue with Ruth and the two proceed to Bethlehem. In a narrative expansion of the law of Levirate marriage,[11] the book foregrounds the interplay between Ruth and Boaz, a kinsman who extends kindness to Ruth by allowing her to glean in his fields. Ruth is surprised by Boaz's decision to help a foreigner in need, but he asserts that he was taken by the kindness she had shown her mother-in-law. He perceives her to be a woman of virtue, in part because she has not sought after younger men. He vows to redeem her (to serve as *goel*) once it is clear that a closer kinsman is not interested in fulfilling his Levirate duty. Boaz and Ruth marry and she gives birth to a son, whose arrival the women of Bethlehem announce, curiously, with the declaration, "A son is born to Naomi." A phrase at the end of the short book identifies this son, Obed, as the father of Jesse, who in turn is the father of [King] David. A genealogy in the final verses explicitly forges links from Perez [son of Judah and Tamar] to David.[12]

Not surprisingly, Ruth conforms perfectly to the conventions of the biblical short story, which are somewhat different from those of its modern counterpart. When reading the book in light of modern definitions of the form, however, we find that it (anachronistically) conforms to many of the modern conventions of the modern genre as well as the ancient. Indeed, in *The Short Story in English,* Walter Allen argues for the short story as a modern form, but does note, "It is not difficult to find stories from the past that approximate to modern stories; the Old Testament story of Ruth is an instance."[13] Is Allen's assessment anomalous? Let us run Ruth through another theorist's framing of the modern form, seeing how it fares in a more circumspect delineation of the genre. In her introduction to

On Writing Short Stories, novelist, essayist, and short story writer Francine Prose offers a much-cited musing of the characteristics of the genre. In sharp contrast to Allen, who readily defines the genre, she thinks that there might be no more difficult question out there than "What makes a short story?"

By Prose's reckoning, "the most obvious answer is the most correct":[14] As discussed in the previous chapter, the short story can be somewhat short (twenty pages, maybe even forty) or very, very short (a page, a paragraph, a single perfect sentence!), but if a short story gets too long (eighty pages, by one accounting) it risks becoming a novella. At four chapters, or eighty-five verses, or about five pages in an English-language devotional Bible, Ruth is decidedly short. So far, so good.

Prose treads carefully forward in her definition, making tentative distinctions between the short story and other forms of fiction—the anecdote, the sketch, the fairy tale, the myth. For each distinction, there is at least a single exception, or perhaps many. Some fairy tales are "as carefully constructed, as densely layered, as elaborated crafted" as the stories of Hawthorne or Poe.[15] Ruth is more sustained, more substantial than an anecdote. Because it is so carefully crafted it transcends its own folkloric beginnings, outstrips the fairy tale literarily. The book perfectly exemplifies Prose's assertion that "unlike most novels, great short stories make us marvel at their integrity, their economy."[16] Short, tight, evocative, even profound: the literary artistry is what sets Ruth apart from so many short tales.

Prose assures us that "this also can be said, of the short story: If we find a way to describe what the story is *really* about, not its plot or its essence, what small or large part of life it has managed to translate onto the page, there is always *something* there—enough to engage us or pique our interest."[17] This condition resonates strongly with Henry James's insistence that the short cannot be a story in the vulgar sense, "it must illustrate something . . . something of the real essence of the subject."[18] So what is Ruth *really* about? Most readers agree that *hesed*—loving-kindness—is the essence of the book.

In Ruth humans and their actions both seem small—they interact with one another on a very local level. But they unfailingly act with *hesed*, one of the book's *Leitworter*, words that are meaningfully repeated throughout a work. It is first mentioned by Naomi, who asks that the Lord display to Ruth and Orpah the *hesed* they have "dealt with the dead and with me" (1:8). Naomi praises Boaz for showing Ruth *hesed* in his concern for her in his fields (2:20). Boaz, who had admired the *hesed* Ruth had shown her mother-in-law, upholds Ruth's "not turn[ing] to younger men" as a form of *hesed* (3:10). As the book moves to its national ending—the birth of King David—we see the transformative power of these small human actions of kindness.

The flow of *hesed* among the three characters brings us to another dimension of the modern short story. Chekhov was concerned that it should not have too many characters: its center of gravity must be in two persons, a him and a her.[19] Prose acknowledges that this rule of thumb is not necessarily true, but that a writer does need limitation, a manageable cast of characters. In this regard, too, Ruth conforms to our modern expectations of the short story. Although there are many actors, they represent different levels of characterization. We find in Ruth, as in much biblical narrative, the type, the agent, and the full-fledged character.[20] The types—the unnamed women of the city and the elders—effectively function as a chorus. Through their deaths, Elimelech and his sons become agents, propelling the motion of the story back to Bethlehem. Likewise, Orpah and Ploni Almoni are also agents, dispensable versions of Ruth and Boaz. As other daughter-in-law, she returns to Moab; as other *goel*, he disappears almost as quickly as he had appeared. Their divergent responses to the same situations faced by Ruth and Boaz heighten our understanding of the full-fledged characters. When we pare all these other figures away, we do not arrive precisely at Chekhov's center of gravity. Rather, the story orbits around two diads:[21] the her-her story of Ruth and Naomi and the her-him story of Ruth and Boaz.

Prose contends that "even the story that lacks a central character should, presumably, limit itself to a single point of view, a controlling intelligence that guides us through the narrative." But then she follows this assertion with the question "Or should it?"[22] Whether or not it should, the Book of Ruth has a controlling intelligence: Ruth herself, the common element in the her-her and the her-him stories. As Christian Brady and others have noted, the narrator constructs the story so that Ruth even drives the action of Boaz and Naomi.

Where we see a shifting of perspective, something of a freeing of Ruth's hold on the story, is in the narrator's reporting of the ways that the different characters understand the role of God in their story.[23] Naomi, in her distress, seems to see the Lord as "a menacing power in her life"[24] who "has made [her] lot very bitter," "has brought [her] back empty," has even "dealt harshly with [her] and ... brought misfortune upon [her]" (1:20-21) As her fortune turns, however, and Ruth returns from the field with grain, she blesses Boaz in the name of YHWH, "who has not failed in His kindness to the living or to the dead!" (2:20). Boaz, by contrast, not only regularly uses figures of speech that mention God ("The Lord be with you!"; "as the Lord lives"), but also understands the Lord to be active in human affairs. He says to Ruth, "May you have a full recompense from the Lord, the God of Israel, under whose wings you have sought refuge!" (2:12) and again "May you be blessed of the Lord, my daughter" (3:10). Ruth pledges herself to the Lord, but it seems she understands him best when his values are manifested by humans. "Your people shall be my people and your God my God," she says to Naomi (2:16). It is as much an expression of total devotion to her mother-in-law as it is to a divine being. Likewise, when Boaz asks that the Lord spread his wings over Ruth, Ruth responds that he should "spread [his] robe over [his] handmaid" (3:9). How each of the characters understands the role of God who is not immanent reveals much about each of them.

The absent but present Creator brings us to one final point about the short story from Prose: "A story creates its own world . . . While reading the story, we enter that world. We feel that everything in it belongs there, and has not been forced on it by its reckless or capricious creator." Here, we can understand "creator" as Prose intends us to—as the author of Ruth, who has, as we have seen clearly, exhibited no recklessness or caprice with his tale. For the reader of Ruth, Prose's next two sentences can also be read as speaking directly about God in the Book of Ruth: "In fact, we tend to forget the creator, who has wound the watch of the story and has vanished from creation. We may feel this world is something like life and at the same time better than life."[25] Much "like life," God does not intervene in the daily goings on of the characters here. But, "better than life" the humans act in his stead, treating one another with kindness, compassion, and mercy.

Prose's not quite final thoughts about the short story seem especially apt in our context: "Everything in the story resonates at its own unique, coherent, and recognizable pitch, along with everything else in the story, creating an effect that Joyce described—quoting Aquinas, and in another context—as 'wholeness, harmony, and radiance.'"[26] Ruth is not merely a near-perfect version of an ancient story, reflecting a former but abandoned aesthetic. Rather, it has fresh currency, appealing to every generation of interpreters. Not just that: it has somehow felt contemporary in every generation. As we have seen in our reading of Ruth, the book achieves what we expect a modern short story to achieve. One can be almost certain that in another century or two, when tastes and expectations have once again shifted, the tiny Book of Ruth will continue to delight its audience. It does not seem naive to imagine that in the years to come, Ruth will continue to speak the language of the contemporary short story, no matter how it comes to be defined. Such is the legacy of its wholeness, harmony, and radiance.

The short-short story in the Bible: The parable

The Gospels acclaim Jesus variously with titles—"the Messiah, the son of David, the son of Abraham" (Mt. 1:1)—and metaphors—"the bread of life," "the light of the world," "the way, the truth, and the life" (Jn 6:35, 8:12, 14:16). They also show him in action as a prophet, a teacher, and a miracle worker. But most intriguingly they depict him as a storyteller who could not only draw a crowd but also keep them riveted: "The same day Jesus went out of the house, and sat by the sea. And great multitudes were gathered together unto him, so that he went into a ship, and sat . . . And he spake many things unto them in parables, saying, Behold, a sower went forth to sow" (Mt. 13.1-3). The Gospels contain thirty-three parables according to a restrictive reckoning, twice that number if figurative analogies in addition to narratives are included in the count.

By etymology, a parable is literally "a throwing beside," a composite of the Greek para- ("alongside") and bole ("a throwing, casting, a beam, a ray"). Parables are often underestimated as simple, one-point short stories designed to illustrate or teach some truth, religious principle, or moral lesson. In Jesus's version of the form, however, they are much trickier (as are those of Kierkegaard and Kafka after him). The story he throws is often a curve ball—more an enigma than an illustration, a problem to be puzzled over, rather than a moral to be learned. Instead of neatly tying things up, his parables often leave the listener with interpretive work to be done. Occasionally, the Gospel writers will have Jesus offer an interpretation that brings closure to a tale that otherwise would stand open-endedly on its own. And so the Evangelist Matthew tells us in chapter 13 what to make of what Jesus otherwise left to the imagination—what the wheat and tares each signify, or who is meant to be understood as seed that falls on rocky ground as distinct from what languishes among thorns.

Sometimes these parables, like those that offer a glimpse of the kingdom of heaven, are "zingers," one-liners that seem meant, like Zen koans, to puzzle or confuse. (How, precisely, is God's reign "like treasure hidden in a field, which someone found and hid; then in his joy he goes and sells all that he has and buys that field"? Isn't this at best shady business?) Others are also short but more fleshed-out narratives that often work against received wisdom, propriety, and even justice. Latecomers to the vineyard receive the same wages as those who have worked in the sun for an entire day; unjust judges and wily stewards become exemplars (but of what?). Such stories seem determined both to mystify and to disturb the peace.

The Gospels give contradictory reasons for Jesus's practice as a storyteller. According to Matthew, his parables were meant to reveal the truth to the multitudes (13:34), whereas Mark says that they were intended to baffle the larger crowd and make sense only to the inner circle of disciples (4:10-12). The Evangelists cite proof texts from the Hebrew Bible that support both understandings, in the former case from the Psalms (78:2), in the latter from Isaiah (6:9-10). The Jewish context is important here. No doubt Jesus spoke in parables not only because he was good at it, but also because doing so was part of Israel's prophetic legacy. Telling difficult stories was part of the calling.

Take, for instance, the stealth tactic of a parable Nathan told when bringing David to his senses in 2 Samuel 12. The king had impregnated a loyal officer's wife and then had him dispatched in battle when he could find no other cover-up for his wrongdoing. At once an adulterer and a murderer, David "displeased the Lord," who prompted Nathan to catch the conscience of the king through the subterfuge of fiction. The prophet's story begins with a comforting "once upon a time" that is designed to lower defenses by engaging the listener in other people's business: "There were two men in a certain city, the one rich and the other poor." In the short narrative that unfolds we hear of a rich man who has everything, who selfishly demands that the pauper hand over his most beloved possession, a little ewe lamb "that was like a daughter to him." Hearing of this injustice, David is incensed. The parable immediately overtakes him; he enters its world and, taking it for truth, cries out for justice. "He said to Nathan, 'As the Lord lives, the man who has done this deserves to die.'" Once those irate words are spoken, however, Nathan tears away the veil of his fiction—the trap he artfully set—so that David is left with the consequences of his own malediction. "Nathan said to David, 'You are the man!'" Like the play in *Hamlet*, the parable holds up a mirror that reveals the errant king to himself.

The most famous of Jesus's parables—commonly known as those of the Good Samaritan and the Prodigal Son—are stories considerably more developed than Nathan's tale of two men; nonetheless, they also work in brief compass to disarm their audience and elicit a personal response. They serve, that is, a heuristic purpose: how you react to them reveals a great deal about who you are. Take the parable of the Good Samaritan. In Lk. 10:25-37, when Jesus is asked by an expert in the Law what the man must do to inherit eternal life, he answers with a summary of the Law as found in Deut. 6:5 and Lev. 19:18: love God with all your heart, soul, and strength, "and your neighbor as yourself." "And who is my neighbor?" the scribe then asks. Jesus's reply is pointed but indirect: a story that describes a crisis and the response of three individuals.

"A man was going down from Jerusalem to Jericho, and fell into the hands of robbers, who stripped him, beat him, and went away, leaving him half dead." Two religious authorities associated with the Jerusalem Temple, a priest and a Levite, show no compassion to their fellow Jew but step out of the way and simply pass him by. A third man, however, is moved with pity and spends both time and money to see to the victim's well-being. What is surprising is that the friend in need turns out to be a Samaritan, a "foreigner" traditionally estranged from Jews and their Temple, and therefore not likely to come to the rescue.

Returning to the lawyer's opening question at the conclusion of the tale—"Who is my neighbor?"—Jesus asks him in conclusion, "Which of these three, do you think, was a neighbor to the man who fell into the hands of the robbers?" The answer is clear, "The one who showed him mercy." So too is the challenge that Jesus poses at the end of the encounter: "Go and do likewise." Thus the story reverses the expectations that a lawyer might be expected to have of priests and scribes, on the one hand, and Samaritans, on the other. A neighbor is not defined by identity but by action. Pious co-religionists show no mercy, but a heretic is a cup that overflows with *hesed*, loving-kindness.

When Jesus tells the parable of the Prodigal Son in Luke 15, he is not responding to an earnest man's question, but rather to a controversy regarding his own piety. Pharisees and scribes take issue with his flagrant consorting with those whose company would, by the standards of their shared religion, pollute him: "This man receiveth sinners, and eateth with them." He then responds to what Luke calls their "murmuring" with three parables that suggest how one might treat lovingly those who are "lost" rather than merely condemning them. A shepherd risks all ninety-nine of his flock for the sake of a single stray; a woman lights a lamp and sweeps her house in search of a silver coin she has misplaced from a cache of ten. In both cases, the story ends with rejoicing. "Likewise," says Jesus after each tale, "there is joy in the presence of the angels of God over one sinner that repenteth."

A third story continues the sequence but alters it as well: it avoids the happy, religious endings that transpose the safe return of sheep and coin into the joy of heaven. Like the beginning of Nathan's parable ("There were two men in one city"), Jesus's opening line gives his listeners the expectation of fiction, a once-upon-a-time in which "A certain man had two sons." Given the problematic history of siblings in the Hebrew Bible—Cain and Abel, Ishmael and Isaac, Jacob and Esau, Joseph and his older brothers—surely a problem will follow. And so it does: the younger son recklessly asks for his inheritance prematurely, before his father's death. There is nothing in the mores of the ancient world that justifies such a request; it is meant to come as a shock. But almost as surprising is the fact that, immediately upon request, the father gives his younger son the share of the property that should only eventually be his.

The windfall, however, does not lead the young man to make careful investment or indeed any prudent move; instead, it launches him into ruin in a "far country" where he ends up scrounging for food in the company of pigs. This downward spiral—"And he fain would have filled his belly with the husks that the swine did eat"— seems inevitable; so, too, does his decision to return home, where even under the worst circumstances of embarrassment and shame he can at least expect to receive regular meals among his father's hired hands. A canny speech is rehearsed that rings the changes on repentance: "'I will arise and go to my father and I will say unto him, 'Father, I have sinned against heaven and before thee; And am no more worthy to be called thy son: make me as one of thy hired servants.'"

When he finally makes it home and begins his speech, however, his father cuts him off with an outpouring of generosity that runs against all expectation or desert. There is a rushing forward, a paternal kiss and embrace; presents are lavished and a party arranged. Using resonant language that soars above the specificity of shoes, robes, and fatted calves, the father makes clear what is ultimately at stake: "For this son of mine was dead and is alive again; he was lost and is found."

The story might well end at this high point—like the parables of lost sheep and coin—but it does not. Instead, focus shifts to the elder son who was lost sight of after the opening line. He is clearly another type altogether, as earnest and diligent as his brother is irresponsible. He is also filled with rage when he learns of the fuss being made over the wastrel who has come home after (or so he surmises) devouring valuable property "with harlots." He notes the gifts that, despite his exemplary behavior, he has never received, the family "living" he has only tended, never wasted. Most of all he registers the injustice of the homecoming festivity, the extravagant welcome for a ne'er-do-well brother whom he will identify to his father only as "this son of thine."

After leaving the feast to search out his firstborn, the father might well have turned on his heels and left the naysayer to stew in indignation. Instead, he opens a door of communication between the two of them just as he did with the returning prodigal. He calls him "son" (*teknon*, child or beloved boy), reminds him not only of the constancy of their unbroken relationship but also of the full extent of the inheritance that awaits him in future ("all that is mine is yours"). Finally, and with an unmistakable echo of words spoken earlier to the household at large, he insists on the importance of joy, of remembering the stakes that are the highest of all—life and death, loss and recovery.

If we take the parable out of its Gospel setting, separate it from the other parables of lost sheep and coin, and view it apart from Jesus's controversy with the Pharisees, what does this intricately constructed short story give us merely on its own? On the simplest level, it is a domestic tale of father and sons, of a single parent and sibling rivalry. The sons are predictable enough in their opposition, embodying as they do the night and day contrasts we recognize in fiction as in life. ("There are two kinds of people in the world.") But it is the father, who serves as the fulcrum between the oppositions, who is truly remarkable. One thinks of his lack of interest in hearing his younger son's extended apology, his patience with the elder's insults and complaints, the way he refuses to deal with anything less than the biggest picture: loss and recovery, death and life.

Other features of the story may come into view thanks to the way we have been instructed by the insights of literary criticism. A feminist would note the absence of a mother in the story, and the extraordinary degree to which the patriarch of this family seems to embody so many of the values we commonly identify as matriarchal or feminine. It is also important to attend to the economic realities at play here, to note issues of property and inheritance, of the elder brother's singular status in a world of primogeniture, the significance of luxury goods (like rings, shoes, and fatted calves), the way possessions broker position and confer status.

The parable also owes an evident debt to the Hebrew Bible, to Genesis in particular, not only in the tension between siblings as well as between fathers and sons, but also in the contested issue of blessing—who gets it and who does not. Yet Jesus's story can be seen as a biblical fiction not only in its deployment of general themes but also in a specific detail that links the father's rush to embrace and kiss the returning prodigal to a moment in the Jacob saga. In Genesis 33, we find Jacob, on the lam, returning to Canaan twenty years after his hasty departure under cloak of night. Now in daylight, he has every reason to fear a reunion with his brother Esau, his older twin, from whom he gained a birthright under dubious circumstances and deviously stole a paternal blessing intended for the firstborn. And yet, instead of fraternal recrimination what greets him on return is the spontaneous, unmerited expression of love. "And Esau ran to meet him, and embraced him, and fell on his neck and kissed him: and they wept" (4). All that Jacob can do in response is realize that his brother's welcome has moved beyond the merely human: "therefore," he tells Esau, "I have seen your face, as though I had seen the face of God" (10).

Does the parable in looking back to this moment in Genesis—and with it a complex backstory of family drama interwoven with divine purpose—likewise bring the reader to an experience of God's presence? Indeed, where precisely does it bring us? If the parable can be said to have any resolution, it takes place only in a hypothetical future *after* the narrative ends. The father issues a pardon to both his sons that is unconditional, that offers a new light in which it may be possible to see everything afresh. Pardon flows from the father's largesse and comes without strings: it can only be accepted or rejected. The question that hovers implicitly at the end of the tale, however, is what either son will make of what the father gives. It remains to be seen—in the imagination of listener or reader—whether any negotiated settlement of forgiveness can take place between the brothers. What will it actually mean for the prodigal to be welcomed back with such graciousness, not as a hireling with limited responsibilities but as a son given another chance? Will pardon inspire him to undertake the hard work of deserving forgiveness? And what about the elder brother: Can he reinvent his own place in the family, not as beleaguered drudge but as what he's been called, *teknon*, "beloved boy"? Will the one son grow in depth, the other in generosity? What is the chance that "forgivingness" will prevail in the end—that is, in the present participle, work-in-progress disposition to forgive in the face of human frailty?

Given the narrative frame of Luke 15, with its fractious double audience of saints and sinners, it seems inevitable that Luke's Jesus intended his listeners to raise such questions, and in answering them, to repent either of shallow contrition or of lingering resentment. If so, then the parable serves to force everyone to come to terms with him- or herself. If you join the feast, whoever you are, what will *you* need to become once you are there? What will those pardoned need to take on, and what will the offended need to give up?

Although the parable has long been identified as the prodigal's story, it is the elder son (and behind him, the scribes and Pharisees) who bears the heavier burden. It is right to rejoice, says the father, but to do so is finally to make a decision. Heaven rejoices over those who come home, tax collectors and sinners though they be; but one must choose to feast with them—or not. So it is in Shakespeare's *Twelfth Night*, when in the closing scene of the play, music and dancing bring together unlikely people in a reconfigured community. Everyone is given another chance to reconcile and live anew, but not everyone joins in. Like Malvolio, the elder brother of the parable may refuse "present mirth" and cling to the notion that he has, in fact, been "notoriously abused." He may cry out, as well, "I'll be revenged on the whole pack of you!". To call for revenge, however, would be to fall into a version of the same "death" that befell the prodigal when he chose the far country over his own home. It would represent another kind of famine, another bout with starvation.

Being willing to eat together after all that has taken place may in fact be the "point" of the parable. The story itself does not work out the terms of reconciliation that true "forgivingness" entails; it does not offer a philosophical exploration, and it lacks the specificity of injunctions about whom to forgive, or how to do so. Instead, Luke's Jesus conjures a fiction in which a *pater familias* forgives both his sons without conditions. In doing so, he gives each an opportunity to become either more responsible or more gracious than he has been until now. In the face of loss and death, he offers the possibility of a new life that can yet be discovered if everyone at odds comes into the feast. Once there, the gathered community will have to work with the prodigal to determine how he is to be reintegrated into the world he abandoned so rashly. The elder son will have to figure out if nurtured grievances against father and brother are worth holding onto, or whether they might in the end actually be manifestations of inflated self-regard that is best let go of, even repented. Hence the urgency of the father's final plea to his firstborn, as if to say: clinging to resentment is a way to die alone, but "forgivingness" is a way to go on living together.[27]

******

A small family drama with implications as large as loss and restoration, life and death: the Gospel parable of the Prodigal Son builds on biblical narrative from the Hebrew Scriptures and in turn inspires a host of later stories. Augustine and Dante were early inheritors, sharing the notion of a protagonist who, like the younger son, is lost in a "far country" of existential disorientation—the "region of unlikeness" of Augustine's *Confessions* and the *Inferno's* "*selva oscura*". The tale of sibling rivalry continues to be played out over the centuries. Poets have drawn on it for inspiration, as with Rilke in "The Departure of the Prodigal Son" and Lea Goldberg in her poem cycle "The Prodigal Son." The parable underlies classic novels like Dickens's *Great Expectations* and Willa Cather's *My Antonia,* and more recent ones like Anne Tyler's *A Spool of Blue Thread.* In terms of short stories, we explore it in Tobias Wolff's "The Rich Brother." Others have identified it in James Baldwin's "Sonny's Blues," which James Tackach describes as having a "biblical foundation."[28] At its heart are the conflicts of Cain and Abel, Ishmael and Isaac, and the elder and younger brothers of Jesus's parable. As is true of the Bible as a whole, Jesus's sibling short story keeps on being retold. It would seem that a man *always* has two sons.

4

Flannery O'Connor

Fresh from the University of Iowa's Writers Workshop, a sojourn at the Yaddo colony, and a spell in New York City, Flannery O'Connor set out to be a novelist. On that score she would succeed twice, with *Wise Blood* (1952) and *The Violent Bear It Away* (1960). And yet after her diagnosis of lupus—the disease that claimed her father and dictated the circumstances of her life from 1950 until her death in 1964—the novel demanded a great deal more sustained energy than she could readily marshall during the carefully guarded three hours of her working day. O'Connor's descriptions of that effort are at once painful and characteristically funny. "I suppose that half of writing is overcoming the revulsion you feel when you sit down to it. All through the middle section of this last novel [*The Violent Bear It Away*] I had to wade through tides of revulsion every day. It's the curse of any long piece of work" (HB 368).[1]

Short stories came easier—they also reveal her true genius as a writer—so that she sometimes turned to them for relief when a novel was at an impasse: "Before Christmas I couldn't stand it any longer so I began a short story. It's like escaping from the penitentiary" (HB 127). Some of them required more time and creative energy than others. It took her only four days' work on "Good Country People," for instance, as opposed to two or three months on "The Artificial Nigger" (HB 160). Both, however, were quick studies compared to the five years devoted to her first novel and the seven to her second.

Quite apart from the burden of her illness, writing itself was hard labor, as she confided to an aspiring storyteller, Betty Hester, known as "A" in her collected letters, *The Habit of Being*. Apart from the two characters that came to her effortlessly—Enoch Emery (*Wise Blood*) and Hulga ("Good Country People")—"the rest has been pushing a stone uphill with my nose" (HB 241). That said, it was her short fiction that by and large gave her joy, affording the confidence she needed to get on with the novels she seemed to take more seriously and value more highly. To mentor and critic Robie Macauley, she wrote after her first collection, *A Good Man Is Hard to Find* (1955), "I am certainly glad you like the stories because now I feel it's not bad to like them so much. The truth is I like them better than anybody and I read them over and over and laugh and laugh, then get embarrassed when I remember I was the one who wrote them. Unlike *Wise Blood*, they were relatively painless to me; but now I have to stop quite enjoying life and get on with the second novel" (HB 80–81).

These confessions from the trenches, candidly personal and often comic, are quite different in tone from the grander reflections found in her essays, most of them worked up from lectures given at colleges and universities posthumously published in *Mystery and Manners* (1969): "For those of us who want to get the agony over in a hurry, the novel is a burden and a pain" (MM 76). The short story makes its demands as well. There is no lingering in the telling, no space for relaxed enlargement when the narrative is "concentrated and circumscribed" (HB 183): "The short story requires more drastic procedures than the novel because more has to be accomplished in less space. The details have to carry more weight" (MM 70). "Less" has to work harder and faster to say "more."

******

In her critical reflections on the art of fiction, O'Connor emphasized the importance of the specific, of fact rather than idea or sentiment. She spoke in particular about the kind of detail that gathers meaning over the course of a story so that gradually an image becomes a symbol— an image, action, or event that moves the reader from surface to depth, from the limited to the limitless. One thinks of the wooden leg in "Good Country People" that starts out as the distinctive feature of Hulga's outward appearance, along with her "yellow sweat shirt with a faded cowboy on a horse embossed upon it" (276); in short order it becomes a way of representing the complexity of her character and motivations. The sweatshirt is a detail that brings a character into view; the wooden leg, however, is an outward and visible sign that expresses an inward and spiritual condition.

O'Connor was especially interested in the symbolic role that a specific gesture could play: the touch of the Grandmother's outstretched hand on the Misfit's shoulder ("A Good Man is Hard to Find"), the impact of a book thrown across a crowded room ("Revelation"), the arc of a swung pocket book that resolutely hits its mark ("Everything That Rises Must Converge"). But gestures need not be motion; they could be static, like the "plaster figure of a Negro" placed incongruously on a city lawn in "The Artificial Nigger." This racist garden "ornament" mesmerizes two warring characters who find themselves standing dumbly before it as miraculously it effects their reconciliation: "They stood gazing at the artificial Negro as if they were faced with some great mystery, some monument to another's victory that brought them together in their common defeat. They could both feel it dissolving their differences like an action of mercy" (269). This figure appears after a series of derogatory references to color that run through the story in rapid succession—a "heart of darkness" that threatens to engulf the two protagonists. But then without warning, the statue's grotesque rendering of blackness—with its one eye white and piece of brown watermelon in hand, the figure "pitched forward at an unsteady angle" (268)— transforms those negative references and makes peace between the two characters. Its travesty is transcended: what had been despised and rejected, the bad joke of a racist cliché, by the story's end becomes a monument to an unnamed other's "victory," a "great mystery," an "action of mercy."

O'Connor spoke of "the redemptive quality of the Negro's suffering for us all" (HB 78),[2] but never expanded upon the assertion; nor did she explicitly identify the ludicrous "artificial Negro" with what St. Paul (1 Cor. 1) speaks of as the "foolishness" of the cross. Much is left between the lines, made present only by inference and association. And yet, given the theological context of the story that blossoms in its closing section—as O'Connor noted, "I have practically gone from the Garden of Eden to the Gates of Paradise" (HB 78)—it does not seem far-fetched to see the statue with its "wild look of misery" (268) as gesturing toward the Man of Sorrows: "Despised and the most abject of men, a man of sorrows, and acquainted with infirmity . . . wounded for our iniquities . . . bruised for our sins: the chastisement of our peace was upon him, and by his bruises we are healed" (Isaiah 53:3–5, Douay–Rheims).

*****

O'Connor emphasized that any writer who wanted to move toward the symbolic had first to do "the highest possible justice to the visible world" (MM 80). This gnomic phrase came to her from Joseph Conrad, one of her literary heroes along with Nathaniel Hawthorne, Henry James, and Edgar Allen Poe (HB 78–79).[3] It was a charge to attend carefully to the particular by making readers stare and puzzle at a setting or event until more was discerned than the merely apparent.[4] To this end some lines she found in Conrad's preface to *The Nigger of the "Narcissus"* came to serve as her own mantra: "My task which I am trying to achieve is, by the power of the written word, to make you hear, to make you feel—it is above all, to make you *see*" (MM 80).

But if vivid description of the visible is essential to any writer, it is not the ultimate goal for someone with designs on the ineffable. For such storytellers, rendering the visible in fiction is always at the service of what "eye hath not seen, nor ear heard" (Isa 64:4, 1 Cor 2:9), something beneath the surface of the story or beyond its near horizon—an "added dimension" (MM 150) that points to the "eternal and absolute" (MM 27). Like Hawthorne in his romances, O'Connor wanted her stories to "lean away from typical social patterns" toward "deeper kinds of realism" (MM 39–40).[5] The natural needed to shade into the supernatural.

To make this transition from earth to heaven, the writer must keep in mind two distinct but related geographies. First, it was necessary to establish a literal countryside of landscape and custom, a world of recognizable manners "grounded in concrete, observable reality" (MM 148). This realistic foreground came easily to O'Connor thanks to the acute skills of observation honed as a college cartoonist[6] and amply on display in her wry Milledgeville letters about life on the farm. Aside from observation, she also drew on a literary tradition of Middle Georgia humor, with its "comic escapades of rural Southern folk, often in conflict with city slickers."[7]

Recognizable manners, however, were meant ultimately to give way to mystery, to suggest a "True Country" that, although not immediately visible, is never cut off from what can be seen. She looked for spirit incarnate in local flesh, blood, and Georgia red clay. In her own narratives, O'Connor thought what pointed the way from one country to the other was often a gesture:

> I often ask myself what makes a story work, and what makes it hold up as a story, and I have decided that it is probably some action, some gesture of a character that is unlike any other in the story, one which indicates where the real heart of the story lies. This would have to be an action or gesture which was both totally right and totally unexpected; it would have to be one that was both in character and beyond character; it would have to suggest both the world and eternity. The action or gesture I'm talking about would have to be on the anagogical level, that is, the level which has to do with the Divine life and our participation in it. It would have to be a gesture that transcended any neat allegory that might have been intended or any pat moral categories a reader could make. It would be a gesture that somehow made contact with mystery (MM 111).

This description of what makes a story "work"—a gesture that makes contact with mystery—was partly a word of advice to aspiring writers; it was also her defense against what she took to be the misinterpretation of her early critics. Reviewers said that she "looked on life as a horror story" (HB 85), that her work was "technically expert but spiritually empty" (HB 108). She felt plagued by "idiot readers" who thought she was a "hillbilly nihilist" (HB 81), or a Catholic who failed to give spiritual uplift or answers to life's problems.

What she intended—as we know from the hindsight provided by *Mystery and Manners* and *The Habit of Being*—was something altogether different from what others often found in her work, or indeed wanted from her: "All my stories are about the action of grace on a character who is not very willing to support it, but most people think of these stories as hard, hopeless, brutal, etc." (HB 275). She wrote everything, she maintained, "from the perspective of Catholic orthodoxy" (HB 147); her first collection was made up of "nine stories about original sin" (HB 68). Her aim was to present encounters with "the God of Abraham, Isaac, and Jacob, and not the God of the philosophers and scholars" (MM 161). If she incorporated violent actions and gestures, therefore, it was to show the impact of grace on characters resistant to change, let alone salvation. Others might woo readers; she would use shock and awe for the sake of the kingdom of heaven.[8]

Take the climactic moment of "A Good Man Is Hard to Find."[9] When in the story's closing pages, the addled Grandmother suddenly touches the Misfit's shoulder, she identifies him not as a killer but as kin: "Why you're one of my babies! You're one of my own children!"[10] This move seemingly comes out of nowhere, perhaps brought on by delirium and the fact that the Misfit is wearing her son's distinctive shirt. Her mistake can be understood, in fact, without an "added dimension" at all; it is completely comprehensible if unforeseen and counterintuitive. But however the old woman's intentions are to be understood, what matters is what happens next. Her gesture has an immediate and lethal consequence: she is shot three times through the chest and her corpse thrown unceremoniously on top of those of her family. Bloodshed wins the day. At the story's end, there would seem to be no exit from life as a horror story.

And yet, although a careful reading does not resolve the enigma of the Grandmother's motives, it suggests what her touch may have effected—a subtle change in the Misfit that marks at least an interruption of his business as usual. It may also hint at something more. Earlier, he spoke about Jesus passionately in the Either/Or way that O'Connor herself favored: "He thrown everything off balance. If He did what He said, then it's nothing for you to do but throw away everything and follow him, and if He didn't then it's nothing for you to do but enjoy the few minutes you got left the best way you can—by killing somebody or burning down his house or doing some other meanness to him" (132). What he chooses is the pleasure of killing, and not only "somebody" but an entire family. And yet he is in some complex way "touched" by the feel of the Grandmother's hand on his shoulder. He is frightened, his recoil "as if a snake had bitten him," is an attempt to preserve life as he has known it, as someone who does not fit in. Hearing himself declared one of her own children—her baby—he is dramatically thrown "off balance."

Whereas once he could say there was "No pleasure but meanness," by the story's final line he has lost everything, even this joy. For him there is now "No pleasure in life" (133). He is left with nothing, which, in the paradoxical world of O'Connor's fiction, may actually be the beginning of something previously unimaginable.

At least this is what she wanted the reader to believe. From her now-published comments on this story, we know that she saw it not reaching a dead end but rather presenting the possibility of there being a door ajar, a next step. The Misfit's loss might well become a discovery: "I prefer to think, however unlikely this may seem, that the old lady's gesture, like the mustard-seed, will grow to be a great crow-filled tree in the Misfit's heart, and will be enough of a pain to him there to turn him into the prophet he was meant to become. But that is another story" (MM 112–13).

*****

"Like the mustard seed." The reference here is to one of Jesus's shorter parables (Matt. 13:31–32): "The kingdom of heaven is like to a grain of a mustard seed, which a man took, and sowed in his field: Which is the least indeed of all seeds: but when it is grown up, it is greater than all herbs, and becometh a tree, so that the birds of the air come, and dwell in the branches thereof."[11] O'Connor's appropriation of this text reveals her sensibility at work, as the parable's lofty "birds of the air" become a familiar flock of local crows. Unlike the birds that have their place in the Gospels—sparrow, rooster, dove, or a hen and her chicks—there are no crows in the world of the New Testament. They are, however, common in the author's Georgia. She surely knew them first hand, for undoubtedly there were not only peacocks that roosted in the trees of her farm.

In using this parable of the kingdom to suggest that there might be a spiritual afterlife for the Misfit as well as yet another tale to be told, O'Connor may also be alluding to her own vocation as a short-story teller. The mustard seed starts out tiny, "the least of all seeds," but grows to be so great a tree that "the birds of the air come, and lodge in the branches thereof." In this regard, it is like the stories O'Connor cultivated against all odds and which she mastered with such brilliance—all of them growing from small to large, each striving to present "moments of mystics expansion" (to recall Steven

Millhauser's "Ambition of the Short Story") "when the macrocosmic flower bursts from the microcosmic seed."

Offhand biblical references like this recollection of the mustard seed parable are not uncommon in O'Connor's prose. In a letter to Andrew Lytle, she recalls a specific biblical narrative when speaking about her desire to do something new in her work. She knew she had mastered the violence of grace in its assault against evil; indeed, this combat had become a trademark. "At the same time I keep seeing Elias in the cave [1 Kings 19:11–13], waiting to hear the word of the Lord in the thunder and lightning and wind, and only hearing it finally in the gentle breeze, that I feel that I have to be able to do that sooner or later, or anyway keep trying" (HB 373). Even without the burden of discovering a new strategy in her storytelling, she knew that writing per se meant wrestling with forces greater than herself. As she told a Georgetown audience with an allusion to Genesis 32:22–32, the storyteller was "like Jacob with the angel, until he has extracted a blessing" (MM 198).

Scripture was central to her imaginary, an aspect of her mother tongue. It came to her early, in church, where as a daily Mass-going Catholic she encountered both Testaments through the "bits and pieces" of Bible that appeared in the liturgy (MM 203). But other Mass-goers—certainly the overwhelming majority—were not as "totally dependent" on the Bible as she. It did not penetrate their consciousness or condition how they understood their experience (MM 203). They might well have committed the catechism's definition of faith to memory, she observed, but were not haunted by the fear and trembling of Genesis 22 or likely to imagine themselves standing with "Abraham as he held the knife over Isaac" (MM 203). She could.

No doubt this was because, as a writer, she had a greater susceptibility to the power of biblical narrative and metaphor than the Catholic rank and file; it may also have been because in addition to attending Mass, she was also a serious student of Scripture. Inventories of her personal library show that she had a well-marked Douay–Rheims version of the Latin Bible as well as the contemporary Ronald Knox translation.[12] There were also works of biblical criticism on her shelves, a number of which she reviewed for two diocesan publications, the *Bulletin* and the *Southern Cross*, as well as for other

Catholic journals.[13] Although by no means a scholar, she nonetheless had scholarly interests. After reading Karl Barth's *Word of God in Words of Men*, she found it "very enlightening" to learn about the trials of biblical scholars in the late nineteenth century: "It's certainly easier to be a Bible reader in 1962 than in 1904" (HB 480).

She wanted other people to be Bible readers as well. She encouraged a nun to pursue a writing project that would assist her order to "read, mark, learn and inwardly digest" the liturgically assigned texts that they might otherwise not pay attention to: "I thought it was good for her and good in general for the sisters to get interested in the Bible" (HB 549). Toward the end of her life, when asked for reading recommendations, she replied, "I don't read anything but the newspaper and the Bible. If everybody else did that it would be a better world" (HB 574).

Therefore, her confession of deficient biblical literacy—"I am plagued by my ignorance of the Old Testament" (HB 145)—rings untrue. (Like other protestations of ignorance, it was no doubt a ploy and a game; at times she enjoyed playing dumb.) She was pleased to acknowledge George Clay's observation that the best of her work "sounded like the Old Testament would sound if it were being written today—in as much (partly) as the character's relation is directly with God rather than with other people" (HB 111). She even placed herself, though sheepishly and indirectly, within a canonical tradition: "The Lord doesn't speak to the novelist as he did to his servant Moses, mouth to mouth. He speaks to him as he did to those complainers, Aaron and Aaron's sister, Mary: through dreams and visions, in fits and starts, and by all the lesser and limited ways of the imagination" (MM 181).

*****

In addition to these scattered revelations, O'Connor articulated more fully what the Bible meant to her in a 1963 lecture given at Georgetown University and later published in *Mystery and Manners* as "The Catholic Writer in the Protestant South." In it she named the two most formative influences on her vocation as a writer, the American South and the Roman Catholic Church. They were birthrights—both the "pure whiskey and coffin and Bible land" region that had famously Lost the War (HB 359) and the religion that gave her the deepest source of identity. From church she got her theology and religious practice; from the region she received not only the particular idiom and landscape of rural Georgia but also an exposure to fundamentalist Protestantism. Because this was not her own faith tradition, its world came to her secondhand from farm workers, neighbors, and the much-relished newspaper reports of Evangelists and their doings.[14] But if not properly speaking her own world, she appropriated it with gusto. Were she not a Catholic, she said, she would not be the next best thing, an Episcopalian, but rather a "holiness Pentecostal."[15]

Apart from the furious excesses we see in many of her fictional true-believers—Mrs. Shortley ("The Displaced Person"), Lucy Carmody (*The Violent Bear It Away*), Rufus Johnson ("The Lame Shall Enter First")—she respected the firmly held convictions of Fundamentalist Christians, especially their belief in a "living God," and in the reality and impact of the supernatural on everyday life. She differed with them radically when it came to the nature of the Church and the question of authority. She was, after all, someone who asked permission to read books on the Index. Nonetheless, she found herself accepting "the same fundamental doctrines of sin and redemption and judgment that they do" (HB 350). For her as for them, Jesus Saves.

With Fundamentalists, moreover, she found more than bedrock Christianity, a shared belief in "the nature of God and our obligation to him" (HB 518). There was also the sheer vitality and all-or-nothing theatrics of their rural religion. Unlike her Catholic coreligionists, about whom she confessed an inability to write well, these country Protestants "express their beliefs in diverse kinds of dramatic action which is obvious enough for me to catch" (HB 517). H. L. Mencken had famously named the South "The Bible Belt" and scorned the flamboyant ignorance of the "Sahara of the Bozarts." O'Connor would have none of this. For her the Bible Belt was golden. She may have been critical from a theological point of view of its "extreme individualism" (MM 206), but not as a writer. In her attempt to address the invincible ignorance of her secular readership, she did not hesitate to practice evangelical zeal in her own way: "to the hard of hearing you shout, and for the almost-blind you draw large and startling figures" (MM 34).[16]

The sawdust trail was a path she was happy to travel down, at least in her fiction. It everywhere bears witness to this embrace: fire and brimstone preachers, child evangelists, theological disputes, blessings and curses, river baptisms, and the roadside piety documented so well in the photographs of Sam Fentress's *Bible Road: Signs of Faith in the American Landscape.*[17] Throughout her fictional landscape there are "signs nailed on the pine trees: DOES SATAN HAVE YOU IN ITS POWER/ REPENT OR BURN IN HELL. JESUS SAVES" ("The Lame Shall Enter First," 450–51).

O'Connor felt privileged to live among these same pine trees, particularly because the territory was underwritten by the Bible. She rejoiced in a region that found in Scripture a story "of mythic dimensions, one which belongs to everybody, one in which everybody is able to recognize the hand of God and its descent, in a region where belief could be made believable" (MM 202). Many of her characters, of course, give it only lip service. Like Mrs. Hopewell in "Good Country People," they may protest, "I keep my Bible by my bedside," but in truth, "It was in the attic somewhere" (278). Likewise, the Bible salesman in that story is all hypocrisy: "'I hope you don't think,' he said in a lofty indignant tone, 'that I believe in that crap! I may sell Bibles but I know which end is up and I wasn't born yesterday and I know where I'm going'" (290). Disbelief in all its banality coexists with the passion of those who proclaim with uppercase conviction, and at any opportunity, THE WAGES OF SIN IS DEATH (Rom. 6:23).

O'Connor relished the mixture. "A half-hour's ride in this region" took her from places where life has a distinctly Old Testament flavor to places where life might be considered post-Christian. Yet all these varied situations "can be seen in one glance and heard in one conversation" (MM 209). She celebrated the fact that in the South the Scriptures were held close not primarily by educated believers like herself, let alone by those who read the Bible "as literature," but by common people with no particular standing or cultivated point of view: "When the poor hold the sacred history in common, they have ties to the universal and holy, which allows the meaning of their every action to be heightened and seen under the aspect of eternity." In the South, moreover, "belief can still be made believable, even if for the modern mind it cannot be made admirable" (MM 203): "What has given the South her identity are those beliefs and qualities which she has absorbed from the Scriptures and from her own history of defeat and violation: a distrust of the abstract, a sense of human dependence on the grace of God, and a knowledge that evil is not simply a problem to be solved, but a mystery to be endured" (MM 209).

*****

Granted that, as O'Connor maintained in "The Catholic Novelist in the Protestant South," it "takes a story to make a story" (MM 202)—and granted that the Bible offered the Greatest Story Ever Told for those who, like her, were after "Christian Realism" (HB 92)—a question nonetheless remained: How might a contemporary writer produce work that was in some way "scriptural"? Although she eschewed the how-to approach, on several occasions she offered advice, as when in both lecture and letter she recommended medieval biblical exegesis as a model for writers (MM 72–73, HB 468–69). She thought that the way the Bible had been read for centuries could help a storyteller tell a tale. There was a literal or historical "sense" to the narrative, but (in the words of Gregory the Great) "every time the sacred text describes a fact it reveals a mystery" (MM 184). Or, for the exegete of Scripture, three different kinds of mystery: the moral, the allegorical, and the anagogical. The latter has "to do with the Divine life and our participation in it" (HB 469). This third *sensus* or level of meaning was the one that most interested her. It pointed to the True Country the writer could glimpse when limning the features of a literal countryside—an eternal realm concealed within the works of time.[18]

Dante made explicit reference to this same exegetical model in order to inform readers that his *Commedia* was "polysemous": like the Bible, the literal level of his poetic text had multiple meanings to be discerned. Without pretending to be in the same league as Dante[19]—or to be writing for an age that, like his, could envision "the image at the heart of things" (MM 186)—O'Connor believed that her fiction also had an anagogical function. It too aimed to explore "the Divine life and our participation in it" in order to give "an enlarged view of the human scene" (MM 72–73). But whereas Dante could present the image of the heart of things by leading his readers to the beatific vision of God at the end of his journey through the Catholic afterlife, O'Connor could not even come close to that trajectory. She never left the earth behind, and the visions she afforded her characters were more sporadic than beatific. Her own divine comedy was at best a matter of "fits and starts"—no heavenly rose but only a reflection of "our broken condition and, through it, the face of the devil we are possessed by" (MM 68).

*****

There are many ways that the Bible itself, and not only the medieval exegesis she recommended to other writers, helped O'Connor toward her goal.[20] Sometimes the bare minimum of a single text could blossom like the mustard seed. In "Good Country People," for instance, a composite of Matthew 10:39 and 16:25 is invoked at the beginning of the story by Manley Pointer, the phony Bible salesman who hopes only to make a sale. "'He who losest his life shall find it,' he said simply and he was so sincere, so genuine and earnest that Mrs. Hopewell would not for the world have smiled" (280).

This verse reappears later on, in paraphrase, in a context where Jesus's deadly serious words inspire not only a smile but also a wince. Thinking to seduce the salesman huckster, Hulga aims to convert this exemplar of the story's Good Country People to her own rigorous nihilism. The hayloft in which the pair end up is meant to be her classroom and Manley Pointer her student. And yet, as is so often the case in folktales, the would-be trickster is soundly tricked, in this case by a man who has improbable designs on her and a fixation on the wooden leg that had long been the key to her identity. With an insight that draws her to him, he says, "It's what makes you different. You ain't like anybody else" (288). Capitulating to his desire to detach the leg and hold it in his own hands, Hulga—allegedly nobody's fool, and with a PhD in philosophy to boot—becomes something like the village idiot. In her surrendering to him completely, the narrator tells us in words that evoke Harlequin romances as well as Scripture, "It was like losing her own life and finding it again, miraculously, in his" (289).

The story's two references to the Matthew text—the first an insincere quotation, the second a fantasized misappropriation—contribute to the mordant humor of the tale. Manhandled Scripture compounds the cruel fun of the story, which in effect is a retelling of the farmer's daughter seduced in a hayloft by a traveling salesman.[21] Like the trickster tricked, it is another O'Connor appropriation of a bad joke. And yet, although the verse is twice played for laughs, in the end "He who losest his life shall find it" lingers in mind as something much more compelling and provocative than merely a laugh line. Indeed, Jesus's saying, for all its ironic permutations in the story, provides O'Connor with a way to intimate theological meaning under the narrative surface of absurdity.

This is the case, however, only if one is on board with O'Connor's convictions about devastation as the beginning of wisdom, of breakdown as the possible agent of breakthrough; only if one goes beyond where the narrative ventures. Hulga loses her leg, which she has long held to be the mark of her singularity and to tell "the truth about her" (289). At the story's close, she has nothing of what formerly made her who she was, especially the arrogance that led her to believe that in the person of Manley Pointer "for the first time in her life she was face to face with real innocence" (289). Because of him she is left alone, her face "churning" with rage at the departing Bible salesman who, as it turns out, has utterly outclassed her as a nihilist: "I been believing in nothing ever since I was born!" (291).

Conventional wisdom would have the story also come to nothing. But then there is the quirky presence of biblical teaching, "He who losest his life shall find it," which even when delivered by a bogus Bible salesman, makes a case for the positive value of loss. To lose may be in some paradoxical way to gain; to end one's old life may possibly be to enter the new world of a beginning. "He who losest his life shall *find* it."

If there is no life-affirming happy discovery at the end of "Good Country People," the biblical saying nonetheless holds out a promise beyond what the storyteller herself can deliver. But then, thanks to the Bible, she does not have to. O'Connor can do here what she did best elsewhere: clear the decks, tear away blinders, leave her heroine high and dry—with only one leg to stand on. What matter if she was able only to reflect our "broken condition and through it, the face of the devil we are possessed by" (MM 168)? A verse from the Gospel, injected twice into the narrative, might very well intimate something more.

*****

In contrast to the single Scripture that "leavens the lump" of "Good Country People," the biblical presence in "Revelation" (which earned

O'Connor a third O. Henry Prize in 1965, a year after her death) is extensive although not explicit—a network of biblical allusions rather than any actual citation.

Set first in a doctor's office and then on a farm, the story reveals from its beginning the compulsion of its protagonist to make judgments. In the opening pages Ruby Turpin sizes up the people sitting all around her according to their race, class, and the quality of their footwear. Even when alone, whether lost in a daydream or locked in a nightmare, she never tires of deciding who belongs where. Along with her sense of what is wrong with everyone else, moreover, is her conviction of how right everything is with her. Interspersed among her negative judgments are outbursts of self-congratulation that often take the form of prayer: "'If it's one thing that I am,' Mrs. Turpin said with feeling, 'it's grateful. When I think who all I could have been besides myself and what all I got, a little bit of everything and a good disposition besides, I just feel like shouting, "Thank you, Jesus, for making everything the way it is!" It could have been different!'" (499).

Mrs. Turpin's alternation between blame and praise finally becomes unbearable for Mary Grace, a dyspeptic raw-complexioned Wellesley college girl who snarls at Mrs. Turpin with every put down, every "Thank you, Jesus" or snide remark (many of them aimed at her). The mounting tension finally breaks when Mary Grace hurls a book at Mrs. Turpin's head—it strikes just over her left eye—and then sinks her fingers "like clamps" into the soft flesh of the woman's neck. More painful than the blow, however, is the curse she snarls in Mrs. Turpin's ear before the girl passes out and is taken away, "Go back to hell where you came from, you old warthog" (500). These words torment Mrs. Turpin for the rest of the story.

In the aftermath of the attack, and with no small measure of irony, O'Connor goes on to present Ruby Turpin as a kind of Job figure. Unable to nap beside her sleeping husband, she is tortured by memories of what Mary Grace called her, mentally "defending her innocence to invisible guests who were like the comforters of Job, reasonable seeming but wrong" (503). Soon those useless imaginary comforters take flesh as her black farmhands, who as usual say only what they think she wants to hear ("'Jesus satisfied with her!'" [205]). Their sham sympathy brings no relief; they are merely, as she growls to herself, "Idiots!" (505).

The Old Testament analogy continues to be drawn out. Just as Job mounts his lengthy self-defense in Chapter 31, so Ruby Turpin brings her virtues to the fore, albeit in much shorter shrift: "'Why me?' she rumbled. 'It's no trash around here, black or white, that I haven't given to. And break my back to the bone every day working. And do for the church'" (507). Job finally reaches his limit and cries out to God demanding a response: "Oh that one would hear me! Behold, my desire is, that the Almighty would answer me" (31:35 KJV); she sputters with exasperation for a reckoning with the Almighty and, perhaps, an apology: "A final surge of fury shook her and she roared, 'Who do you think you are?'"

Answers in both cases are forthcoming. Job gets more of a response to his demands than he might have bargained for: the Lord speaks to him from the whirlwind over the course of four chapters, posing a series of questions that he, not God, is meant to answer: "Where wast thou when I laid the foundations of the earth? declare, if thou hast understanding" (38:4). On the other hand, Ruby Turpin receives a less direct reply from the heavens, but nonetheless the equivalent of the Lord's "Where wast thou?" But in this case it is only the echo of her own question, "Who do you think you are?" Her words return to her "clearly like an answer from beyond the wood" (508).

The aftermath in both stories is swift. Confronting God's onslaught of authority, Job repents in "dust and ashes"; he is, after all, only a mortal and has no business going up against the Almighty. In O'Connor's version, by contrast, Mrs. Turpin has nothing at all to say for herself. Instead, she experiences a sequence of insights that bring the story to its close. With "Who do you think you are?" echoing as the sun begins its long setting, she takes the measure of her own human mortality by accounting for two quite different aspects of it. First, there is her fear as she imagines how easily her husband Claud could be killed in an accident, his truck on its evening return to the farm easily crushed "like a child's toy" (508). Then she takes in a sight that suggests birth rather than death: an old sow nursing her hungry offspring on the cement floor of the "pig parlor" she hosed down with a vengeance. "A red glow suffused them. They appeared to pant with a secret life" (508). As the evening sun goes down we are left with a sense of anticipation: surely something is about to happen.

O'Connor's level of diction continues to rise in the story's final paragraphs when Ruby Turpin is accorded a full-blown vision that takes the story far beyond the confines of the doctor's waiting room or her modest farm's cement "pig parlor." The author grants her protagonist an epiphany—or, to recall the story's title, a "revelation"—that revisits the judgment calls made so relentlessly earlier in the story. What Mrs. Turpin sees unfolding before her across the evening sky is a surprising (and also gently humorous) reversal of her earlier assignment of places. Hierarchy remains—this is Mrs. Turpin's vision, after all—but is suddenly inverted. At the head of a procession that stretches before her "like a vast swinging bridge extending upward from the earth toward a field of living fire," she sees that "a vast hoard of souls were rumbling toward heaven" (508).[22] Looking at these figures more closely, she sees all sorts and conditions of black folk brilliant in white robes, and then "trash clean for the first time," but also "battalions of freaks and lunatics shouting and clapping and leaping like frogs." In this company she also finds her own kind, the very best sort of Good Country People, who, like her and Claud, had a little bit of everything "and the God-given wit to use it right." But it is precisely they, until now resolutely at the head of any line she could imagine, who bring up the rear rather than lead it. She sees them in their great dignity, notes that they alone were singing the corporate Hallelujah on key. Nonetheless, it is clear that Mrs. Turpin's cohort is "bringing up the end of the procession"; they are the last in line, not the first. Earlier she had raged at God, "'Put that bottom rail on top. There'll still be a top and bottom!'" (507). Now she sees *sub species aeternitatis* where she and her kind are "put." Renowned for their virtue, especially in their own eyes, they are being gradually delivered from their pride. In this foretaste of purgatorial flames, "even their virtues were being burned away" (508).

In this reordering of top and bottom—of who sits in the front of the bus and who goes to the back—O'Connor recalls several New Testament texts that enlarge her frame of reference by bringing "Revelation" into contact with the Bible, "a story of mythic dimensions, one which belongs to everybody, one in which everybody is able to recognize the hand of God and its descent" (MM 202). The most apparent of these is found in all three of the Synoptic Gospels, when Jesus tells his disciples that a sign of the kingdom is precisely a reversal of the way things are in the world. "So the last shall be first shall the last be first, and the first last" (Matt. 20:16); "If any man desire to be first, the same shall be the last of all, and the servant of all" (Mark 9: 35); "And behold, there are last which shall be first, and there are first which shall be last" (Luke 13:30). The vision's processional line-up, therefore, is at once a rebuke to Mrs. Turpin's calculus of worth and a necessary reorientation for any who would "rumble" to heaven. Until now she has got it all wrong; she needs to be set straight by being turned around.

Another text that also hovers in the air of the story (although without the specificity of the procession's "last shall be first") is Jesus's teaching in the Sermon on the Mount when he speaks on the peril of judging. Throughout the story it comes to mind whenever Ruby Turpin comments on the quality of a person's shoes or assesses where she and her husband stand in the social order. When she runs aground in her construction of this hierarchy, it is only because of the sheer complexity of placement. Where is she to locate, for example, "a colored dentist in town who had two red Lincolns and a swimming pool and a farm with registered white-faced cattle on it" (490–91)? On the other hand, what might well have given pause to any "respectable, hard-working, church-going woman" (502) is this dominical caution against judging:

> Judge not, that ye be not judged, For with what judgment ye judge, ye shall be judged: and with what measure ye mete, it shall be measured to you again. And why beholdest thou the mote that is in thy brother's eye, but considerest not the beam that is in thy own eye? Or how wilt thou say to thy brother, Let me pull out the mote out of thy eye; and behold, a beam is in thine own eye? Thou hypocrite, first cast out the beam out of thine own eye, and then shalt thou see clearly to cast out the mote out of thy brother's eye. (Matt. 7:1–5)

These words speak directly to Mrs. Turpin's condition, although they do not seem once to have given her pause throughout the story. But just as relevant is the resonant conclusion to Jesus's parable in Luke 18:9–14, his story about "two men [who] went up into the Temple to pray." One is a Pharisee who, like Mrs. Turpin in her mode of self-congratulatory thanksgiving, reminds the Almighty of all that he is and has done: "'God, I thank thee that I am not as other men are . . . I fast twice in the week: I give tithes of all that I possess.'" The other figure, a publican (tax collector) and therefore a person of no repute, knows that he has nothing to offer other than heartfelt repentance. Striking his breast, he asks only to be forgiven: "'God, be merciful to me a sinner.'" After this sharp contrast between pride and humility, the parable hurtles to a quick conclusion. Jesus puts the last in front of the first, the publican before the Pharisee, "for every one that exalteth himself, shall be abased; and he that humbleth himself shall be exalted."

*****

Unlike "Good Country People" with its overt citation of a saying in Matthew, the biblical world of "Revelation" is at once more diffuse and more pervasive. There is no text within quotation marks to alert the reader to a source; instead, the biblical frame of reference is just under the surface, out of sight if never out of mind—at least for those readers who have (to quote a metaphoric formula that occurs in both Testaments) "ears that hear and eyes that see."[23] O'Connor was clearly pessimistic on this score. "I don't believe we shall have great religious fiction until we have again that happy combination of believing artist and believing society" (MM 168). Expecting little, she resorted to shock tactics ("to the hard of hearing you shout, and for the almost-blind you draw large and startling figures" [MM 34]), to endings that soared to an articulation of the "added dimension," or to oblique references that only hinted at what she did not say more plainly.

On at least one occasion, however, she waves a Scriptural flag in the story's closing line to insure that the reader would understand what the story meant, all appearances to the contrary notwithstanding. This is no simple task. In "A Circle in the Fire," three adolescent boys terrorize one of O'Connor's several imperious but anxiety-ridden farmwomen, resisting her attempts to control not only them but the world. After setting fire to Mrs. Cope's woods, the flames "widening unchecked inside the granite line of trees" (193), the boys are said to dance with "a few wild shrieks of joy." They are rebels with little cause, adolescents caught up in Dionysian frenzy. The narrator, however, wants us to see them as something not only more but also wholly different: they are not dark angels of destruction but servants of the Lord. And so to their shrieks of joy O'Connor appends one of her trademark similes: It was "as if the prophets were dancing in the fiery furnace, in the circle the angel had cleared for them" (193).

Nothing in the story prepares us for this transformation of hooligans into prophets: it comes solely on the basis of the simile's reference to the Book of Daniel, Chapter 3, with its account of Shadrach, Meshach, and Abednego in the fiery furnace of Nebuchadnezzar.[24] The King demands these pious Jews worship in his image; when they refuse, they are incinerated. O'Connor's simile draws attention to what Nebuchadnezzar sees when, looking into the furnace, he expects to find only charred remains. Instead, "they walked in the midst of the flame, praising God and blessing the Lord" (3:24); "Behold I see four men loose, and walking in the midst of the fire, and there is no hurt in them, and the form of the fourth is like the Son of God" (3:92).

"As if" Dionysian whelps and frenzied dancing can become, as by fiat, "men walking in the fire, praising God and blessing the Lord." Any such transposition of value seems arbitrary on the literal face of things: it simply would not come to mind without the Scriptural gloss and authorial stage direction. The explicit biblical subtext, in other words, reveals a "mystery" heartfelt by the author but not otherwise apparent to a reader unable to make anything of interpretative clues carefully left behind unless told to look for them retrospectively. They are planted in O'Connor's text, to be sure, but narrative details become clues, and dots stand to be connected, only when we are prompted to see "A Circle in the Fire" in the light of Daniel 3.

With the biblical narrative in view, the boys become agents of transformation rather than of doom, angels rather than devils. The story also enters familiar O'Connor territory, where an agent of havoc and destruction—the Misfit, Manley Pointer, Mary Grace—breaks down a character in order to enable what we are led to assume (or hope) is a spiritual breakthrough. The Grandmother is murdered but in dying she rises to the occasion however unwittingly: "She would of been a good woman . . . if it had been somebody there to shoot her every minute of her life" (133). Mrs. Turpin is assaulted and cursed in order that she might have her enlarging vision of the first being last. Hulga is "freed" of her leg so as to exchange one identity for another, because "He who losest his life will find it." Along these lines, then, Mrs. Cope's woods are turned to ash so that grace may more abound, even as hooligans become prophet-arsonists who speak truth to power when they say, rightly, "Man, Gawd owns them woods and her too" (186).

Now that O'Connor's intentions for her fiction are so well known—indeed, since 1988 they have been canonized by the Library of America along with her fiction—it may have become almost too easy to read her. Knowing what she meant to say, we've lost a feeling for her struggle in doing so and, perhaps, made the work more transparent than it really is. Her auto-exegesis is compelling, encouraging an awareness of the presence of grace when what actually strikes us may be its absence. (What *really* shines through her broken images? Is it, as she suggested, the face of the Devil rather than of God?) Like the Gospel writers when they "make sense" of parables that do not themselves resolve difficulties or offer satisfying closure, O'Connor's clarification of her work, luminous though it often is, also tames it, makes the rough places plain. Her intentions can also forestall interpretation on terms other than the author's own, so that she ends up having not only the first word but the last as well.

With "A Circle in the Fire" it is easy to feel strong-armed. Not so with "Good Country People," with its sly, funny deployment of a verse, or "Revelation," in which Scripture is like the radio hymn tune playing in the story's background—easy to take for granted but key to everything: "When I looked up and He looked down" (490). And yet, whatever the measure of her success in this or that story, there is no other contemporary American writer who has made more of the Bible than Flannery O'Connor or brought the short story itself so close to the paradoxical, often bewildering world of Jesus's own parables.

5

Allegra Goodman

In 1977, Irving Howe famously predicted the end of Jewish American literature: "My own view is that American Jewish fiction has probably moved past its high point. Insofar as this body of writing draws heavily from the immigrant experience, it must suffer a depletion of resources, a thinning-out of materials and memories."[1] Leslie Fiedler had sounded his own death knell for the genre a decade earlier in response to the movement of writers like Saul Bellow, Bernard Malamud, and Philip Roth into the American mainstream: "The moment of triumph for the Jewish writer in the United States has come just when his awareness of himself as a Jew is reaching a vanishing point, when the gesture of rejection seems his last possible connection with his historical past; and the popular acceptance of his alienation as a satisfactory symbol for the human condition threatens to turn it into an affectation, a fashionable cliché."[2]

We can put these prophecies into historical context. After the "period of arrival" (Jews coming from Europe between 1640 and 1880) there followed the first major generation of Jewish American writers. These were European-born Jews who explored the immigrant experience—the *Norton Anthology of Jewish American Literature* describes this as "The Great Tide (1881-1924)." The writing of the second generation, from 1945 to 1973, was marked—in Norton's terms—by achievement and ambivalence. This was literature that struggled with the pulls of assimilation and American belonging and reflected an increasing decline in Jewish identity. Therefore, it was hard for critics in the late 1960s and 1970s to imagine Jewish American writers doing anything other than becoming merely American writers as Jews became absorbed into the mainstream.

Sociologists familiar with Marcus Lee Hansen's principle of third generation return, which is "derived from the almost universal phenomenon that what the son wishes to forget, the grandson wishes to remember,"[3] would likely have raised their eyebrows at Fiedler and Howe's dire predictions. And they would have been right: Jewish American literature has not disappeared. Not at all. Rather, in the latter decades of the twentieth century and the beginning of the twenty-first, it has enjoyed something of a resurgence. In a 2000 interview, author Rebecca Goldstein noted, "There is not just a revitalization of Jewish life, but also of Jewish letters, going on. Young writers, younger than I, writing authentically Jewish pieces of fiction; not about assimilation, not about wanting out, but instead writing about a Jewish sensibility."[4]

A key part of this new sensibility is its religious dimension. Whereas the concerns of mid-twentieth-century Jewish literature were largely ethnic—marked by themes of alienation, assimilation, intermarriage—those of the third generation turn on questions of ritual, memory, and tradition. In particular, we find a renewed interest in Jewish religious thought and values, the reexamination of orthodoxy, and the role of gender in Jewish practice. Perhaps most notable is what has been perceived as a widespread return to traditional Jewish texts—especially the Bible.

From Genesis to Deuteronomy—from the exploration of the ways that Eve (Gen. 2–3) is refracted through Yiddish poetry in Dara Horn's "Reader's Digest" to the meditation on the impossibility of the *Shema* (Deut. 6) as a legitimate expression of devotion to God in the wake of the Holocaust in Norma Rosen's "What Must I Say to You?"—Jewish American short-story writers return again and again to the Torah. But they do not stop with the Five Books of Moses. We find short fiction writers like John J. Clayton and Steve Stern wrestling head-on with narratives from across the biblical canon. As Ezra Cappell argues, "Despite the seemingly limited role the Bible and biblical themes would within the wider scope of twentieth-century literature written in America, biblical themes do in fact animate much of Jewish American fiction."[5] In terms of our own bailiwick, the modern Jewish American short story is animated by the Bible in a wide variety of ways.

Sometimes, as in Melvin Jules Bukiet's "The Golden Calf and the Red Heifer,"[6] the appeal to the Bible is made in the title. It alludes both to the golden calf, an idol made by the Israelites in the absence of Moses, who is with God on Mount Sinai (Exod. 32), and to the red heifer whose sacrifice enabled ritual purification (Num. 13:2). The biblical encounter is not merely titular, mind you: Scripture propels the stories. The first centers on Kleinberg, the only kosher butcher in a fictive Orthodox suburb of New York, who is undergoing a crisis of faith: he has begun to think that the killing of animals as delineated in the laws of kashrut is unethical. Much of kosher law is codified post-biblically—it is part of the Oral Torah—but it is also toward the written Torah, the Book of Leviticus, that Kleinberg directs much of his skepticism. In his period of disavowal of the law, Kleinberg is visited by a red-headed female golem who leads him astray both through illicit slaughter (he kills a pig to make her bacon) and illicit sex. Just as he understands his community's obsession with correctly slaughtered meat to be a form of idolatry—they have made of the laws of kashrut a golden calf—so too does he understand the woman symbolically: she is the red heifer that ancient Jews followed out into the desert for sacrifice. He is roundly condemned by the community, whom he himself condemns for their mechanical observance of the law (in this regard, the story can be read as a midrash on the Book of Jeremiah)[7] and ultimately sacrifices himself to absolve them of their sin (after the golem has sacrificed herself). He cuts his neck as he would that of an animal for kosher slaughter, using a swift knife stroke from a perfect blade which "was as straight as the line from Adam to Moses"[8]—from sin to the law.

Then there is Max Apple's engagement with Jewish law and its biblical origins in "The Eighth Day."[9] Here again the title is biblical, although more obliquely so: the reference is to God's commandment that Abraham and his people circumcise their sons on the eighth day (Gen. 17:12). In this story, the Jewish protagonist undergoes "primal therapy" in an effort to connect more deeply with Joanne, his gentile girlfriend, who is an avid proponent of this new age technique that regresses practitioners backward through their lives to the moment of their birth. The protagonist can't get all the way back to his birth because in his regression he becomes stalled at the eighth day, his circumcision, because—as a Jew—there is no "past that point." In keeping with Jewish law, his life began on the eighth day. At the girlfriend's urging, the couple locates Hyman Berkowitz, the *mohel* (a self-described "ritual slaughterer") who performed the circumcision, and asks him to re-enact the rite. The story is alarming, funny, crude, and fully engaged not only with Jewish themes (identity, assimilation) but also with biblical ones. Berkowitz hesitates as the protagonist lies naked under a sheet on his dining-room table, reflecting on the connection between God and blood. Joanne has suggested that he take only a drop of blood, but the *mohel* replies, "Down there there's no drops. It's close to the arteries; the heart wants blood there. It's the way the Almighty wanted it to be."[10] Indeed, in the Bible, God directs and controls blood. We see this in his injunctions to Noah not to eat an animal with its blood in it and to slay a man who sheds the blood of another (Gen. 6); his commanding circumcision (Gen. 17); his legislating the flow of blood in kosher law (Lev. 7) as well as in family purity laws (Lev. 15), among other places. Berkowitz's declaration that this is how the Almighty wanted it to be underscores the deep biblical connection between God and blood. Ultimately, the *mohel* cannot proceed: "I can't do this, even symbolically, to a full-grown male. It may not be against the law; still I consider it an abomination."[11] Like the emphasis on blood, the language of abomination is profoundly biblical. Berkowitz processes the contemporary world—this very peculiar situation—through the language and experience of the Bible.

The deployment of biblical imagery in this way can deepen a story. In "Dancing on Tisha B'Av" (1985), Lev Raphael, one of the first observant Jewish American writers to be out, describes the developing relationship between Mark, an older gay Jewish man, and Nat, a younger observant Jew just beginning to act on his attraction to men. The third significant character in the story is Brenda, Nat's older sister, who is worried about her brother's reputation—and, in the age of AIDS, his health—but not as much as she is about her own. She realizes with brazen clarity while talking with Mark "even though she felt warmer to Nat after his crying confession, she didn't love him, still, and feared what people would say about *her* more than what might happen to Nat."[12] Brenda is trying to understand why the two are so unconcerned with what people think—a woman at the synagogue had just asked if Nat was gay; later, a man at the synagogue will forbid them from touching the Torah scroll his grandfather had donated to the shul and banish them from the service. Mark responds in biblical terms: "You know it doesn't bother me now. . . . But for years I thought God would get me, like Aaron's sons when they offer up 'strange fire' and get zapped?" In invoking a narrative about God directing his quick and unequivocal wrath at the sons of Aaron who have transgressed his law (Lev. 10:1), Mark understands his experience through the Bible. Even more, he is undertaking what Harold Bloom says has "always has been the function of Jewish writing, or rather its burden: how to open the Bible to one's own suffering."[13] The expectation is not only that Brenda's appreciation of his suffering will be deepened by her fully understanding the reference, but that the reader's will be as well. Such a use of the Bible is only fully effective "if the Bible is regarded as the basic text of Judaism and as a source of the world-view and values of Judaism, and if one assumes that the reader is familiar with the original."[14]

The engagements we have considered so far turn on a particular biblical phrase or allusion. We also find plenty of instances of the use of a biblical name to convey meaning. In Grace Paley's "Zagrowsky Tells,"[15] the recurring character Faith Darwin (in case one needed convincing that Paley is deliberate in her choice of names) strikes up a conversation with Zagrowsky, a retired Jewish pharmacist who is playing in the park with his black grandson, Emanuel. Emanuel's mother, who had become pregnant by a black gardener at a mental institution to which she had been committed, chose the boy's name. For the biblically minded reader, the allusion to Isaiah is clear: "Behold, a virgin shall conceive and bear a son and call him Emanuel" (Isa. 7:14). Even to the Jewish ear, which hears the word "maiden" rather than "virgin" in the Hebrew of Isaiah 7:14, the naming of the child is clearly understood to be an assertion of the mother's innocence. Paley's "Samuel" is likewise about a name chosen by a mother that sheds light on her sense of maternal identity. Samuel is a boy killed in a subway accident, and his story foregrounds the great loss felt by his mother. Through the name and other cues, Paley links the story to that of Hannah, who pledged her firstborn son Samuel to God (1 Sam. 1:27). The force of the biblical allusion comes in the divergent role of solace in the two tales. Hannah finds solace in community—in her husband, in Eli the priest, in God and his promise of future children for her—but Paley's mother, her Hannah, finds solace in neither community nor the promise of continuity. She and her husband have other children, "but never again will a boy exactly by Samuel be known."[16]

So far our examples of the use of the Bible by Jewish writers have turned on titles, verses, names. We turn now to Allegra Goodman as our exemplar of a Jewish writer who engages the Bible not here and there through the use of occasional biblical references but through an ongoing literary commentary. Raised Jewish in Hawaii (truly the periphery of American Judaism), Goodman locates herself religiously between Orthodox and Conservative movements. She has come uneasily to accept the label "Jewish American writer"—a term eschewed by many authors who seem to meet all three criteria but view the ethnic designation as marginalizing—in large part because a lot of her work is not merely "culturally Jewish" but religiously so. One critic summarized Goodman's project (evident particularly in her earlier works) as an "expressed desire . . . to be part of a Jewish literature that in the post-assimilationist era can recapture the spiritual and religious dimensions of Judaism."[17]

In addition to publishing two collections of short stories and five novels (along with many essays and a book for young adults), Goodman has appeared in the *New Yorker, Commentary,* and *Ploughshares* as well as being anthologized in *The O. Henry Awards* and *Best American Short Stories.* Her short fiction often grows into longer work. Sharon, the flighty protagonist of "Onionskin" becomes the central figure of the novel *Paradise Park*; Cecil Birnbaum, the Orthodox English professor in "Variant Text," recurs as a secondary character in *Kaaterskill Falls.* Both of these novels are engaged with questions of Jewish religious identity, exploring what Goodman calls "a living unself-conscious tradition" where "ritual and liturgy are a natural part of my fictional world and not anthropological objects to be translated and constantly explained."[18] The first novel follows self-absorbed seeker Sharon Spiegelman on a two-decade-long spiritual journey that begins with Israeli folk dancing in Boston and moves to a reform congregation in Hawaii, to the Greater Love Salvation Church, and to an Ultra-Orthodox community in Jerusalem. The second, *Kaaterskill Falls* is set in a New York State enclave where Hasidic families summer. Though all are members of a single community, the characters vary widely in their personal understandings of Judaism. One critic notes, "At the heart of the novel is a quiet reexamination of the talmudic ethos that Torah is pluralistic, lending itself to be seen from a myriad of perspectives and in turn supporting those perspectives."[19] The same themes dominate *The Family Markowitz,* a collection of related short stories that has sometimes been described as a novel. Here the Markowitz family members express their respective Judaisms in light of the Holocaust and the State of Israel, with history and politics both examined in the religious and ritual sphere. All these explorations of Jewish identity are part of Goodman's quest to "recapture the spiritual and religious dimension of Judaism."[20] Not surprisingly, this pervasive concern with the lived religiosity of her characters has led critics to liken Goodman to Flannery O'Connor, even though Goodman's characters exist within religious community and O'Connor's without.[21]

Like O'Connor's fiction, Goodman's novels and stories are permeated with Scripture.[22] The Song of Songs, for instance, is the particular thread that weaves together the diverse parts of Sharon Spiegelman's spiritual odyssey in *Paradise Park* (although the vision of God she experiences on a whale-watching boat naturally calls to mind the Book of Jonah). The biblical stories of Sarah, laughing when God tells her she will bear a child in her old age, and the many narratives of fraternal conflict (Cain and Abel, Isaac and Ishmael, perhaps especially Jacob and Esau) lurk just beneath the surface of *Kaaterskill Falls.*[23] Quite unlike those Jewish writers who do not have "full awareness of being under the scriptural sway," Goodman is familiar with the interpretive tradition. Writing about the biblical matriarch Rachel, she observes of Genesis overall, "It does not matter how much commentary has been written; questioning and speculation are a part of reading this text. The questions cannot end, because gaps are integral to the story; the text will never be exhausted, because it can never be filled."[24] Goodman's assertion brings to mind the rabbinic dictum about the Torah: "Turn it, turn it again, for everything is in it" (*Pirkei Avot* 5:22). The Bible is an unending source of wisdom, inspiration, even of complexity and consternation.

Goodman, as we have begun to see, returns repeatedly to the well of Torah. Here we will look at a handful of the stories in *The Family Markowitz* to see the varied ways she engages Scripture. She has described these stories as focused on "characters who are far more assimilated" than those in the earlier collection. Two collected in *Total*

Immersion are explicitly biblical. "And Also Much Cattle" describes a hectic Yom Kippur service in a makeshift home synagogue in Hawaii. Despite the importing of yeshiva students to impart a sense of holiness and authenticity to the service, it is far from solemn or introspective. A senile grandmother calls out from time to time, brothers swear and fight in front of the ark, the local beach bum who has taken up residence in the home arrives in a straw hat and lei, the hostess natters nonstop through the prayers, and a dog runs through the "sanctuary." In one of the distracting sidebars, one congregant turns to another:

> "Look at this." Avi thumbs his machzor. "Elliott," he calls downwind, "it says here that Jonah was bummed because God killed the gourd shading Jonah's head. But look at what God says!" Avi points a dirty fingernail at the passage: "Then the Lord said: You would spare the gourd, though you spent no work upon it, though you did not make it grow; it sprang up in a night and perished in a night. Should I not then spare the great city of Nineveh with more than a hundred and twenty thousand human beings, who do not know their right hand from their left, and also much cattle?'

The invocation of these verses from Jonah, which is the prescribed reading for the Day of Atonement, allays any skepticism on the part of the reader that God will heed the prayers of this ragtag band, gathered in their unfinished, unclean, utterly improvisational synagogue. The gathered worshippers, made reference to in the story's title, aren't even as worthy of God's forgiveness as the people of Nineveh who knew not their right hand from their left. Rather, they are more like the cattle of these gentiles. But what of it, the story seems to say? God spared the cattle as well as the Ninevites. Unlike the forgiveness of humans, which is conditional—the mother of the house concludes the service with threats that she will never forgive her sons for their behavior—God's mercy is total, independent of the quality of the petitions of those who seek it. It even extends to those who make no petition at all, who behave like cattle in his house of worship.

"The Four Questions," an especially memorable story in *The Family Markowitz*, also turns on proper behavior in a ritual setting. It is Passover and Sarah and Ed Markowitz have gathered their four children (all young adults) to observe the holiday at the home of Sarah's mother. Like the four sons in the Passover Haggadah, the younger generation represents four different stances toward the tradition. Miriam, the eldest, has become increasingly observant as well as rigid. Ben, a senior at Brandeis, is the antithesis of his older sister: "No one is worried about Ben becoming too intense. . . . He has no thoughts about the future. No ideas about life after graduation. No plan. He is studying psychology in a distracted sort of way."[25] Though the second oldest, he seems to be the child of the family—the one in the Haggadah who is too young to ask a coherent question about Judaism. The wicked child, if there is one, is the assimilationist Avi, studying at Wesleyan, who has a non-Jewish girlfriend, "Methodist Amy." The youngest, Yehudit, is a Stanford student who has returned east for the holiday despite being "sick as a dog." An ardent vegetarian who volunteers to work with seniors at the Jewish Community Center, she seems to embody an ethical rather than religious Judaism. The story is about negotiation of these Jewish identities against the backdrop of the Passover seder, the ritual commemoration of the Israelites' exodus from Egypt.

There is much to be said about the religious dimensions of this work. It marks precisely the imaginative return to religion that Dara Horn describes in her response to Paul Elie: "The Jewish practices most rooted in collective memory, which are coincidentally those most accessible to the least observant (family-oriented holidays and text study in various forms), are less about believing in a supernatural reality than about appreciating the metaphor of the past's presence." Goodman herself seems never to have been far from Judaism, but her characters all stand in differing relationship to it—the crux of this story.

Our interest, however, lies in the explicit biblical dimensions of "The Four Questions." The names of the children have biblical meaning that suggests something about their personalities. Avi and Yehudit, names popular in modern Israel, are Jewish rather than specifically biblical (there is a biblical Yehudit / Judith, but her story resides outside the Jewish canon). Nonetheless, their names seem significant: Avi means "my father" (often referring to God) and Yehudit "Jewess." Benjamin, as we have noted, seems to function as "*le benjamin*" of the family: the indulged youngest child. Miriam most vividly lives out the biblical nature of her name. The sister of Moses and Aaron, she is a strong female figure who, timbrel in hand, leads the Israelite women out of Egypt singing her "Song of the Sea" (Ex. 15:1-18). The prophet Micah remembers her in this liberating role: God declares, "For I brought you up from the land of Egypt, and redeemed you from the house of slavery; and I sent before you Moses, Aaron, and Miriam" (Mic. 6:4). In Deuteronomy, however, she serves a cautionary function: "Remember what the Lord your God did to Miriam on your journey out of Egypt" (Deut. 24:9). She and Aaron had spoken against Moses's wife, a Cushite, so that God punished her by making her white as snow (i.e., leprous). Aaron, on the other hand, was unharmed. Miriam was cast out of the congregation of Israel for seven days, and the people stayed in camp that whole time waiting for her return (Num. 12). The complicated biblical portrait of Miriam helps shed light on the complexity of Goodman's treatment of the character.

The dramatic tension in "The Four Questions" is primarily between Miriam and her father, Ed, a liberal professor of Middle East politics at Georgetown. In his leading of the seder (which, Miriam complains, he shortens every year), he draws out themes of social justice and focuses on those "who have not yet achieved full freedom; those discriminated against because of their race, gender, or sexual preference."[26] Miriam asks him to focus on "the original context" instead. "As in the Jewish people?" asks her mother Sarah. "As in God," Miriam replies.[27] Like Sharon Spiegelman, Miriam is one of Goodman's seekers, one her "characters [who] are inevitably engaged in a cultural conflict in their attempt to transcend the quotidian of contemporary American society and connect to some deeper theological meaning."[28] Unlike Sharon, Miriam has found what she sought religiously: traditional Judaism. She contests her father's humanist Judaism and insists on one focused on the relationship between God and Israel. Ironically, because of her move toward a Judaism more observant than that of her parents, she is perceived as the Haggadah's stubborn child. She tunes her father out and retreats into the Orthodox Haggadah she has brought with her, reading and singing to herself long after the rest of the family has completed its ritual.

Miriam would likely frame this struggle between Orthodox and progressive Judaism as a battle between the secular and the religious;

Ed, on the other hand, sees a contest between hide-bound tradition and responsible innovation. However one casts it, their struggle is mapped onto a biblical backdrop. Miriam has strong affinities with her biblical namesake, whereas Ed, notably, has a non-Jewish name. Scriptural Miriam spoke out against her brother Moses, the leader of their tribe; Miriam Markowitz speaks out against her brothers, whom she finds juvenile, and against her father, the Markowitz pater familias/ ostensive leader of their family. In her act of rebellion, modern-day Miriam turns to a different liturgy, effectively singing her own song. Exodus gives us two accounts of the departure from Egypt: the prose version, featuring Moses and Aaron, and the verse version, featuring Miriam's song (Exod. 15:20–21). Likewise, the Markowitz seder gives us two accounts of the family's relationship to the past: Ed's version and Miriam's. Additionally, if the punishment for Miriam's subsequent speaking out against Moses is her banishment and isolation from the community, Miriam Markowitz enacts her own parallels: she banishes herself from the community of the table, turning instead toward her own Haggadah, choosing to eat off paper plates rather than off her grandmother's china, which is not sufficiently "kosher for Passover."

Just as Miriam internalizes her own Exodus experience story through private recitation and personal food, so too does Ed internalize the story of Israel and Egypt. Asleep on the pullout in his mother-in-law's den, he dreams of another Exodus, "Sarah's parents, along with the Rothmans, the Seligs, the Magids, and all their friends, perhaps one thousand of them walking en masse like marathoners over the Verrazano Bridge. They are carrying suitcases and ironing boards, bridge tables, tennis rackets, and lawn chairs. They are driving their poodles before them as they march together. It is a procession both majestic and frightening." In this "comic reenactment of the exodus," the older Jewish generation "bring[s] with them not the 'flocks and herds . . . the unleavened cakes of dough' which the Israelites 'driven out of Egypt' carried (Exodus 12:39–41), but rather the accouterments and extravagances, the necessities and indulgences, the amenities and the material features of American life."[29] The experience is overwhelming. Ed "wants to turn away; he wants to dismiss it, but still he feels it, unmistakable, not to be denied. The thundering of history."[30] Ed can no more shake the Jewish particularity of the Exodus than can Miriam.

"Sarah," the final story we will consider, is about Ed's wife, Sarah. The story, ostensibly *about* midrash, is itself a midrash—a reflection on the biblical Sarah's having a child in her advanced old age, and a commentary on the relationship of Ruth and Naomi. As a story about Jews who write midrashim about Jewish experience, as a story written by a Jew, it thus falls squarely within the contemporary understanding of "midrash" as a Jewish American literary genre.

Sarah had published a novel, which provides her with the necessary credentials to teach creative writing at the local Jewish Community Center:

> The class is called Creative Midrash, and it combines creative writing with Bible study. Like the commentators in the compendium the Midrash, the students write their own interpretations, variations, and fantasies on Biblical themes. Sarah developed the concept herself, and she is happy with it because it solves so many problems at once. It forces the students to allude to subjects other than themselves, while at the same time they find it serves their need for therapy—because they quickly see in Scripture archetypes of their own problems.[31]

The design of Sarah's class brings to mind Harold Bloom's notion of the eternal relationship between the Jewish writer and Scripture: "What Jewish writing has to interpret, finally, and however indirectly, is the Hebrew Bible, since that always has been the function of Jewish writing, or rather its burden: how to open the Bible to one's own suffering."[32] (Like other scholars who explore the literary return to the Bible as a response to Jewish catastrophe, Bloom is specifically interested in Jewish suffering.) In Sarah's class, engagement with the Bible forces the students to consider the suffering of others. At the same time, it affords them the opportunity to see themselves in the pages of Scripture, thus offering them a therapeutic exercise.

Initially, Sarah seems unaware of the ways that her own story might be mapped onto Scripture. Her biblical namesake was barren for years, despite every expectation (and divine ordination) that her husband would have offspring as numerous as the sands on the shore and the stars in the sky. Sarah Markowitz is hardly barren in any literal sense: as we have seen, she has four children. But she is creatively dry. She wrote one novel long ago and fears that there are none left in her. As God had promised (a promise at which she had laughed), biblical Sarah bears a child in her advanced age—Isaac is born when she is ninety. Perhaps there is also hope for Sarah Markowitz? She too laughs at the thought of conceiving (of) a new novel so late in her life. In keeping with the Yiddish proverb that "man plans, God laughs," God also seems to laugh. Sarah does not bear new creative fruit, but rather ends up becoming a mother anew. She brings Rose, her increasingly dependent mother-in-law, into her home, thus taking on mothering duties in her mid-age. Goodman inverts the biblical story of Sarah: there, it is the mother who is advanced in years; here, it is the child.

Because of these relationships of mother-in-law and daughter-in-law, it is clear that the Book of Genesis is not the only biblical narrative to underpin "Sarah." The themes of the biblical Book of Ruth echo throughout the short story and there are explicit recalls to the scriptural novella discussed earlier in this book. One of Sarah's students writes a midrash about losing her own daughter:

> My daughter and I are like Ruth and Naomi, but with a twist. When my husband passed away, may he rest in peace, and we went on the way, as it says in the Bible, I said to Ellen, "Don't stay with me, go and live your life." "I want to stay with you and take care of you," she said. "No, you need to live your own life," I said. "Okay," she said, so she went back to New York where she was attending NYU film school.[33]

The daughter then moves in with a non-Jewish man, which pains the mother:

> This is what I want to ask her—"How do you think you can live in New York like a Ruth gleaning the alien corn? How do you think you can come to him and lie at his feet in the night so that one morning he will marry you? How can you go on like this living in his apartment for five years? If I had known this would happen when we went on the way I would not have told you to go. I would have said, 'Stay.'"[34]

The student knowingly deploys the Book of Ruth, when she sees the suffering of the women in Moab in the light of her own suffering. She knows how the biblical story goes, and she therefore knows how her story should go. But her daughter is not the steadfast Ruth who cleaves to her mother-in-law. She takes at face value her mother's dispatching her to go and live her life.

As Sarah reads her student's work, she is moved in ways she cannot understand. *She* cannot understand it. We readers know, however, that her story is reflected in Scripture: we know her better for seeing her as another Sarah, another Naomi. She is no longer the aged matriarch who might still bear a novel, but the Ruth who must bear her mother-in-law. Her ambivalence about tending her mother-in-law stands in contrast to Ruth's devotion and willingness to "go" with Naomi. Her empathy for the Naomi in her class illuminates her own shortcomings as Rose's Ruth. Goodman's story is built not on one scriptural archetype, but on two, and its truth is revealed through both.

In her repeated returns to the books of Genesis and Exodus, the scrolls of Jonah, Ruth, and the Song of Songs, Allegra Goodman in effect makes her fiction a running commentary on Scripture. Her characters are all contemporary Jews, fully formed and alive today, and yet many of them are best understood through a biblical lens. In light of the Song of Songs, the already complicated Sharon Spiegelman becomes richer still: she is at once lover and beloved, church and Israel. Miriam Markowitz is the Miriam warily remembered in Deuteronomy and proudly extolled in Micah. Sarah Markowitz is Sarah and Ruth.

By virtue of their belatedness, Allegra Goodman and the other Jewish writers mentioned here are forced "to return time and again, whether consciously or not, to a centering text in their work"[35]—the Hebrew Bible. In many cases, as we have shown, the return is more conscious than not. It is also a return that engages Scripture, that possesses it. But if for many contemporary Jewish writers the Bible is inescapable, it is hardly immutable. These writers play with the Bible, turning it over and over again, finding everything within it. They make abundantly clear to the audience who knows what to look for, that "*Lo beshamayim hi*"—the Torah is not in heaven (Deut 30:2); rather, as Ezra Cappell asserts, "It is alive and well and being written in the American diaspora."[36]

6

John Updike

Given the *New Yorker* magazine's reputation for secular urbanity—its easy "Talk of the Town" sophistication—it is surprising to note how many of its leading short story writers have in fact been seriously engaged with "the varieties of religious experience." The roster should be enough to make heads spin: J. D. Salinger, J. F. Powers, John Cheever, John Updike, Andre Dubus, John L'Heureux. Some of these have even been branded "*New Yorker* writers" because of their close and longtime association with the magazine. Salinger, for instance, had thirteen stories published between 1945 and 1965, John Cheever more than a hundred, and John Updike over two hundred appearing over the course of his fifty-five-year relationship with the weekly.[1] The religion represented by its storytellers is primarily Christian, although Salinger's "Franny" and "Zooey" famously presented an eclectic Upper West Side blend of Judaism, Christianity, and Buddhism. The major players, however—Cheever and Updike—were both churchgoing WASPs when it was no longer fashionable to be so. Together they offered different takes on what Updike spoke of, with reference to Cheever, as "the deep melancholy peculiar to American Protestant males."[2]

With the possible exception of Flannery O'Connor, no twentieth-century American writer has been as preoccupied with Christianity and its contemporary discontents as John Updike. Certainly no one else has been as disconcertingly prolific in his considerations of the faith in so many diverse genres. There is his open engagement with religion in the form of critical essays, interviews, lyric poetry, and his one self-proclaimed memoir, *Self-Consciousness* (1989). But then, of course, there is the huge output of fiction, his often heavily autobiographical short stories, and his novels.

By Updike's own admission, his short stories are especially "personal." This is easily seen in retrospect, say, in the teenage David of "Pigeon Feathers" (first published in the *New Yorker* in 1961), after one has read about Updike's own religious crisis as a young man freely confided in *Self-Consciousness* and elsewhere.[3] The short story genre he turned to so often (although with less notoriety than his novels) provided him with a way to join his narrative gift to the self-disclosures of both lyric and autobiography: "Situated between the novel and the poem, and capable of giving us the pleasure of both, the form also has the peculiar intimacy of an essay, wherein a voice confides its most and important secrets to the reader's ear."[4]

Updike first came by his religion as a family inheritance—a Presbyterian minister grandfather, Lutheran parents—that bequeathed to him the weekly rituals of small-town Sunday School and church that remained with him after he left Pennsylvania for Ipswich and Beverly Farms in Massachusetts. Unlike many others who came from a similar religious background but who quickly "put away childish things," this legacy became a lifelong habit, lived out over the years in a succession of three Mainline Protestant denominations: Lutheran gave way to Congregationalist, and finally to Episcopalian. Unusual as this ongoing practice was his willingness to identify himself as a Christian in elite cultural circles when doing so put him at no advantage. He was, by his own account, an anomaly, a Gentile "pet" at the *New Yorker* and its "token Christian."[5] Despite his ongoing church attendance, however, he often claimed very little for himself as a believer. Faith was his "curious hobby": "I've never quite escaped the Christian church. . . . I suppose I'm just one more of the millions of more or less lukewarm, but not quite cold, Protestants that fill this country."[6] He inherited a religion, he said, and was "too timid to discard it."[7] Ian McEwan described him as the "most Lutheran of writers" who was constitutionally unable "to make the leap of unfaith."[8]

Many others of his ilk seem to have had no difficulty abandoning ship, as he observed ruefully in his turn-of-the-millennium *New Yorker* essay on "The Future of Faith": "A Protestant Christian on the eve of the third millennium must struggle with the sensation that his sect is, like the universe itself in the latest cosmological news, winding down, growing thinner and thinner as entropy works an inevitable dimming upon the outspreading stars." In the same piece, he reports wandering with increasing fatigue through Italian churches and museums that were brimful with biblical iconography, all deliciously described in vintage Updike prose. He wonders if what had for centuries formed a paradigm to live and die by—"whose details in hasty summary I profess to assent to every time I attend church"—had finally reached a point of exhaustion. "How much more mileage could be squeezed from those darkened, crumbling images?" With those images, he hastens to add, crumbles the Bible they largely come from: "Adam and Eve and the serpent," the Annunciation and Visitation, "the denouement of the Crucifixion."[9]

There is nothing to suggest, however, that "unfaith" was something he ever wanted to leap toward, or that he thought the "God hole" could be filled by anything else.[10] He could imagine the alternative to belief—indeed, his fiction is replete with those whose faith is shaky, dying, or dead—but the personal loss of it held no attraction for him. On the contrary, as he writes in *Self-Consciousness*, it was a horror analogous to extinction. His disclaimers of piety do no justice to his sustained reflection (more or less intense depending on the decade) on the theologians Soren Kierkegaard, Paul Tillich, and most especially Karl Barth.[11] Nor do they honor the fact of his own religious experience—"The Future of Faith" ends with two very moving "personal testimonies"—or his lifelong relationship to the Bible.

His strong engagement with Scripture, like church attendance, was also an inheritance, an accident of birth that he was ready to make his own. Although he grew up in a household of only "average Protestant piety," it was a place nonetheless where biblical characters "were as familiar, and as frequently mentioned, as relatives on a distant farm." Elijah's chariot of fire and Joseph's coat of many colors "brightened our stock of mental imagery"; Christ's parables of the talents and Paul's contentious advice on the position of women particularly "stimulated our thoughts and familial conversation."[12]

Those dinner table discussions in the three-generation Updike household later made their way more or less directly into his fiction. The stories are especially rich in these autobiographical recollections.

One can easily imagine, for instance, how Lutheran *Tischgespräche* over Pauline advice in 1 Corinthians 11:3 went on to generate "Sunday Teasing," whose protagonist, the curmudgeon Arthur, proudly self-describes himself as "Eleventh-generation German. White, Protestant, Gentile, small-town, middle-class." (These are markers of the author as well, and one thinks of Updike's description of himself, at least early in his career, as a "literary spy within average, public-school, supermarket America." [13]) On this particular Sunday, Arthur has decided not to go to church. Rather than listen to some "servile, peace-of-mind-peddling preacher," he will "stay at home and read St. Paul." His wife, Macy, dreads these "Sunday-morning club" moments when invariably he excludes her. Picking up his grandfather's King James Bible, he turns to the old man's favorite passage and reads it out loud: "First Corinthians eleven, verse three, 'But I would have you know, that the head of every man is Christ; and the head of the woman is the man; and the head of Christ is God.' He loved reading that to my mother. It infuriated her." With that gauntlet thrown down—not directly to his wife but in memory to his mother—the narrator continues:

A mulish perplexity ruffled Macy's usually smooth features. "*What?* The head? The head of every man? What does 'the head' mean exactly? I'm sorry, I just don't understand."
   If he had been able to answer her immediately, he would have done so with a smile, but, though the sense of "head" in the text was perfectly clear, he couldn't find a synonym. After a silence he said, "It's so obvious."
   "Read me the passage again. I really didn't hear it."
   "No," he said.
   "Come on, please. 'The head of the man is God . . .'"
   "No."

And then there is the afterlife of the other biblical text Updike recalls from the family table talk of his youth. The parable of the talents in Matthew 25:14–30 appears in his 1996 loss-of-faith novel *In the Beauty of the Lilies*, where it provides the text for a sermon that Clarence Wilmot, a preacher plagued by doubt, finds he cannot deliver. The parable is also featured in an essay on the Gospel of

Matthew, where Updike, despite allegedly having been a mediocre
Sunday School student, vividly recalls the peculiar power of this
New Testament story for him. Unlike other of Jesus's parables that
"puzzled or repelled" him—"like those in which foolish virgins or ill-
paid vineyard workers are left to wail in outer darkness"—this one
spoke to him, "bore a clear lesson": "Live your life. Live it as if there
is a blessing on it. Dare to take chances, lest you leave your talent
buried in the ground." At this point in the essay, Updike delivers his
own version of a homily. (Unlike Clarence Wilmot, the preacher in
distress, the text does not silence him.) But then he gives the kind
of close observation for which he was justly celebrated as a stylist.
In the course of doing so, he retells Jesus's story of servants and
investment as if it were his own. "I could picture so clearly the hole
that the timorous servant would dig in the dirt, and even imagine how
cozily cool and damp it would feel to his hand as he placed his talent
in it."[14]

As is clear in this essay on Matthew, Updike was by no means
daunted by the "mild-mannered commentary of the Sunday-school
teacher" that almost always turned biblical gold into straw. Instead,
he found in his early exposure to the messy tumble of biblical narrative
a universe on which to draw as a writer, albeit one that was starkly
different from our own. It was "a robed and sandalled world of origins
and crude conflict and direct discourse with God." Before it, he says,

> I seemed to stand on the edge of a brink gazing down at polychrome
> miniatures of abasement and terror, betrayal and reconciliation.
> Jacob deceiving blind Isaac with patches of animal hair on the back
> of his hands, Joseph being stripped of his gaudy coat and left in
> a pit by his brothers, little Benjamin being fetched years later by
> these same treacherous brothers into the imperious presence of a
> mysterious stranger invested with all Pharaoh's authority.[15]

These memories that date "from more than sixty years ago" are
recalled by Updike in his 2004 New Yorker review of Robert Alter's
translation of the Pentateuch. Although as a youth he may have
"failed to win the little perfect attendance pin in May," he clearly
learned what the Bible has to teach about storytelling: God is always
in the details. Wily, smooth-skinned Jacob has the presence of mind

to deceive blind Isaac by putting "patches of animal hair on the back of his hands"; the Egyptian Joseph stands "imperious" before the brothers who years before left him for dead. Updike learned from Scripture as well as from the novelists he esteemed (Proust and Henry Green), that the great abstractions which form the backdrop of our lives—abasement and terror, betrayal and reconciliation—always spring to life only in the form of a gaudy coat or a youngest brother.

*****

As we see in these stories and essays, the Bible is present in Updike's work in a variety of ways. In addition to its appearance as a citation (like 1 Cor. 11:3 in "Sunday Teasing"), or in an autobiographical recollection in the midst of biblical criticism, or in his frequent use of biblical epigraphs at the head of his fiction,[16] there is also another point of entry in his novels: minister characters whose lives are intimately connected to the Bible and whose sermons, delivered to the reader in one way or another, amount to set pieces within the text. In addition to *In the Beauty of the Lilies*—where Wilmot's failed preaching is contrasted to the "success" of cult leader Jesse Smith—there is *Rabbit, Run* (1960), where Christ's temptation in the Wilderness is preached to Rabbit Angstrom by the Reverend Jack Eccles. In *Of the Farm* (1965), there is a substantial and thoroughly Barthian sermon on the creation of Eve that sets off conversation about the relationships of men and women that are as thorny as those that were no doubt generated by St. Paul in Updike's boyhood.[17] In *A Month of Sundays* (1974), which is punctuated by four homilies prepared but not delivered by the disgraced cleric Thomas Marshfield, the preacher draws on both the Gospel of John's account of the woman taken in adultery and the raising of Lazarus. In *The Witches of Eastwick* (1984), the narrative also moves along from one sermon to another, essentially offering an extended parody of the whole homiletic enterprise in contemporary liberal Protestantism. (The final one is delivered by a Satan figure, showing that indeed, even the Devil can quote Scripture.)

*****

Religion was a preoccupation in Updike's short fiction, although less in his later short stories than in the earlier collections; with that preoccupation also came the Bible. He is drawn to ordained or would-be clergy. In "Dentistry and Doubt," it is an American priest in Oxford researching the "judicious" Elizabethan theologian Richard Hooker; in "The Life Guard," a lustful, suntanned narrator who for nine months a year is a pasty seminarian buried in the "immense pages of Biblical text barnacled with fudging commentary" and, like Updike himself in the sixties, plowing "through the terrifying attempts of Kierkegaard, Berdyaev, and Barth to scourge God into being."[18] In "The Deacon" and "Believers," there are dyspeptic churchgoers for whom it is all "indeed a preparation for death" (669) or who recognize that in the end, for all the earnest committee meetings and stabs at edifying reading, busy piety comes to very little: "crushed beneath the majesty of the Infinite, believers and non-believers are exactly alike" (770). Stories that Updike admitted were strongly autobiographical— "Pigeon Feathers," "Packed Dirt, Churchgoing, A Dying Cat, a Traded Car," "The Christian Roommates"—were about, he said, "religious belief under siege" and evidence of "the crisis of faith that new knowledge brings."[19] The fading of belief is recounted in terms of a married couple in "Made in Heaven," in which a husband's practice waxes as a wife wanes.[20] In "The Music School," the narrator cycles between one Eucharistic memory and another: a Roman Catholic priest's new ideas on the sacrament, memories of "a grave, long service" in a Lutheran boyhood. He realizes that in the Gospel accounts of the Last Supper, "Christ did not say, *Take and melt this in your mouth* but *Take and eat*" (522): No, "it was necessary, if not to chew, at least to touch, to embrace and tentatively shape, the wafer with the teeth" (526). From this he moves to a larger thought that expresses Updike's own theology: "The world is the host; it must be chewed" (527).[21]

The later fiction is not so overtly theological. Updike's aging characters are less involved in church or in the unsuccessful pursuit of the Infinite; instead, they attend to irregularities in their own heartbeat, pay attention to receding gums and hairlines. At best, they are like the octogenarian narrator of "The Full Glass," who is "drinking a toast to the visible world, his impending disappearance from it be damned."[22] The protagonist of "Short Easter," a 1988 *New Yorker* story collected in *The Afterlife* (1994), is Fogel: retired, financially well-off, with an enviable amount of worldly security, who also knows himself to be well past his prime. He finds that on the highway other cars seem frequently to tailgate his Mercedes, as if he were falling behind, losing time rather than making it. This sense of loss is made explicit on a particular Easter Sunday when Daylight Savings makes time "spring forward, and, thereby, steal an hour": "Because the clocks had been jumped ahead, the day kept feeling in retard of where it actually was. It was later than he thought."[23] Even Fogel's house seemed to participate in this entropy, as its creaks, decay, and "irreversible expenditures of energy" mirror his personal sense of running down and out.

We are told from the outset that Easter had always been "a holiday without punch," an occasion for disappointing Easter egg hunts and boozy champagne brunches. The one in question is, in fact, more memorable as the anniversary of a particular love affair decades earlier than as a reminder of Christ's resurrection: it is a sign that "all things end" (414). Nonetheless, he is miffed when his wife proposes a morning of yard work rather than entertaining the possibility that he might want to go to church, even if only for the sake of nostalgia. Christianity has no deep hold over his life, and yet unlike his wife, the fact that the day is Easter means something to him, something he can neither name nor get out of his mind.

When at the end of the story he wakes from an afternoon nap in blank fear, he realizes that, although everything in his world seems to be in place, "yet something is immensely missing" (419). Such a realization is a far cry from the disciples' Easter discovery or the angel's announcement, "He is not here, he is risen!" (Matt. 28:6). Nonetheless, it represents for Fogel a moment of truth. Nothing he possesses can make up for what he lacks, nor can anything in his comfortable suburban world fill the need for something more.

*****

Unlike the more sustained appearance of the Bible in Updike's novels, especially those that involve a minister's preaching, references in the short fiction are often simply witty or ironic. For instance, the title of a story from 1969, "I Will Not Let Thee Go, Except Thou Bless Me," comes from the Hebrew Bible's account of Jacob wrestling with the angel in Genesis 32:26: "And he said, Let me go, for the day breaketh. And he said, I will not let thee go, except thou bless me." The title is precisely King James, right down to the comma and archaic diction. And yet the relevance of the passage, which is highly important in Genesis—Jacob is at once wounded and blessed; he receives a new name, "Israel," meaning "the one who strives with God"—is negligible, merely cute, in the story. Tom corrals Maggie onto the dance floor, sentimental about an affair that ended, badly, five years ago. "The music stopped. She tried to back out of his arms, but he held her until, in the little hi-fi cabinet with its sleepless incubatory glow, another record flopped from the stack." Once again he grabs her: "Tom, let go of me."/ "I can't." He persists nonetheless until she breaks free with a devastating put down: "You're *nothing*, Tommy." This time, wounded, he relents: "Tom backed off from Maggie, relieved to let her go, yet hoping, as he yielded her, for a yielding glance. But her stare was stony" (674–75). It's unclear if the title's biblical reference is meant to make an ironic comparison, one that contrasts the monumentality of a biblical turning point with a bitter but finally unimportant leave-taking of former lovers. Is Updike comparing small things to great so as to savor the difference?

A biblical phrase can also be used to signal a character's sensibility. The near octogenarian in "The Full Glass" prepares for bed clutching his pills and other medications, his Xalatan drops to stave off glaucoma and Systane to ease dry eye. Suddenly the Bible breaks through the surface of the story, not only in the character's choice of words but by his explicit identification of their source: "In the middle of the night, on my way to the bathroom, my eye feels like it has a beam in it, not a mote but literally a *beam*—I never took that image from the King James Version seriously before" (903). The passage alluded to comes from Jesus's Sermon on the Mount in Matthew: "And why beholdest thou the mote that is in thy brother's eye, but considerest not the beam that is in thine own eye?" (7:3). There is no indication in the story that we are dealing with a Ruby Turpin, whose judgmental eyes are bristling with beams and who brings to mind the injunction against judging. Updike's dry-eye sufferer is not in any way reproved or even contextualized by the biblical allusion. It merely suggests his breeding, his age, and a world of eighty years ago where people of a certain sort could not only drop Scripture's "mote" and "beam" into common speech but also recall the King James attribution.

From early to late, Updike's short stories are part of a lifelong project "to give human behavior theological scrutiny," "to examine the human predicament from a theological standpoint."[24] In particular, he was interested in describing what it meant to be a religious person at a time when it has become increasingly difficult for many to believe. The Bible is very much a part of this exploration as the foundational Christian text, which, like the faith itself, is both remembered and forgotten. "Pigeon Feathers" is the perfect case in point, with its exploration of a teenage believer appalled by disbelief, on the one hand, and, on the other, by "fusty churches, creaking hymns, ugly Sunday-school teachers and their stupid leaflets" (276). Obsessed by a need to believe in a life after death, disappointed by the demythologized evasions of the Reverend Dobson and his humanist mother, David Kern (a recurrent character in the short fiction) looks for reassurance in Jesus's words from the cross in Luke 23:43, "Today shalt thou be with Me in paradise." He searches for the verse in his grandfather's Bible: "It was a stumpy black book, the boards worn thin where the old man's fingers had held them" (276). The words are there with their promise, but "Nowhere in the world of other people would he find the hint, the nod, he needed to build his fortress against death. They none of them believed. He was alone. In that deep hole" (279).

If Christian faith seems at permanent ebb in 1960's "Pigeon Feathers," it faces an even more devastating challenge when the fortress crumbles on 9/11. "Varieties of Religious Experience" opens with a salvo that cries out in upper case italics: "THERE IS NO GOD: the revelation came to Dan Kellogg in the instant he saw the World Trade Center South Tower fall" (753). The story moves from one religious point of view to another. It opens with Dan, "a sixty-four-year-old Episcopalian and probate lawyer," who once shared Updike's own early recourse to "ingenious and jaunty old books—Kierkegaard, Chesterton," but who has more lately joined "the run of mankind in its stoic atheism" (754). Close by him on the "brutally clear" morning of 9/11 is his granddaughter Victoria, who asks him, "Why does God let bad men do things?" (755). In a following section, those "bad men" are given their voice, along with verses from the Qur'an, before the story turns to those who died at the hands of the terrorists. First, there is the World Trade Center office worker Jim Finch on the phone with his wife ("My blessing, for Chrissake, Marcy. I'm giving a blessing on anything you want to do. It's all right,

Feel free" [766]). Then in the airplane hijacked and brought down over Pennsylvania, there is Carolyn who prays: "*Mercy*, Carolyn managed to cry distinctly inside her pounding head. *Dear Lord, have mercy*" (773). In conclusion Updike returns to Dan Kellogg, who changes his mind half a year later: although the Towers have gone to dust and ashes, he "was here, and God with him; his conversion to atheism had not lasted" (775). There is nothing resounding in his return to the church's "mild-manner fellowship," its "stream of Cranmer's words in which the mind could lose itself," "the taste of the tasteless wafer in his mouth" (775). What matters, however, is that "He was alive, and a shadowy God with him, behind him" (776).

Unlike David Kern in "Pigeon Feathers," who searches for comfort in his grandfather's stumpy, black, well-worn Bible ("Today shalt thou be with Me in paradise"), Dan Kellogg turns to liturgy rather than to Scripture. Updike ends his story, however, at a time months after the attack on the Towers with a biblical reference put in the mouth of Victoria, the granddaughter who earlier had asked on 9/11 why God "let bad men do things." She hopes that in time the gleaming towers will be rebuilt, even though counseled by her grandfather that they were always provocative, asking for trouble: "Those towers were taller than they needed to be." A certain kind of reader might think here of the doomed immensity of Babel skyscraping its way to heaven in Genesis 11 and thereby inspiring God's wrath. Scripture may or may not be in the offing with this reference to overweening towers, an allusion detected only by those with the most sensitive of "ears that hear." It most certainly is recalled—though subtly—in Victoria's reply, to which Updike gives the story's last words: "My teacher at school says the lights are like the rainbow. They mean it won't happen again" (776).

At the end of the Flood story in Genesis (9:8–17), God provides a rainbow to follow the lethal world-destroying deluge. He says to Noah—four times over in the composite authorship of the text—"I do set my bow in the cloud, and it shall be a token of a convent between me and the earth. And it shall come to pass, when I bring a cloud over the earth, that the bow shall be seen in the cloud: And I will remember my covenant, which is between me and you and living creature of all flesh; and the water shall no more become a flood to destroy all flesh" (13–15). It is no doubt significant that whereas Dan Kellogg as a child would probably have heard these words in Sunday

School or church, perhaps proclaimed from a lectern under a vaulted Neo-Gothic ceiling, Victoria gets them at school, from a teacher, in a handing down of tradition that has probably been made "appropriate for children" and cut loose from its original setting. God may be a shadowy figure in the post–9/11 world, and holy books most often quoted by those distorted by a passionate intensity for revealed truth; nonetheless, the Bible lingers on—if not in a place of religious study or worship then, as we have seen in our chapter on the Bible in America, in a classroom. Whoever the bearer of good news may be, the city lights have a message worth passing on to the young. "The lights are like the rainbow. They mean it won't happen again."

7

Jamie Quatro

Like Flannery O'Connor—the writer to whom she is often compared, and whom she references most often in interviews—Jamie Quatro's debut collection of short stories, *I Want to Show You More* (2013), is permeated with the Bible. The Scripture came to her through an upbringing (first in California, then in Arizona) within the Church of Christ—"no instruments in worship, adult baptism by immersion, literal interpretation of the scripture; layman as preachers, able to administer the sacraments."[1] From that Bible-centered background she took away a conviction that language mattered: "Words, written in a book, could be of life and death importance."[2]

Words that "matter" to her, however, are also literary, as one might expect from someone with graduate studies in English as well as an MFA degree. Quatro is widely read in current contemporary fiction but taken aback when she talks to fellow writers "who've all read their contemporaries but have never read Milton or Wordsworth or Dickens."[3] She has also acknowledged the importance of Donald Barthelme, Kafka, Camus, and Beckett, whose collective influence can be seen in her more experimental or fantastic moments.[4] But apart from the familiar contemporary American "masters of the short story form" whom she names at the conclusion of her Acknowledgments,[5] Quatro is quick to identify the importance of those working within a theological tradition congenial to her own: Flannery O'Connor ("of course"), T. S. Eliot, Graham Greene, Walker Percy, Marilynne Robinson, and Thomas Merton. To this list she adds Christian Wiman, author of the 2013 spiritual memoir *My Bright Abyss: Meditation of a*

Modern Believer ("which has unlocked the universe for me. My soul sang alongside every word").[6]

Whereas Flannery O'Connor was a Southern writer by birth, born and buried in the Bible Belt (albeit in ground consecrated by Roman Catholicism), Quatro is a transplant from other places. Before assuming her present location on the Georgia side of Lookout Mountain, she lived in San Diego, Tucson, Malibu, Los Angeles, Williamsburg, VA, and Princeton. The stories in *I Want to Show You More*, although set in borderline Georgia, are indisputably part of a New South seemingly in another universe from that of O'Connor's post-Second World War farmers, backwoods evangelists, embattled matriarchs, and criminal interlopers.

There are still signs of the old religion: "Pastor Murray oiled a thumb print on the woman's forehead and prayed that God would 'strangle the tumors'" (86). Church camps continue to look for dramatic ways to "introduce God" to teenagers ("Sinkhole"); troubled adults call prayer hotlines, memorize Scripture, take prayer walks, place hope in anointing.

But there is nothing backwoods about the milieu of Quatro's Lookout Mountain. Women go to hot yoga classes or, dressed in black spandex, set out for ambitious runs. They find Lifestyle magazine ways to bring comfort—"Chicken broth, lit candles, hot baths, Enya's Winter album" (7)—before the pastor comes for prayer and counseling. Whereas no television appeared in O'Connor's fiction, and scarcely a mention was made of a commercial brand—Hulga's "Vapex" perfume is one exception to the rule—Quatro's stories are replete with twenty-first-century things: pastel Skittles and protein bars, cellphones and laptops, not to mention all the wares that can be purchased from lubricious online offerings: "One day you click on the pop-up ads for the Jackrabbit, Silver Bullet, Astroglide for Beginners, Butterfly Kiss. The next day you order the Classic G Natural, which arrives overnight in an unmarked box" (17). Quatro is adept at using the internet and smartphone, to the point that in a whimsical mood she can imagine what it would look like were God to "text" the Ten Commandments.[7]

Aside from a Battle of the Chickamauga restaging in the story "Ladies and Gentlemen of the Pavement," it is difficult to remember that in Quatro's fiction we are in Dixie. Except, that is, for the presence of the Bible in this fictional landscape. The references are easy to find. A woman confessing her long-distance adultery ("the recordings of your voice you created using GarageBand, the nude photos you emailed. The phone sex") is likened by her pastor to Jacob who "wrestled with God and overcame. But make no mistake: those who wrestle come away wounded. You will walk with a limp for the rest of your life" (9). Another woman—or perhaps the same woman refracted several times over in the collection—is almost taken in an adulterous kiss but then heeds an admonishing voice that comes to her straight out of Genesis: "*Joseph and Potiphar's wife—flee*" (100). A mother trying to reassure a child that she may well "beat" cancer falls back on "the story of Hezekiah, God prolonging his life, making the sun retreat up the steps" (132). A boy who wants to heal a dead infant brother thinks twice about extending his hand: "I remember how God strikes people down for trying to mess with his decisions: Adam and Eve kicked out of Eden, Pharaoh and his army drowned in the Red Sea, Herod eaten up by worms" (149).

The story "Holy Ground" is especially rich in Bible banter. At an urban shelter for women in Chattanooga—named "The Oak Project" after Isaiah 61:3, "They will be called oaks of righteousness, the planting of the Lord, to display his glory"—a woman named Danielle reads from the first epistle of John. The story's narrator says, "The translation is edgy and full of slang: *I'm not writing anything new here, friends. Whoever hates is still in the dark, doesn't know which end is up.* When she closes the book I see the cover: The Rainbow Bible."[8] The women in the Oak Project may be down on their luck but are able to speak with one another freely, often humorously, in the language of Scripture. "If you call out a verse I can find it in ten seconds" (191). When the addled narrator confesses to any number of youthful sins—sex in ninth grade, shoplifting in college while on a Young Life mission trip—the women remind her that she is "God's girl" nonetheless. Why? "No one is righteous, not even one, Jade says" (198). Her response comes from Paul in Romans 3:12, who is himself quoting the Psalmist (14:3, 53:2).

New Yorker literary critic James Wood framed his influential review of *I Want to Show You More* by placing Quatro's literary engagement with adultery—her obsession "with almost-errancy: the long distance, not quite infidelity"—in the context of the New

Testament's oscillation between judgment and forgiveness, between sins committed and those only contemplated "in the heart" (Matt. 5:28). Quatro writes, Wood says, "in the shadow of Christian belief and Christian prohibition."[9] It is certainly true that many of her female protagonists—or, again, the same troubled figure who shows up in several stories—are burdened by a sense of sin reinforced by Bible verses and Calvinist theology ("I can recite the Westminster short catechism and explain Calvin's TULIP" [191]). Scripture and tradition cast their shadows, but it is precisely in Christianity's uncertain territory that Quatro writes her fiction, with a cast of characters who discover in the aftermath of their sinning that, while No is as necessary to the religious life as Yes, grace abounds—and Yes prevails in the end.

It is in this spirit that the collection's final story reaches its conclusion. Now ended, a passionate long-distance affair three years earlier haunts a woman as she stands lakeside with her loving husband, both admiring their children at play. Her former lover comes to mind, and in particular their dalliance over the telephone about a particular kind of apple: "I said, 'Best thing about fall: the Honeycrisp, and you said, I adore the Honeyscrisp, and in the silence that followed, there was between us—what else to call it?—something like joy." Recalling that moment, and the near occasion of sin it represented—if disembodied, and only over the telephone—the narrator finds herself traveling back in time to Genesis and Eden, to the first man and woman, and to the sharing of forbidden fruit. But instead of "all our woe," as Milton would have it in the opening lines of *Paradise Lost*, she retrieves "something like joy" from her "fall": "I was thinking of Eve and her apple, or whatever kind of fruit it was; how she was driven by delight to share the taste with one she loved, and it ruined them both, but God, knowing this in advance, loved them anyhow" (204). Adultery, even if kept in the heart and out of bed, turns out to be adultery after all. But, as Jade at the Oak Project might put it to this new Eve, "You'll still be God's girl."

*****

Quatro, although still in the early stages of a career, has been warmly celebrated by many writers and critics alike, praised for what Jill McCorkle calls "amazing stories [that] explore human boundaries between the physical world and the spiritual—lust, betrayal, and loss in perfect balance with love, redemption, and grace."[10] Not all her readers have been so happy with the "perfect balance," however, especially those who have found her mixture of spirit and flesh not only unsettling but even obscene.[11] Her response has been to invoke the witness of O'Connor: "I'm with Flannery: the role of the artist, even—no, especially the Christian artist—is to present the world as it is, in all its complexity and ugliness."[12] One might note, however, that sex is largely absent from O'Connor's fiction, or if present, then largely an aspect of the grotesque. Her readers were disturbed for other reasons, not the celebration of sensuality at play in *I Want to Show You*, whether in the mind or on a cell phone.

But Quatro's real defense of her stories against her conservative critics is not the witness of O'Connor, it is none other than Scripture. In one interview she imagines her disapproving readers flanked before her. With the Bible at her fingertips, she can beat them at their own game:

> Have you read the Bible? Abram and Sarai use Hagar, then rid themselves of her and the child they forced her to bear; Lot was an alcoholic and had sex with his own daughters; Moses killed an Egyptian and cowered behind his brother Aaron, who did all the talking for him; David committed adultery with Bathsheba and had her husband, Uriah the Hittite, murdered; Saul held Stephen's garments while overseeing his stoning, then went from church to church, dragging followers of "The Way" off to prison. These are the heroes of the faith.[13]

The upshot here is also biblical: There is none that doeth good, no, not one.

But Quatro does not appeal to the Scripture only for its warts-and-all truth telling or for its flawed heroes. The Bible animates her work more positively, and perhaps especially the Old Testament Song of Songs once it is shorn of the allegorical interpretations that have been imposed upon it by Jews and Christians alike. The text itself is alluded to only sparingly by Quatro's erstwhile lovers in the two-page story "Imperfections," but nonetheless makes an impression. The Song's "set me as a seal upon your heart" (8:6) becomes "*Like you put a seal on my forehead*, I wrote him later, *and hot wax dripped*

down into my eye" (100); so too the Song's delight in cataloguing
body parts (cheeks, mouth, neck, breasts, thighs) is recalled in the
man's long-distance request, "won't you please send me a picture of
your foot, breast, ear, some part of you."[14] But more than citations like
these, the spirit of the Song is what makes it Quatro's Gospel, her
biblical inspiration for bringing together "the erotic and the spiritual,
the sexual and the sacred"[15]:

> I'm often flummoxed by religious strictures on sexual behavior on
> the one hand and the rampant scriptural use of sexual imagery
> and metaphor on the other. . . . It seems there's something
> inherently erotic about the way we're supposed to think about
> God (bridegroom; unless you consume me, you have no part
> in me) and the way he thinks about us (the return of Christ as
> "consummation," the church as his Bride, et cetera).[16]

Although that Christian tradition has often separated Eros from
Caritas, sexual from spiritual love, Quatro is convinced the two are
closely aligned—at least they are for her as a writer: "Of course this
alignment has been distorted and subverted in a myriad of ways, and
I find this endlessly fascinating and worth exploring."[17] Indeed, her
probing of such distortion and subversion is much of what her fiction
is about, even as it explores the impulse toward union that prompts
her characters—and herself as an avowedly Christian writer—to take
risks. As one of her narrators confesses in a letter to her sister, "I
think I want to have an affair with him [Jesus] because I'm in love
with God. My body is so mixed up with my soul I'm not sure there's a
difference anymore."[18] Whether or not Quatro has herself experienced
this kind of fusion is irrelevant: it is what she wants to write about:
"An artist must probe these moments. She cannot look away. In the
act of creation, she must ask herself—*require* herself—to suspend all
judgment. She must beg the same of her readers."[19]

*****

In "Caught Up," the opening story of *I Want to Show You More*, the
collection's tormented adulteress-in-the-heart (and over-the-phone)
recalls a recurrent vision from childhood "It was always the same":
she stands on the brick patio of her house as the sky's clouds turn

shades of red and purple, forming a kind of tornado: "Whirlpool, hurricane, galaxy." The wind picks up, whips her hair across her face, and sets the stage for what will surely be a cataclysm: "Then came a tugging in my middle, as if I were a kite about to be yanked up by a string attached just below my navel. Takeoff was imminent; all I had to do was surrender—close my eyes, relax my limbs—and I would be catapulted, belly-first, into the vortex." The reader is primed for something like Yeats's vision of things falling apart and coming together: "Surely some revelation is at hand, / Surely the Second Coming is at hand. / The Second Coming!" Or maybe "Leda and the Swan": "Being so caught up, / So mastered by the brute blood of the air, . . ."[20] Instead, in a new paragraph, Quatro gives us a two sentence anti-climax: "The vision ended there. I never left the patio."

In the absence of any actual rapture into the realm of "up," the narrator's mother gives a religious interpretation of the vision that affirms, "God speaks to his children in dreams." And so God does, from Jacob and Joseph in Genesis, to another Joseph in the Gospel according to Matthew (1:20–25) and to Peter in the Acts of the Apostles (9:9–16), not to mention the seer in the Revelation to John, who goes from one heaven-opening vision to another. In Quatro's story, the child is told that she is being prepared (one might almost say groomed) for the end time: "[her mother] said, we should always be ready for the Lord's return: lead a clean life and stay busy with our work, keeping an eye skyward."

The biblical warrant for this advice, which combines expectation with admonition, comes from Saint Paul's first letter to the Thessalonians. The Apostle begins by instructing his "brothers and sisters" in how they should live "through the Lord Jesus": "For this is the will of God, your sanctification: that you abstain from fornication; that each one of you know how to control your own body in holiness and honor, not with lustful passion like the Gentiles who do not know God" (4:3–5). Instead of fornicating, they are to love one another as siblings, "to aspire to live quietly, to mind your own affairs, and to work with your hands" (11). For good reason, therefore, the nine-year-old girl imagines her mother taking her own counsel to heart by positioning herself skyward, "up on our roof, sitting in a folding chair, snapping beans" (1).

Paul follows his charge to the faithful of Thessalonica with a vision of what they might expect to occur at some future but unknowable time when "Whirlpool, hurricane, galaxy" (1) will precede Christ's Second Coming:

> For the Lord himself, with a cry of command, with the archangel's call and with the sound of God's trumpet, will descend from heaven, and the dead in Christ will rise first. Then we who are alive, who are left, will be caught up in the clouds together with them to meet the Lord in the air; and so we will be with the Lord forever. Therefore encourage one another with these words. (4:16–18)

This end-time event is only adumbrated, never actually described, in Scripture. It is a "day of the Lord" that will come like a thief in the night (1 Thess. 5:2, 2 Pet. 3:10), when two men will be in a field, one taken up and the other left behind (Matt. 24:37–42, Luke 17:35–37). This "Rapture" has long been the preoccupation of Evangelicals, who have debated the sequence of events following upon the Second Coming.[21] Since the 1970s, the sudden disappearance of the blessed "caught up in the clouds" with Christ (with the reprobate abandoned to the Great Tribulation), has been popularized by Hal Lindsey's *Late Great Planet Earth* (1970) and Tim LaHaye's *Left Behind* series of novels, both of which have been turned into film.[22]

In Quatro's "Caught Up," the nine-year-old visionary finds that, as she matures, her dream fades away.[23] In lieu of the Lord's return, she has the advent of a devoted husband who cherishes her flesh as well as her soul, who, she confides, "never goes to sleep without kissing some part of my body. He says he wants to know, on his deathbed, that his lips have touched every square inch" (2). It is not with her lawful bridegroom, however, that she experiences rapture. It is the man on the phone who brings her to something very like the former visionary "take off." After she hangs up the phone, the heavens open: "the light sped down the street" toward her; the road seemed to be moving on its own, "a conveyer belt that would scoop me up from underneath": "The old vision returned. The upward tug in my belly. I recognized the feeling—what I felt every time the other man, the faraway man, told me what he would do if he had me in person, my wrists pinned over my head" (2–3).

What Would Saint Paul Say? This is all fornication, the lustful passion of Gentiles "who do not know God." But in the story, the woman and man (to recall Quatro's own terms) unite "the erotic and the spiritual, the sexual and the sacred." The woman is unsure, but the man is not: "It would be devotional, he'd said. I would lay myself on your tongue like a Communion wafer." He also co-opts her vision: "Above us the sky rips open and God is there, smiling down, and what he is saying is *Yes*" (3).

It is unclear whether the couple ever actually meet. The affair, such as it is, moves to the past tense, but the desire for the ecstasy— of being caught up and taken away—remains. The woman tells her mother that she wishes the phone sex had never happened, because then they might have been able to save a friendship, have a future: "I told her that something inside me was weeping all the time, and that I hoped there would be a literal Second Coming and Consummated Kingdom because then the man and I could spend eternity just talking" (4). The mother, however, will have none of this. Unconsummated adultery, although limited to the phone and kept in the heart, is adultery nonetheless. She is guilty, in fact, given the story's last words, "It's all the same in God's eyes."

But is it? Perhaps; and certainly so, if one stands by Matthew 5:27– 28. But then there is in the plenitude of Quatro's biblical resources, what James Wood refers to as "the softer Song of Solomon"[24]—"I sat down under his shadow with great delight, and his fruit was sweet to my taste" (2:3)—as well as Jesus's comment to those who would stone the adulteress in John 8:7, "Let him who is without sin cast the first stone." Quatro negotiates her way through the Scripture, finding in its various voices a way to allow No and Yes to be heard at the same time, with *Yes* ringing clear if not loud throughout *If I Could Show You More*.

8

Steven Millhauser

Although Steven Millhauser has written four novels—including the Pulitzer Prize-winning *Martin Dressler* (1996)—he holds short fiction in higher esteem. In an essay (another of Millhauser's preferred forms) on the short story, he imagines the sense of the inferiority the latter must feel. "I'm not a novel, you know. Not even a short one. If that's what you're looking for, you don't want me," the short story cries out to its potential reader. It goes on: "rarely has one form so dominated another. And we understand, we nod our heads knowingly: here in America, size is power."[1]

It is precisely the diminutive size of the short story that so captivates Millhauser. "Large things tend to be unwieldy, clumsy, crude; smallness is the realm of elegance and grace. It's also the realm of perfection." If "the novel is the Wal-Mart, the Incredible Hulk, the jumbo jet of literature," the short story is something entirely other—a single grain of sand. A world in miniature. No, more. The whole universe in miniature, for "in that single grain of sand lies the beach that contains the grain of sand. In that single grain of sand lies the ocean that dashes against the beach, the ship that sails the ocean, the sun that shines down on the ship, the interstellar winds, a teaspoon in Kansas, the structure of the universe."[2]

Millhauser's predilection for the very short accounting is exemplified in the response he gave to the *New York Times* editor who requested a brief biography in preparation for a *Times* review. Millhauser knows the form well. He has written two books that one critic has dubbed "apocryphal biographies"—a choice term for us, with our interest in all things biblical—"(rather than mock or fictional biographies), since apocryphal texts are not always considered completely false or lacking in truth. Rather, their existence often invites us to reconsider an established truth or even the authenticity of an original text."[3] Millhauser's response to the editor? "(1943–)."[4]

Millhauser's autobiography is not even a single word, only a single date. It is the shortest of short stories, and perhaps the closest to perfect. For Millhauser, at least: "The short story apologizes for nothing. It exults in its shortness. It wants to be shorter still. It wants to be a single word. If it could find that word, if it could utter that syllable, the entire universe would blaze up out of it with a roar."[5] "(1943–)" is maybe not the syllable that will cause the universe to roar, but it certainly stops the reader short—and makes the literary critic quest for something more expansive.

Critics and reviewers typically mention a few salient facts about Millhauser— he's lived most of his life in Connecticut and New York, where many of his stories are set; he began a PhD in English at Brown but ended up writing a novel, *Edwin Mullhouse*, not a dissertation; he is a professor of English at the City College of New York, not unlike his father who was a professor of English at City College NY and the University of Bridgeport. Only one of them, however, has offered any sustained analysis of what we know (and don't know) about the span of time between "(1943–)" and now. In an article that treats at some length the apparent failure of critics to pick up on cues laced throughout *Edwin Mullhouse* that the protagonist is, in fact, Jewish, Josh Lambert probes Millhauser's own Jewish roots. He notes that *everyone* has read Millhauser "as an American, and not Jewish, writer."[6] Reviews of his work never note that he is Jewish nor do Jewish anthologies ever include his work. Lambert sees this is a major oversight, one that closes off certain interpretive avenues:

> Critical readings that assume Millhauser to be an American-and not-Jewish-writer and *Edwin Mullhouse* to be an American-and not-Jewish-text suppress these historical, cultural, and personal contexts to the point of erasure, intentionally or not. Critics and scholars have of course not been wrong to read Millhauser into other interpretive frames as, for instance, a contemporary fabulist, or miniaturist, or American postmodernist, as the heir to a Nabokovian or Borgesian program, but it does not belittle

Millhauser's achievement to recognize that the novel is also a masterful distillation of what the professional study of literature could mean to Jews in the postwar period.[7]

No one but Lambert, it would seem, has dared to plumb the depths of Millhauser's biography.

This critical disinterest may come from the fact that Millhauser is regarded as a private person who has sought out neither publicity nor celebrity. The New York Times called him "a playfully reticent man [who] is rarely heard from outside his fictions."[8] Perhaps as a result, Millhauser has suffered somewhat from what Alicita Rodriguez, in the Review of Contemporary Fiction devoted to his work, calls a "lack of notice."[9] For a writer so esteemed by the literary establishment, and one who has written so much and been so appreciated by reviewers, he has not received serious scholarly attention much less a mainstream following. In recent years, reviews of his work in both the popular and literary press have proliferated, but academic articles have not followed suit.

If Millhauser scholars are few in number, they all comment on the recurrence of certain entities in his work: museums, hotels, amusement parks, and especially miniatures. Millhauser himself has written somewhat theoretically on the miniature, which he describes as "an attempt to reproduce the universe in graspable form"[10]—not unlike the grain of sand that is the short story. "The gigantic seizes my attention with a force equal to that of the miniature, but it does not awe me," he says.[11] "I am under the spell of the miniature. Galaxies and supernovas turn at the end of my kaleidoscope. I gratify my secret desire: I become a giant. I draw out leviathan with a hook, I play with him as with a bird." Millhauser is God, speaking to Job from the whirlwind: "Can you draw out Leviathan with a fishhook? Can you press down his tongue by a rope? Can you put a ring through his nose or pierce his jaw with a barb? Will you play with him like a bird, and tie him down for your girls?" (Job 40:25–32, JPS). Millhauser can. To create or even to engage the miniature is (to catch another biblical echo, from the serpent in Genesis 3) "to be like God." To Millhauser, the miniature "represents a desire to possess the world more completely, to banish the unknown and the unseen. We are teased out of the world of terror and death, and under the enchantment of the miniature we are invited to become God."[12] Ultimately, it is not enough to be Creator: He closes his essay expressing his desire also to be his own creature.

Until recently, this was as close as Millhauser would come to talking directly about God and the Bible. Occasionally others would do the honors for him, as when Daniel Orozco began his introduction to Millhauser's short story "Flying Carpets" in the *Paris Review*'s anthology *The Art of the Short Story*, by quoting 1 Corinthians 13:11, in which Paul writes about the giving up of childish things. By and large, however, these are not concerns that often appear in his fiction. Reading through the index of the single critical study of Millhauser, one encounters a wide-ranging list of other common themes (among them we find "lists" which are one of the writer's delights. As Arthur Salzman points out, Millhauser, like Borges, is in love with catalogues.[13]) Topics include (but are not limited to): American dream; animation/cartoons; architecture; automaton; boredom; childhood; gigantism; illusionism/magic; infidelity; medieval world; suicide; and superstore. Nowhere in the long list of recurring motifs do we find subjects that have direct bearing on our work here. No Religion, Christianity, or Judaism. Nor do we find Bible, Old Testament, New Testament, God, Jesus, Mary, or Joseph. But then, suddenly, "Moses" appears. That name warrants notice. Why? Earl Ingersoll reads Martin Dressler's father as coming "to America seeking the Promised Land, but like Moses he gets no more than a Pisgah view because he is too timid, too beaten down the Old Country to do more than beget a son who will dream the Dream."[14] Maybe other people read him that way too. It's not clear that Millhauser does.

To the contrary, when Millhauser truly wants you to think Bible, he will tell you so. He will call a story "The Tower" and in it he will make reference to a place called the Plain of Shinar. Genesis 10:10 tells us Shinar is the beginning of the kingdom of Nimrod, while Genesis and Zechariah 5:11 tell us it is the location that God commanded a house be built for an ephah, but more to the point, Genesis 11 tells us this is where the people who migrated from the east settled and built a tower. The tower of Babel, in case it needs be said—which it might. In his *New York Times* review of the 2008 short-story collection *Dangerous Laughter*, D. T. Max reads the city and the tower as a New Yorker might, noting, "the city in 'The Tower' lives in the shadow of an ever-growing edifice, an embodiment of its ambition to free itself from mortality and physicality that, in the final moments of the story, comes crashing down. This last story has overtones of both the Bible and, of course, 9/11."[15] Millhauser himself emailed Ingersoll as he was writing *Understanding Steven Millhauser* to clarify, "I think early in the discussion of this story, the reader needs to be told that the tower is based on the Tower of Babel. Jehovah destroyed that tower before it reached heaven—I imagined its successful completion."[16] Preempting the possibility that the reader might focus only on the echoes of the World Trade Center towers in the story, Millhauser set the record straight: this is foremost a story about the Tower of Babel.

Beyond the reference to Shinar, there are other clues, of course, that Millhauser is thinking about the Bible. His tower is made of bitumen, which is true of the Genesis tower too: its builders said, "'Come, let us make bricks, and burn them thoroughly.' And they had brick for stone and bitumen for mortar" (Gen. 11:3). The pseudepigraphic book of Jubilees tells us the bitumen came from the sea of Shinar (10:20), but in Millhauser's account there is no sea in sight. The people of Shinar seem decidedly terrestrial—so much so that they develop a weariness of the earth and a desire for air, which translates into their impulse to build upward.

Millhauser's architectural details are specific. Like God, with his instructions to Noah about the construction of the ark, Millhauser provides dimensions: the tower is enormous, a feat of architecture unlike any before it. Its continuous growth upward requires frequent emendations to the design. Two circular ramps wind their way up and down the structure. Off of these are hollows and chambers, and eventually permanent residences. At the top is a high court. At the bottom, a city, populated at first, then abandoned to the lure of the tower, then repopulated when nostalgia for it swept through the tower dwellers. All the specific images are concrete, and yet the whole is impossible to visualize. It is another instance of Millhauser's "impossible architectures"[17]—a tower so tall that no person can reach the top of it in a lifetime. So tall, in fact, that a person can only aspire to have a grandchild or a great-grandchild reach the top.

There is a slow and certain movement of people across the distant plain, into the surrounding city, and up along the ever-growing tower, which comes to be counterbalanced by a similar movement in the opposite direction. For many inhabitants, the weariness of earth and desire for air turn to a weariness of air and a desire for earth. The edifice is a "testimony to human overreaching,"[18] the story a reflection on human striving and human insatiability. It is also a meditation on the human tendency to self-segregate based on ideology. The horizontalists (people who organize their lives around others and activities that occupy the same level of the tower as they do) do not interact with either of the two branches of verticalists. One of these was oriented upward, longing "to reach the top, or to settle on a level that would permit their children or their children's children to reach the top"; the other branch, oriented downward toward the plain, is pulled by "a sudden yearning for the familiar world."[19]

"The Tower" has been read as a compelling account of the vicissitudes of human faith. Even those faithful who orient themselves toward the heavens, who lead lives directed to getting them there, do sometimes find themselves confronting the irrationality of their desire, the almost inevitable doubt—is it really possible to get to heaven? Does it even exist? On the face of it, in Millhauser's story faith is rewarded: the tower actually pierces heaven and people gain entry. But even this is not satisfying, as reports of heaven passed down are perceived to be untrustworthy, inaccurate, or ultimately underwhelming. In an interview Millhauser notes, "Here, among other things, I was trying to present a heaven that is desperately longed for but is finally less interesting than the world far below. But the most vital place of all is the structure that joins the two worlds: the ephemeral tower itself, the embodiment of desire."[20] The tower is a manifestation of human yearning for a sustained connection with heaven.

If we turn from religious impulses more generally back to the Bible specifically, the story is also about the human failure of language. God views the success of the tower as a reason to confound the people's language, as he does in Genesis, so that they can no longer speak easily to one another and therefore will not conspire against him. Paul Auster's return to the Tower of Babel in his *City of Glass* trilogy involves a quest to rebuild the edifice and reconstruct the original language. This contemporary version departs from Genesis: the concern is not how we get back to that time when we all spoke one language, but how it is that we all speak one language but cannot understand each other. Millhauser's tower is allowed to reach heaven, and humans are allowed to communicate freely with one another about what they find there. Even without divine intervention, however, their language becomes confounded: "Meanwhile reports of heaven continued to sift down through the tower, and reports of the plain drifted up, at times mingling and growing confused."[21] The swirl of messages, of "downward nostalgia and upward longing" gives rise to one sect asserting that heaven lay not up in the heavens but down below, "a wondrous place of twisting streets, marketplace stalls heaped with fruit, and two-story houses with wooden galleries running along inner courtyards."[22] This becomes part of the babble—"an extreme instance of the many common confusions of that time. Reports of heaven by actual visitors often seemed unconvincing or deceptive, while people who have never left the Tower began to add colorful touches and even to invent journeys of their own."[23] The imagined heaven surpassed the real in every way, and the distortions led some to strive harder to achieve heaven, but brought upon others "a tiredness, a spiritual heaviness" that put an end to their striving and enabled them to live mostly contentedly where they already were. God, it seems, did not need to intervene for humans to miscommunicate.

Neither, it seems, did he need to intervene by bringing down the tower. Nonetheless, Millhauser's Babel story ends ominously. Amid all the conflicting reports, doubts arise that the tower even exists. No one, after all, had ever seen the whole. Any one person could only take in a portion of it—the whole would vanish from sight "no matter where you stood. Except for a handful of visible bricks, the whole thing was little more than a collection of rumors, longings, dreams, and travelers' tales."[24] The people become listless, disenchanted. They turn their attentions to new towers, neglecting the old. "In this atmosphere of weariness and restlessness, of sudden yearnings that collapsed into torpor,"[25] cracks appear in the bricks, piles of rubble amass around the outer ramp, strange creaking sounds grow louder. The last notes of the story come just before the fall:

On a table in a high chamber, a bowl of figs began to slide. Down below, on one of the buttresses, a row of sparrows rose into the air with beating wings, like the sound of a shaken rug. A wine cup rolled along the floor, smacked into a wall. A wagon, beside a sack of grain, fell through the air. Far away, a shepherd looked up from his flock. He bent his head back, shading his eyes.[26]

Human striving alone undoes itself. God does not interfere.

In Genesis, when God comes down to see the city and the tower that man has built, he muses aloud, "If, as one people with one language for all, this is how they have begun to act, then nothing that they may propose to do will be out of their reach" (Gen. 11:6, JPS). He scatters the people over the face of the earth and thus they cease from their building of the city. Unlike in Genesis, where God must come down to assess the tower, Millhauser's tower is so great that it pierces the very heavens. Presumably, the Creator—who is only mentioned but does not appear in Millhauser's story—has seen the people's creation and is apparently unperturbed by it. Their impossible architecture is, after all, impossible. God does not need to punish hubris: sheer hubris will be its own undoing.

*****

Millhauser, our ostensibly secular writer, makes a second sustained turn to the Bible, albeit in an even less direct fashion, in "People of the Book," one of the short stories in *We Others* (2011). Reviewers and bloggers seem not to know what to make of it. One critic describes it as "a one-note joke that doesn't land,"[27] another asserts that it "apes a biblical tone with none of Scripture's richness and complexity,"[28] a third readily admits, "I really have no idea what 'People of the Book' is supposed to be about."[29] And perhaps their ambivalence is warranted: it *is* a peculiar story. An address to an assembly of "dear young scholars," it is an explication of what precisely it means to be the "People of the Book."

In Millhauser's imagining, this phrase turns out to be quite literal—the speaker's audience consists of people who not only love books, for whom "every moment spent away from books [is] a punishment and desolation of spirit," but who in fact "originate from books." The speaker expounds on a passage from something called The Book of Legends that has until this moment been withheld from the young scholars in their study of the work: "The Excursus in the seventh volume, which in its full title is known as the Excursus on the Copulation of Books." It is a creation story, an accounting of the first book, set in a time before there were humans, when "the Creator breathed the breath of his incomparable being" into Twelve Tablets of stone. "As living things they possessed the powers that rightly belong to living things, among which are numbered locomotion and copulation," and the tablets proliferated.

As did man, once he was created: "it happened one day that a scholar, reading in a garden, under the shade of a pomegranate tree, grew tired in the warmth of the afternoon." As he slept (deeply), "it chanced that a maiden, the daughter of the house at which the young man was staying, entered the garden." Curious about the stone tablet lying in the grass next to the drowsing scholar, she sits down beside him, places the tablet in her lap and also falls asleep in the afternoon sun. "And behold, the divine spirit, which breathes through the generations of books, was present in that tablet of stone, and passed into the womb of the maiden. Thus she grew big with child." The speaker proclaims, "In this manner our race was born," going on to explain to his young scholars that "as we grow fruitful and multiply, we who derive, however slantwise, however remotely, from those first tablets of stone on the first day of creation, so we participate in the animating spirit of the universe, of which we are the guardians and the perpetuators." Their race, he says, has "spread to every corner of the earth, where [they] mingle with ordinary men and women," but they can recognize one another "by the outward signs of our inward devotion: the intense application to study, the habit of inattention to the physical world, the rejection of external distraction, a fanaticism of the desk."

So "fervent [is our] devotion to books, my dear ones, it is necessary that our relations with them be clearly established by law," which is outlined in the vast Book of Laws. There is to be no destroying, injuring, or maiming books—all are criminal acts to be punished by death. No copulation with books, no lying lasciviously atop or under them. These misdeeds are punished by "mutilation of the sexual parts." The aim of the speaker here is not to frighten the young scholars but to impart a deep sense of the sanctity of books— and also to introduce, obliquely at first, the topic of death.

The final portion of the address treats the "meaning of death, for us who burn with a desire to find our way to life, to the breath of the Creator breathed into the First Book of all." These young scholars, only thirteen years old, "already lie on [their] deathbeds" for they are older than Adam, older than Noah, older even than Methuselah— three venerable figures from Genesis, each associated in his own way with death.[30] From the moment of their birth they have been dying:

> You are born wailing, and why? Because when you open your eyes, Death grins at you from your mother's face. You come into the world with a knife in your neck. Your mother rocks you in your coffin. You learn to crawl inside a grave. The worm is your brother. Dead men's bones are your sisters. Who is the bridegroom? Who is the bride? Behold the two skeletons, kissing under the canopy. What is life? A sickbed in a hospital. The nurses are busy. The doctor is dying. No one will ever come.

Not only are the scholars dying, so too is their race.

In the Book of Prophecies, "We read that our people, so rich in wisdom, so rich in suffering, chosen above all others to find the undiscovered words, are destined to come to an end. There we read that the mountains will fall. The sky will grow dark. All mankind will cease." Books also come to an end, but ultimately their lot is hopeful: in the Seventh Paradise there is a Paradise for them. "There you may find the eternal and unchanging shape of every book that has ever been born." Moreover, as the People of the Book, these scholars have an ordained place in this heavenly realm: "When you complete your dying, you will ascend to the Paradise of Books and live in joy forever."

Having shown the scholars the meaning of death revealed the secret of their people—"for before the beginning was, the First Book is. That is the sum of all wisdom. That is all you need to know"—the speaker sends them on their way. "Tomorrow you will begin your long journey through the commentaries," he says. It is a journey of seven years that will tire and perplex the scholars, but they will overcome any sense of hopelessness if they remember what has just been revealed:

> Remember the secret of our people. Remember the Paradise of Books. And when you rise from the study-room, bowed down with weariness, then I say unto you, my dear ones: Lift your eyes to the heaven-shelves on every wall, lift your eyes to the living and breathing words that surround you, to the books that soar over you, lift your eyes in rapture, and know who you are: for behold, they are the Ancestors, row on row.

On some level, the story could simply be about people who love books—about people who "spend every spare moment bent over a book," who are "known by their signs" (a reference to Mark 16:17): "the back laboriously bent, the neck frozen, the head immobile, the eyes burning, the arms still as stone." Their affection for books is so strong that it is *as though* they are descended from them. But Millhauser uses a metaphor, not a simile. He is not speaking of people who love books, but people who are actually descended from them.

The idea of books as generative shows up in an interview with Millhauser about his influences, his use and refraction of other people's writing: "My book came from something deeper, more personal, more intimate, more ungraspable, more obscure than other people's books, though at the same time it was pleased to make use of those books in order to become itself, in order to give birth to itself. Books as midwives—maybe that's what I mean."[31] Is this how he intends us to understand that books are our ancestors?

It is no surprise that even those critics who praised the story were confused by it. In his *Boston Globe* review, Max Winter describes "the most intriguingly unhinged of the new works . . . [as] a commencement speech in which the speaker tells a crowd of 13-year-olds the origins of their race: human copulation with books."[32] A commencement speech? Do Jews not collectively self-identify as the "People of the Book," taking the term from the Qur'an and consciously appropriating it for themselves? Do they not have as a central rite the bar mitzvah, at which the 13-year-old male reads from the Torah—the Five Books of Moses—as part of his ritual passage from childhood to adulthood?

Kirkus Review understands that there is something explicitly religious—biblical, even—going on in the story, which it describes as "a religious allegory complete with a virgin birth."[33] The narrator gives us other reasons to read the story in light of Mary (and by extension, Jesus)—"the union between a tablet and a maiden . . . [is a union] between the spirit and the body, the word and the flesh." These are binaries articulated in the writings of Paul and the Gospel of John. Ingersoll, for his part, recognizes some echoes of the Hebrew Bible as he observes, "This 'Book' narrative begins to remind readers of the Old Testament's textuality, what with Jahweh (*sic*) speaking Creation into existence and later writing the Ten Commandments on the tablets Moses accepts on Mount Sinai."[34] But there is much more going on than Ingersoll suggests.

It seems clear that "People of the Book" is a subversion of the creation stories in Genesis. Set on the first day of creation, "before the light was divided from the darkness," it describes the Creator "breath[ing] the breath of his incomparable being" not into the first man but into tablets that are able to reproduce, creating more and more books. There is in this a suggestion of something before, of stages of creation prior to the sixth day in Genesis, when God created humans, a flicker of the Lilith story (which is treated in more detail in Chapter 11), as well as a strong trace of the Jewish mystical tradition.[35] In Millhauser's account, humans are created (presumably on the sixth day, as his story fleshes out rather than displaces the canonical version) and begin to "multiply and spread throughout the land," just as they are commanded to do in Genesis. One day, in a garden, there is a pomegranate tree—whose fruit, it should be noted, not only represents the Torah in Judaism (613 seeds for the 613 *mitzvot*), but is also thought, by some scholars, to have been the fruit Eve gave Adam. With it there is a woman curious about a stone tablet she finds in the grass. A curious woman, in a garden? The echoes of Eden are strong. She falls into a deep sleep—much like the sleep into which God put Adam before he created Eve from his side.

But to focus only on these biblical allusions is to fail to consider—as Lambert suggests always happens—that Millhauser is a *Jewish* author. Certainly, Jews write about Christian traditions. In this book, we read Nathan Englander as making a nod to Paul's conversion on the Damascus Road in Acts of the Apostles. But so many of the references in "People of the Book" are not merely biblical, but are specifically Jewish. The references to the Book of Laws and the Book of Legends seem to point to the two parts of rabbinical discourse—*halakhah* (law) and *aggadah* (lore). Those people of the book who were such gifted readers that they were "able to pursue their studies without worldly distraction, at long tables in communal libraries, interrupted solely by two sparse meals taken in silence, and by four hours of sleep at night"—are these not *yeshiva buchers*? The speaker describes foretellings of the end of the People of the Book found in the Book of Prophecies, but counters these with a promise of Paradise after death, one the speaker asks his audience to envision: "See the study-room. See the long tables. See the scholars at their books. Do you see them, the scholars in their clothes of black and white?" This is a picture of the yeshiva, the house of study, where Orthodox Jewish men in their black suits and white shirts spend their days. But it is also a picture of the world to come, as envisioned by these Orthodox communities: the image of *ha-olam ha-ba'* "as a great Yeshiva where those who are worthy merit the right to sit at the table studying Torah, is a popular image. The story is told of one man who was given a glimpse of the World to Come. Just a bit disappointed, he asked, 'Are these people in heaven?' His host said: 'These people who are studying Torah are not in heaven; rather heaven is in them!'"[36] The ceremony in the thirteenth year, the locus of the story, is not the end of study for the audience. The speaker makes clear, "Tomorrow you will begin your long journey through the Commentaries." This is precisely the curriculum of the observant Jew.

*****

The reference to the commentary tradition brings us to a third Millhauser story—one that is at once his most biblical and his most autobiographical. In "A Voice in the Night," Millhauser toggles between a retelling of the biblical story of God's call to the prophet Samuel (1 Sam. 3); the musings of a young Jewish boy in Stratford, Connecticut, who lies awake at night wondering if God might call him as he had long before called Samuel; and, the interior monologue of an older man, unable to sleep, his insomnia flooded by memories of his childhood self, awake in bed and open to the possibility of a voice in the night, despite his father's best efforts to dissuade him from belief. The story returns to each character four times, juxtaposing one boy's faith with another's attempt at faith and an old man's disavowal of that young faith. The oscillation forms a repeating pattern.

Millhauser does not need to write an e-mail to a literary critic to make sure that the reader of "A Voice in the Night" understands that there is something biblical going on here. Even the biblical illiterate will understand quite quickly that Millhauser is retelling a biblical story. He begins, "The boy Samuel wakes in the dark. Something's not right."[37] There is no reason yet to think we might be in biblical times. Indeed, the casualness of "something's" hints at the present. But by the third sentence we have left the story, and are in a meta-story, "Most commentators agree that the incident takes place inside the temple, rather than in a tent outside the temple doors, under the stars. Less certain is whether Samuel's bed is in the sanctuary itself, where the Ark of the Covenant stands before a seven-branched oil lamp that is kept burning through the night, or in an adjoining chamber." Temple, Ark of the Covenant, seven-branched oil lamp: the biblical clues are inescapable. Milhauser also invokes the commentary tradition— here, "most scholars say" and later, "according to Flavius." His narrator is going to tell us the story of young Samuel as he imagines it, inflected from time to time with insights from the Jewish commentary tradition and anchored in quotations from the King James Version—the Bible of American letters.

Millhauser's imagining of Samuel's experience is utterly midrashic. Little detail is given in the biblical version itself, but the thrust of the story is this: Elkanah, an Ephramite of Ramah has two wives, Peninah and Hannah. Peninah bears him children, but Hannah bears him none, so that Peninah taunts her. In great distress, Hannah goes to the Temple at Shiloh and prays to the Lord, who rewards her and her husband with a boy, Samuel. They dedicate him to God and bring him to the priest Eli, with whom he comes to live. Every year, Samuel's mother, since blessed with other children, brings him a handmade coat when she and Elkanah come to worship. Samuel ministers at the Temple at Shiloh with Eli—in that day the word of the Lord was rare and visions not widespread (1 Sam. 3:1). One night, when an older Eli's sight has begun to fail, Samuel hears a voice calling "Samuel." Thinking it is the priest, Samuel goes to the older man, who seems to be asleep; when the younger tries to wake him, he dispatches him back to bed. The voice comes again; the interaction between priest and boy happens again. The third time, Eli perceives that it is the Lord who calls to Samuel, and instructs him how to respond to God's call.

Millhauser's narrator takes the bones of a story and fleshes it out in a way that is far more self-conscious than the ancient rabbis' aggadic retellings. He gives details, then almost retracts them: "A curtained doorway leads to the chamber of Eli, the high priest of the temple of Shiloh. We like such details, but they do not matter. What matters is that Samuel wakes suddenly in the night." The story is what matters, not the embellishments. And yet the narrator here cannot resist the details that the narrator of Samuel omitted—the settings, the physical characteristics:

> Eli's head rests on a pillow of goat's hair and his long-fingered hands lie crossed on his chest, beneath his white beard. His eyes are closed. "You called me," Samuel says, or perhaps his words are "Here I am; for thou calledst me." Eli opens his eyes. He seems a little confused, like a man roused from sleep. "I didn't call you," he answers. Or perhaps, with a touch of gruffness, since he doesn't like being awakened in the night: "I called not; lie down again."

The terseness of the biblical narrative is insufficient. We need to know more, to envision where the characters are, hear what they are thinking, understand what they are doing. No more of the storytelling that Auerbach describes as "fraught with background":[38] Everything here is made plain.

There are four textual strands in Millhauser's story of Samuel: snippets of verses from the King James; the new fleshed-out story of Samuel with firmly established setting and more complete characterization; the commentary of the older man, the Author, on his new version; and the commentary on the canonical version produced by biblical scholars. We see them all in play in the final turn to the Samuel story:

> *And the Lord came, and stood, and called as at other times, Samuel, Samuel.* Commentators disagree about the meaning of the word "stood." Some say that the Lord assumes a bodily presence before Samuel. Others argue that the Lord never takes on a bodily form and that therefore the voice has drawn closer to Samuel, so that the effect is of a person drawing closer in the dark. In one version of this argument, the boy hears the voice and imagines a form standing beside him. All this, the Author thinks, can be left to the interpreters. What matters to us is that the voice of the Lord calls Samuel's name. After all, Eli had said, "If he call thee." For it was not inevitable that the voice, which had called three times and not received an answer, would call again. Now the boy Samuel has heard the voice a fourth time and knows who is calling him. He doesn't yet know why the Lord is calling him, but he knows how to answer, for Eli has told him exactly what to say: "Speak, Lord; for thy servant heareth."

The move from Scripture to commentary, to commentary on Scripture, to retold Scripture—the weaving together of four strands—reminds us on the one hand of the nature of the Torah itself, with its patchwork of different authors (J, E, P, D) sewn together to create a story quilt. The four threads remind us too of the commentary tradition itself, for in traditional Judaism, as in Christianity, the biblical text is traditionally understood to operate on four levels, to be understood in four different ways simultaneously. These are the plain sense (*peshat*), the allegorical (*remez*), the imaginative (*derash*—from the same word as midrash), and the mystical (*sod*). *Peshat, Remez, Derash, Sod*: the acronym is Pardes, from which we get the word Paradise. In the Jewish imagination, as we have just seen in "People of the Book," paradise is a place where Jews study Torah and commentary when they depart this world.

The second strand in the repeating series takes a step back from the Bible, but engages it deeply as well. A young boy lying awake on a summer night in Stratford, Connecticut, 1950, listens for the voice of the Lord. He has heard the story of God's nighttime appeals to Samuel in his Sunday school class at the Jewish Community Center. The story "has made him nervous, tense as a cat. The slightest sound stiffens his whole body. He never thinks about the old man with the beard on the front of his 'Child's Illustrated Old Testament,' but now he's wondering." Could he too receive a call? Might he somehow also be one of the elect? Although some part of him hopes so, he suspects not: "He knows he won't hear the voice. Why should he be chosen? He's no Samuel. He's a good speller. He plays the piano with two hands, he can write a poem about George Washington and draw a picture of a kingfisher or a red-winged blackbird. But Samuel opens the doors to the temple when the sun comes up, Samuel fills the lamp with oil so that it burns all night." He knows he should not believe these stories. His father does not, but somehow, the boy yearns for them to be true. He does not believe, and yet "his unbelief upsets him as much as belief would." He imagines Scripture to be more than stories; he wants, in some way, to live in it.

In the third cycle, the Author, aged sixty-eight, also lies awake. He remembers his boyhood self, his desire to be chosen like Samuel. He is an atheist, like his father, for whom the Bible was merely more stories, like "Tootle" or "The Story of Dr. Dolittle." Not mere stories, mind you, because for his father, stories are everything. "Did you see that? Not a book in the house!" he exclaims in the car on the way home from a visit to someone's home. Of Eisenhower, in disgust, "He doesn't open a book!" For the son, too, all stories matter. He lies awake and thinks of:

> all those old stories, wonderful and terrible: the voice in the night, the parting of the Red Sea, Hansel in the cage, the children following the piper into the mountain. "Hamlet" and "Oedipus Rex" as pale reflections of the nightmare tales of childhood. Everything connected: David playing the harp for Saul, the boy in Stratford practicing the piano, the cellos and violins behind the closed doors. The boy listening for his name, the man waiting for the rush of inspiration. Where do you get your ideas? A voice in the night. When did you decide to become a writer? Three thousand years ago, in the temple of Shiloh.

For the boy and his father, the Bible is not The Greatest Story Ever Told. Rather, it is among the many great stories. But it has a particular stature in their lives: The Author measures his family against it. "His father and Samuel, two of a kind. Samuel: 'Thou art wicked.' His father: 'You are ignorant.' A special sect: the Jewish atheist." He measures himself against the narrative: "I am the one whose name was not called in the night." His father is Samuel, he is not Samuel. And yet, somehow, he must be. "When did you decide to become a writer? Three thousand years ago, in the temple of Shiloh." He is both in and not in the Bible, but the Bible is absolutely within him, whether he wants it there or not. The Bible is somehow inescapable.

There is much to say about how Judaism features in this story, about the older man's internal struggle over the desire of his younger self for the Lord and the assertions of his "God-scorning" father and his own convictions that there is no God.

> He thinks of the boy a lot these days, sometimes with irritation, sometimes with a fierce love that feels like sorrow. The boy tense, whipped up, listening for a voice in the night. He feels like shouting at the boy, driving some sense into that head of his. . . . But why yell at the boy? What'd he ever do to you? Better to imagine the voice calling right here, right now: Hello, old atheist, have I got news for you. Sorry, pal. Don't waste your time.

The memories of the Author map closely onto many of the biographical details Lambert gives of the Jewish Millhauser he has studied. Lambert notes in a footnote, "While this essay was being revised for publication, Millhauser published a short story, 'A Voice in the Night,' that reflects in fictional form some of the details of his childhood that he shared in private correspondence with the author in 2009 (Oct. 25)." Reviewers have noted that this story is "as close to straightforward autobiography as Millhauser has ever come—and it feels like a key to his whole narrative universe."[39] Certainly, far more of a key than the supposed life story "(1943–)."

Exactly how autobiographical, however, might this most autobiographical work be? We might be wise to recall a few lines from Millhauser's 1977 novel, *Portrait of a Romantic*: "A work of fiction is a radical act of the imagination whose sole purpose is to supplant the world. In order to achieve this purpose, a work of fiction is willing to use all the means at its disposal, including the very world it is plotting to annihilate. Art imitates Nature as Judas imitates Christ."[40] The degree to which Millhauser's story is a story of himself may be in question, but as this quotation suggests, the extent to which the Bible ripples through his stories is not.

9

Kirstin Valdez Quade

At the heart of a Christian Scripture is the New Testament's account of Jesus's death: All four Evangelists (along with generations of Jesus moviemakers from Cecil B. DeMille to Mel Gibson) are riveted by it.[1] Spanning several chapters in each Gospel, the Passion begins with Jesus's triumphal entrance into Jerusalem and ends with his death and burial. Between those extremes are several major scenes: a supper with his disciples, his betrayal in the Garden of Gethsemane by Judas (and one later by Peter), his double trial (first by Jewish authorities, then by the Roman Pontius Pilate), his torture and humiliation at the hands of both soldiers and the crowd, and an agonizing three-hour crucifixion. The sequence is a study in extremes. What starts off with a joyful messianic acclaim—"Hosanna to the Son of David!" (Matt. 21.9)—ends with a dying man's cry of dereliction, "My God, my God, why hast thou forsaken me?" (Matt. 27:46, Mark 15:34).

At least a cry of dereliction is what the dying man gives up in his last words according to Mark and Matthew. The other two Evangelists recall the event otherwise, with Jesus hopefully resigned in Luke ("Father, into thy hands I commend my spirit" [23:46 quoting Ps. 31:6]), and fully in charge in John ("It is finished" [19:30]). In none of these accounts, however, does death have the final word. Accorded a lengthy telling, Jesus' Passion has a highly abbreviated sequel in the resurrection. In Mark there is only the discovery by three terrified women of an empty tomb; in the other three Gospels, there are post-resurrection appearances by Jesus to the eleven remaining disciples (in Matthew and Luke) as well as to Mary Magdalene (in John). All four Evangelists, then, complete the story of the Passion with a resonantly happy ending: "he has been raised; he is not here" (Mark 16:6), "Why seek ye the living among the dead?" (Luke 24:5).

Just as the Hebrew Bible allows two quite distinct creation stories in Genesis 1 and 2, so the New Testament allows four Gospel accounts. The Greatest Story Ever Told could be told in different ways. Jesus's "last words" did not have to be the same in every version, because each saying led to a different insight. Nor was there any attempt to hide the fact that for Christian storytellers there could be no New Testament without the Old. Therefore, throughout the Passion accounts there is the constant echo of the Psalms in Jesus's speech—his last words are largely quotations—and an emphasis on events as the fulfillment of earlier Scriptures. It always "came to pass," no matter how terrible, for a purpose. From a Christian point of view, the old story required it.

*****

The Church turned biblical narrative into both liturgical time and ritual practice by constructing a Holy Week that annually re-presents, in the worshiper's present tense, the Gospels' narrative sequence. Palm Sunday recalls the entry into Jerusalem, Maundy Thursday Jesus's Last Supper with his disciples, Good Friday the crucifixion, and Holy Saturday Jesus's burial in the tomb. Moreover, as early as Egeria in the late fourth century, pilgrims to Jerusalem could cultivate a devotion to the Passion entirely apart from the annual services of Holy Week. The sites for the narrated events were all there to be venerated: the Passion could be re-experienced in situ.[2]

But location did not limit devotional practice any more than the liturgical year limited when the faithful could experience the events of Good Friday. Those who did not go to Jerusalem to follow in Christ's footsteps along the city's Via Dolorosa could keep track along the Stations of the Cross set up in local parishes, or visit churches throughout Europe that explicitly "recalled" the Church of the Holy Sepulcher, or venerate relics from the Holy Land that had been transported to shrines in Paris (the crown of thorns in Saint Chapelle) or in Rome (the marble staircase leading up to Pilate's praetorium, the pillar of Christ's flagellation). Built environments, objects, and devotional practices found different ways to keep recalling the Greatest Story.

Perhaps the most elaborate of these re-presentations—and certainly, in a literal sense, the most dramatic—were the mystery plays that flourished in some English towns during the two centuries between the mid-fourteenth century and the mid-sixteenth, that is, between the time of Chaucer and the lifetime of Shakespeare.[3] The fullest extant record we have of these outdoor civic spectacles dates from late-fifteenth-century York, where various guilds of the city brought the Bible out of church and into the streets, out of Latin and into the vernacular, and out of the hands of clergy and into those of the laity. Held in midsummer at the Feast of Corpus Christi, this cycle of plays offered the Christian epic narrative from Creation to Judgment. At the core of its canonical sweep, however, was the Passion, which formed the subject of twelve plays out of almost fifty.

Of these, eight are ascribed to an anonymous author known today as the "York Realist," who adapted an alliterative verse form taken from the literary world of the Anglo-Saxon epic and brought it into his own West Yorkshire vernacular. Six of his plays are devoted to the Passion. The most striking among them is the Crucifixion commissioned by the guild of Pinners, craftsmen who fashioned wooden pegs for construction and who undertook to perform the drama written for their company. In this rendering they become four soldiers given the task of nailing Christ to the cross and then of raising up the entire structure—and the man crucified upon it. In the Church Year, both East and West, there is a feast day (September 14) set aside for the commemoration of the Exaltation Cross as the instrument of salvation. In this play, however, the raising up of the cross suggests nothing of a final triumph. It is a gruesome bad joke played for laughs.

The soldiers are concerned about doing their job on time ("He must be dead needlings by noon"), about increasing Christ's pain as they "lay him down / In length and breadth as he should be," and about dividing up their work equitably as a team: one will nail his right hand, another his left.[4] They are also perturbed by practical difficulties that arise from shoddy construction and miscalculation. The holes of the cross have not been drilled properly; the mortice or hole into which the cross must stand is too large: it will need to be wedged in tight in order to stand up. Stretched on the ground and nailed to the cross, Jesus must first be elevated and then plunged down—a feat that causes unspeakable agony. "Now raise him nimbly for the nonce / And let him by this mortice here, / And let him fall in all at once, / For certes, that pain shall have no peer." The soldiers huff and puff complain about their own aches and pains ("My shoulder is in sunder"), with no thought about the suffering of their victim.

To their annoyance, Christ speaks twice from the cross, in words that are gracious and disarmingly forgiving. To the soldiers, however, he only "jangles like a jay . . . patters like a pie." Once their job is done, they leave him to "make faces at the moon," to experience a suffering that "shall have no peer." As the play draws to a close, their only concern is to decide which of them will get to keep the dying man's garment. Anything else is a waste of effort: "This travail here we tine."

The York Realist portrays the banality of evil committed by unthinking men just doing their job. They are utterly oblivious to their role in a drama of redemption meant to "save mankind" and "from the fiend them fend." Echoing Luke 23:34, Jesus prays on their behalf to "Almighty God, my Father free" even as the four soldiers blather around him, revealing that, clearly, that they know not what they do: "What they work, wot they not." The combined effect of both the horrific subject matter and its burlesque treatment—of high tragedy and low comedy—is disconcerting. Despite the grotesque cruelty of the scene it is difficult for the onlooker of the play not to laugh at the solders' oafish vulgarity or to smile at the familiar discourse of "Men at Work" on a hot afternoon.

And yet, whatever does it mean to smile at such goings on? Perhaps we know not what we do. And perhaps this is precisely what the York Realist wants from us—an uncomfortable realization of our own bystander detachment from the horror not only of a crucifixion but also of what is routinely in front of us. As the actors lumber off, would the medieval audience have applauded the Pinners' play?

*****

Although there is no specific evidence that Ernest Hemingway knew this medieval dramatization of the crucifixion, the correspondence between it and his story "Today is Friday" is striking: the latter seems like an even shorter version of what is to begin with a very short play. Its precise genre is something of a puzzle. Ostensibly a Passion play, its three pages open with a stage direction that recalls a standard script: "*Three Roman soldiers are in a drinking-place at eleven o'clock at night. There are barrels around the wall. Behind the wooden counter is a Hebrew wine-seller. The three Roman soldiers are a little cock-eyed.*"[5] Likewise, the piece ends conventionally with a single word, "CURTAIN." The work itself consists almost entirely of dialogue distributed among three enumerated but unnamed Roman soldiers and George, the "Hebrew wine-seller," "a kike just like all the rest of them." It is also marked by a pervasive use of theatrical language, as if to underscore the dramatic nature of everything that transpires: "That's not his play," "I was surprised how he acted," "The part I don't like."[6]

On the other hand, throughout its publication history "Today is Friday" has always appeared in collections of Hemingway short stories, whether initially in *Men Without Women* (1927), or later in *The First Forty-Nine* (1938), until its final inclusion in the posthumous publication of *The Collected Stories of Ernest Hemingway* (1987). The author also speaks of it as such in the 1958 *Paris Review* interview, when asked about "the simple circumstances" under which, on a single day in Madrid, he produced three stories, "The Killers," "Today is Friday," and "Ten Indians."[7] Given all of this, it is best to think of the work as a hybrid that bridges two genres, at once a miniature Passion play and a very short story. Some of Hemingway's most renowned stories—"Hills like White Elephants" (1927), "A Clean, Well-Lighted Place" (1933)—also share similar café settings and consist almost entirely of dialogue. Lacking only the formal theatrical configuration of "Today is Friday," they are already dramas in the making.

Hemingway sets his Passion play after the events of the killing day are over. It is Friday night at eleven o'clock. Jesus's broken body has long been laid to rest in the tomb, leaving the soldiers exhausted and in need of some kind of reckoning. What really happened? In this retelling, there is no recollection of biblical details: the earthquake, the sky turning dark, the two thieves on either side of the crucified Christ, or a report that the veil of the Temple was rent. Nor is there any recollection of words spoken from the cross. Instead, as might be expected of Roman soldiers marooned "out here too long" in Palestine, the men primarily recall the desertion of Jesus's "pretty yellow crowd" of disciples—traitors all—as well as the lingering, faithful presence of his women ("they stuck all right").

Hemingway's primary interest lies in how the soldiers variously respond to the events of this particular Friday. There is no indication that the men were actively involved in executing the crucifixion— which was quite openly the case in the York play—or that they in any way enjoyed the proceedings. Instead of being participants, they appear to have been afternoon observers now turned eleventh-hour commentators, as red wine loosens their tongues and gets them ready for sleep. Soldier One repeats his admiration for Jesus six times and almost verbatim. An experienced soldier, he has seen more than a few crucifixions in his time but insists that this one was different: "He was pretty good in there today." Soldier Two is disappointed: Despite all the messianic build up, Jesus was "That false alarm!" But how different was he, really, when the moment of truth arrived? Like any other man, he must also have wanted to "get down from the cross": "When they first start nailing him, there isn't none of them wouldn't stop it if they could." The two go back and forth, with the second soldier accusing the first of being "a regular Christer" on account of his enthusiasm, of his insistence that "He didn't want to come down from the cross. That's not his play."

As they continue in this manner, one notices the quieter presence and growing discomfort of Soldier Three. Unlike his drunken comrades, he cannot abide the cheap red wine they want to keep downing: "I can't drink the damn stuff. It makes my gut sour." He concedes that, yes, "Jesus Christ!" was "all right"; he alone names the man on the cross. But the whole business sickens him: "The part I don't like is the nailing them on. You know, that must get you pretty bad" and again, "It takes some of them really bad." Whereas his comrades would willingly have gone on drinking, he wants only to return to the barracks. What he says three times in the closing lines of the play in effect brings down the curtain on the story: "Let's go. I feel like hell tonight."

Whereas Soldier Two believes that what ails him is simply the place where all three are stuck—the ordeal of being Roman soldiers in Palestine, dealing with conflicts in which they have no personal stake, and from which they want only to be freed—Soldier Three understands that it "ain't that." For reasons he cannot articulate, he knows (as he feels forced to repeat) that he is in hell. Being "out here" is not the problem.

But what is it, then? After being in the "theater of war" in Spain, Hemingway may well have understood this third soldier's plight as collateral damage. There are only so many battles, so many crucifixions that one can witness. (Says Soldier Two, "When the weight starts to pull on 'em. That's when it gets 'em.") Whereas the first two men can get through the night with the fortification of another round of red wine, a third is sick to his stomach. He cannot carry on.

Or maybe there is something more specifically related to the Christian story at stake here. In the Gospel accounts, the Roman soldiers have their fun with the Man of Sorrows, dressing him up like a king crowned with thorns, flogging his body, jeering at his condition, and then forcing him to carry his cross to Golgotha. Yet in Matthew, Mark, and Luke, there is also a single Roman centurion—the commander of one hundred men—who comes away from the spectacle with an altogether different appraisal: "Truly this man was God's Son" (Mark 15:39), "Certainly this man was innocent" (Luke 23:47).

It would do violence to the bare bones of Hemingway's story to claim too much for what Soldier Three is suffering or the particular hell where he finds himself. Were Flannery O'Connor the author in question, we might be advised to look for the intrusion of grace in the midst of violence, to see in the soldier's wretchedness the beginning of a breakthrough rather than something like a PTSD breakdown. This does not seem likely here. Despite Hemingway's adult conversion to Roman Catholicism, epiphanies of this sort are not his stock and trade: He gives us no moment of recognition. Nonetheless, it is interesting to note that two draft titles of "Today is Friday" were "One More for the Nazarene" and "Today is Friday, or The Seed of the Church."[8] Soldier Three may well be that "one more" in some imagined sequel to this compact drama—if not a follower of Jesus then at least someone who cannot get him out of mind.

*****

Just as we do not know if Hemingway was in any way familiar with the York Realist's Crucifixion play, so we have no indication that Kirstin Valdez Quade knew of "Today is Friday" when she wrote "The Five

Wounds," a story that first appeared in the *New Yorker* in 2009 and was then included in her debut collection, *Night at the Fiestas* (2015). What is clear, however, is that she is steeped in the Catholic culture of the Hispanic American South West—northern New Mexico, in particular—whose faith is Passion-centered. In Octavio Paz's description of Mexican piety, it is "the contemplation of horror."[9] Valdez Quade's family has seventeenth-century roots in this region that can be traced back to the *conquistadors*; it is also where she spent high school and college summers at her grandparents' homes. The landscape of her chosen region—whether in Santa Fe, outside of Estancia, or in the fictional village of Cuipas—has been described as being as "opaque as Scripture," as "Biblical in . . . the near-moral clarity of the dry wind, the desert places, the towering sky."[10]

The stories are also rich in local detail. In the Cuipas village church described in "The Manzanos," "Jesus looks down on us from the cross, mournful and distant and preoccupied with his own story" (265). In another town, Corpus Christi processions are vitally important, especially to the young girl who hopes to recite Psalm 38 perfectly and therefore be chosen to lead the procession "with baskets of petals to cast before the Body of Christ": "the blessed sacrament in its gold box held high by the priest under the gold-tasseled canopy, the prayers at the side altars along the way" (11). In this part of the United States there is also a strong Mormon presence, as reflected in the story "Family Reunion." But the spirituality that engages Valdez Quade most deeply is what she has called "the miracle-laden, medieval Hispanic Catholicism practiced in the region where my family is from."[11] For *Atlantic* book editor Ann Hurlbet, this sensibility is what makes her work distinctive: "If Quade ever yearned to escape her archaic Catholic heritage and redefine herself, let's be glad she didn't. Her vision has thrived on its fierce, flesh-conscious desire for transcendence."[12]

Inevitably, reviewers of her work—as well as Valdez Quade herself—have likened her to Alice Munro (because of her early mastery of the short-story form) as well as to both Graham Greene and Flannery O'Connor (because of her Roman Catholic-inflected spirituality).[13] "O'Connor is a lodestar for me," she told an editor at *Commonweal*. "She's a funny writer. And she has so much compassion for her characters, even when they can feel grotesque.

She says that she liked to write about 'freaks and folks,' and she gives them deep inner and spiritual lives, and allows them to achieve grace. So many of these characters are people that might be overlooked."[14]

Indeed, *not* overlooking anyone or anything is the wisdom she took away not only from O'Connor's celebration of "freaks and folks" but also from *The Power and the Glory*, first encountered in high school and the source of what has become a treasured insight. In one interview she pointed to a particular passage where Graham Greene's Whisky Priest discovers the value of other people when he finds himself surrounded by them in a packed Mexican jail cell. He reflects,

When you visualized a man or a woman carefully you could always begin to feel pity . . . that was a quality God's image carried with it . . . when you saw the lines at the corner of the eyes, the shape of the mouth, how the hair grew, it was impossible to hate. Hate was just a failure of the imagination.

Valdez Quade says, "I think about this passage all the time when I'm writing." Except, she adds, it is not pity but empathy that is at stake for her in "the project of fiction": "our job is to keep looking, and to keep looking closely. . . . It's a job I often fail at. But in my fiction that's what I am most interested in doing."[15]

*****

Asked if she thought actively about her New Mexico heritage when she first envisioned a short story, Valdez Quade said she did not, at least not at first. "I never have a plan that's that clear. I start with a character in a situation—there's a mystery, and the story builds out from there. But I am interested in families. People in families have so much knowledge of one another—how to love one another, how to wound one another. Small actions and gestures can become larger betrayals that have long-lasting consequences. I'm interested in that kind of intensity, the intensity that can arise within families."[16]

This general statement of intent could easily serve as an introduction to one story in particular, "The Five Wounds," which is very much in the spirit of both Greene and O'Connor; it is also the work that has inspired most critical commentary thus far.[17] Its setting is a hardscrabble New Mexican village during *Semana Santa* as the narrative moves from Holy Tuesday to Good Friday. The story centers on a thuggish character who might easily be "overlooked," whose "deep inner and spiritual life" is explored in the context of a family wounded by betrayal but also redeemed by love.

"The Five Wounds" reanimates the biblical Passion in a disconcertingly vibrant way—an updated retelling that takes liberties with The Greatest Story Ever Told precisely in order to extend its implications. Unlike both the York Realist and Ernest Hemingway, Valdez Quade does not go back in time and place to revisit a certain Friday in ancient Jerusalem. Instead, she locates her action in contemporary northern New Mexico and imagines what it would be like, on a hill not all that far away, for a completely unlikely Jesus—"pockmarked and bad-toothed," lazy and no account—to be, in the words of Hemingway's First Soldier, "pretty good out there today."

"Amadeo Padilla is Jesus," reads the story's opening line. With just a few vivid details Valdez Quade conjures the social context in which such an outlandish identification might take place: the close-knit, somewhat underground world of the Penitential Brotherhood of New Mexico, or *Los Hermanos*, with its lay hierarchy, private meeting place (*morada*), ascetic use of the *disciplina*, and the annual Holy Week processions that culminate in a Good Friday reenactment of the crucifixion. This year, "Amadeo Padilla is Jesus" partly because his great-uncle Tivo, mayor of the village's Hermanos, has the power to declare him such; he does so convinced that his famously lazy, n'er -do-well nephew "could use a lesson in sacrifice" (59). But aside from being given yet another undeserved break by his family, Amadeo "is Jesus" this year because he wants desperately (and against all expectations) to prove himself worthy, to be "the best Jesus they've had in years."

Thus far in his life, he has done nothing of value: "Thirty-three years old, the same as Our Lord" but not a single good deed to his credit. On the other hand, "You name the sin, he's done it: gluttony, sloth, fucked a second cousin on the dark bleachers of the high school" (58–59). This trail of haphazard ruin is suggested through flashbacks to when he was eighteen and courting the pregnant Marissa, only to desert her and their child Angel a year later after a violent argument over his fecklessness. He called Marissa "*dirty, dirty whore*," struck her hard, and realized (with some degree of self-satisfaction) that "he has it in him to do this again." Feeling his power to destroy, he walks away from the world he only halfheartedly started to create and moves back to his mother's house—relieved to be free of the obligation to raise a child and "lucky to have been let off the hook" (65).

But in this particular Holy Week, he wants to become a new man, to become the Man of Sorrows by becoming (to recall the Suffering Servant of Isaiah 53) "acquainted with grief." To this end he "builds the cross out of heavy rough oak instead of pine" (59) and decides to make it heavier by studding it with nails. When threatened by impure thoughts, he focuses on "Christ's pain." In short, he does everything he can to prepare for the role of a lifetime: "Each day, Amadeo practices his face in the bathroom mirror . . . spreads his arms, makes the muscles in his face tighten and fall, tries to learn the nuances of suffering" (66).

These rehearsals for the Passion play are designed to make him its leading man, to garner rave reviews and applause. It is his chance "to prove to them all—and God, too—everything he's capable of." But Valdez Quade also makes clear that the role means something more to him than simply being a star: "It's *not* a play—it's real. More real." Others can articulate what he himself cannot. His great-uncle Tivo, for instance, tells him that taking on the part of Christ on Good Friday is "more real even than taking Communion"; "You got a chance to thank Jesus, to hurt with Him just a little" (68–69).

There are two complicating factors in his plan of rehabilitation. One is Manuel Garcia, the man who forty-five years earlier had made himself a legend by demanding that his hands be nailed to the cross. His body then ruined, and living ever since off the village through his public display of suffering, he will do anything to stand in the way of Amadeo's bid to replace him, to be "the best Jesus." In addition to Manuel there is also Angel, the child Amadeo abandoned, who returns to him on Holy Tuesday, on the verge of her fifteenth birthday, which in this particular year—in a stroke of bad fortune—also falls on Good Friday. If Manuel Garcia stands to block his rival through sustained contempt—made palpable in the spit that several times lands at Amadeo's feet—Angel threatens to ruin him simply by her presence: "White tank top, black bra, gold cross pointing the way to her breasts in case you happened to miss them. Belly as hard and round as an adobe *horno*" (61). Pregnant at fourteen and now eight months great with child, she stands to deflate her father's would-be grandeur in the eyes of community by making a joke of him. Embarrassed by "the fervor that being a penitente implies," he tells her, "I'm carrying the cross this year. I'm Jesus." "And I'm the Virgin Mary," she replies in a sassy, perfectly timed comeback (62).[18]

Two scenes bring these three characters together and prepare for the Good Friday climax at the summit of the Calvario. On Holy Wednesday—throughout the story Valdez Quade is careful to mark the passing days of *Semana Santa*—Angel convinces Amadeo against his better judgment to allow her to enter the morada with him. To be more precise, she lays on a guilt trip: "You think I'm too dirty for your morada. Isn't that it? Too dirty for your morada, too dirty for prom, too dirty for everything" (70).

The morada is a former gas station: its interior is bare, with nothing to draw the eye but a wooden Christ nailed up on the wall, "ancient and bloody." Transfixed by it—half expecting the statue to move, to tilt its head—Amadeo looks back and forth between the crucifix's "living witness to his transgression" (73) and the pregnant girl at his side. She is his transgression incarnate, now fourteen years after he abandoned her. As Angel traces a trickle of painted blood down the bound wooden feet, she asks him why he wants to know "what it feels like" to suffer like Christ. He can't say, but his answer is this: he needs to know if he has it in him to ask for the nails, if he can get up there in front of the whole town and do a performance so convincing he'll transubstantiate right there on the cross into something real. He looks at the statue. "Total redemption in one gesture, if only he can get it right" (74).

The following day, on Holy Thursday morning, it becomes apparent that Manuel Garcia—now parked in a lawn chair in front of Amadeo's house and "scratching his balls with his stiff-curled claw"—knows about last night's visit. Not only had Amadeo brought a woman into the santuario, but an unmarried pregnant one at that: "The puta whore. No Jesus never lived in a house of putas." This observation leads to a threat. "I'm thinking what your uncle will say when he finds out a whore has been in the morada. . . . You watch how quick they cut you down from that cross. . . . They'll cut you down fast" (75). Amadeo directs the fury he rightly owes Manuel against his daughter. She has given the old man something to sneer at, "tainting his Passion Week with her pregnancy and her personality" (76). It's all her fault. And yet what Angel actually does, rather than destroy him, is save him. As Amadeo watches from the safety of home, she walks barefoot down the drive in front of the house to the place where Manuel keeps his punishing vigil. We are not made privy to what transpires between them, but only see what happens as a result. Angel stands before the seated man, stony faced and silent. She raises her shirt above her huge belly—"Her breasts are too big for the black lace bra, her maternity jeans low"—as Manuel extends his gnarled brown hand and places it against her stomach (and her unborn child within). With his other hand he cups her belly, moving both "claws" back and forth, all around. As he does so, with eyes closed, she looks beyond him to the neighbor's yard. Amadeo watches the entire scene from behind the pink lace of the bathroom curtain, knowing that at any point he could "put a stop to the terrible thing that is happening" (78–79). In fact, he does nothing. He remains the coward he always was.

Later that Holy Thursday night, when he is to transport himself mentally to the Garden of Gethsemane "thinking about his soul and his salvation," Amadeo sits on the couch imagining the Hermanos in the act of their yearly fervor, "murmuring about suffering and gratitude, yearning for pain" (79). Already given a telephonic blessing by the priest who will otherwise stay clear of the next day's events, he knows that the Bible's Passion story should be foremost on his mind: the betrayal of Judas, the cock crowing a third time as yet again Peter denies his Lord. Instead—and drunk—he can only sit on the couch and stare at the wall. Angel joins him, at last breaking the silence between them by saying what he is desperately waiting to hear but will not ask for ("I never asked you for nothing"). She says, "He's not gonna tell. You can have your Jesus day." Sacrificing the integrity of her own body so that he can turn himself into Christ, Angel—for all her pregnancy and personality—saves that day.

*****

When it finally comes, it is Angel who gets her father out of bed to assume his role in the Good Friday drama. "They gather at the base of the Calvario. Nearly two miles to the top, and Amadeo will walk barefoot, dragging the cross" (80). The Hermanos play their part,

first with soft punches, then with slugs, "shouting the worst curses
of two languages and two thousand years." Crowned with thorns,
Amadeo then leads the way along this Via Dolorosa, the brotherhood
behind him in two lines, followed by Manuel Garcia "bearing no load
except his own hands," "huffing and stinking like a dying man." He
spits at the new Christ as he grinds his way up the sharp stones
of the Calvario's pathway. Angel is there too, of course, repeatedly
offering her father sips of water that he rejects in order not to lessen
the suffering he has taken on. "He calls between heavy breaths to
the hooded men behind him, 'Whip me!' And then because they do
not respond, louder, 'Whip me!'" (82).

As Amadeo stumbles and falls, just like Jesus along the fourteen
Stations of the Cross, he comes to see both Manuel and Angel in
a new light. Manuel's mockery is a gift that can make him stronger,
more Christ-like in his replay of the Passion: "The filthy old man is
playing his part and doesn't even know it." And Angel, rather than
being a distraction—too dirty for the morada or for Good Friday—
"she's the *point*! Everything Jesus did He did for his children!"; "For
the first time he's glad she's here: more than anyone, he realizes,
she's the one he wants with him today" (82–83).

The pace of the story slows as Valdez Quade sets the scene at the
top of the Calvario—the "moment of truth" we have been waiting for.
The Hermanos bind him to the cross, his feet placed on the block of
wood that will be all he has to stand on. As they do so, Amadeo finds
himself enacting other Scriptures in addition to the Passion: "lines
once memorized surface: *With a word He stilled the wind and the
waves.*" The reference here is to the story in Matthew, Mark, and
Luke of Jesus calming a windstorm on the Sea of Galilee, "Who is
this, then, that even the wind and the sea obey him?" (Mark 4:41,
with its echo of Psalm 89:9, 25). In the Gospels the disciples hail
Jesus's power over the elements. As the Hermanos raise the cross,
and Amadeo along with it, he feels his power grow too. In every
sense he is rising to the occasion. He will be the "best Jesus they've
had in years."

What will insure his victory is the specific moment the village has
been waiting for, when they will see whether or not they were "right
about this Christ," whether he is truly willing to "put himself through
Hell for them" (84). "The People" in the story have been there from

its opening, the men watching Amadeo in the dirt yard behind the morada as he "upgraded" his cross. On the Calvario, however, the entire village is assembled, the Hermanos in their white pants and black hoods, the women and children in "bright clattering colors" (81). Their hope is that he will give them an experience that they and their children "will remember their whole lives" (84)—something beyond the splatter of blood they already see, or the flies that land on his cheeks and neck that he's too exhausted to shake away. He knows that, finally, what they want from him is proof: they want the nails. And so, answering his own desires as well as theirs, they begin the wounding: "They pound the nail through Amadeo's palm" (85).

*****

The Evangelists take us inside Jesus's mind through the recollection of his last words. In the Gospel of John, moreover, Jesus has sufficient strength to take care of those he holds most dear: "When Jesus therefore saw his mother, and the disciple standing by, whom he loved, he saith unto his mother, Woman, behold thy son! Then saith he to the disciple, Behold thy mother!" (19:26–27). Valdez Quade's narrator, at one with her protagonist, goes further than this: she tells us what Amadeo thinks and feels as the story draws to its close:

In a moment, pain, but for now he thinks, *This is all wrong*, and has time to clarify the thought. *I am not the Son*. The sky agrees, because it doesn't darken. Amadeo remembers Christ's cry—*My God, why hast thou forsaken me?*—and he knows what he is missing. It's Angel who has been forsaken.

All at once he sees her. He is surprised by the naked fear on her face. It is not an expression he knows. And she feels not only fear—Amadeo sees that now—but pain, complete and physical. Nothing he can do will change this, and soon it won't be just her suffering, but the baby, too. Angel cries out and holds her hands aloft, offering them to him. This is when the pain makes its searing flight down his arm and into his heart. Amadeo twists in agony on the cross, and below him the people applaud. (85)

In one sense, Amadeo's Imitation of Christ is a failure. The whole attempt to be the best Jesus in years is "all wrong." He's not the Son of

God, even in a play; and it is not God about whom he thinks in his hour of greatest need nor even about his own forsakenness. On the other hand, what Valdez Quade gives us, if not Jesus redux, is quite another Amadeo Padilla—an inveterate narcissist who now "all at once" sees someone else, sees someone other than himself reflected back at him in the mirror of his self-regard. First and foremost he sees Angel, who has been forsaken by everyone in her short life, but most especially by him. He sees her not as she has been until now—brash, quick witted, angry, know-it-all—but as she is, terrified: "He is surprised by the naked fear on her face. It is not an expression he knows." Her pain overwhelms him. And perhaps most remarkable of all when he looks at her, he sees not the mark of her shame inside her huge belly ("The puta whore"), "but the baby, too." Until now he had only put up with her talk about child-rearing classes and diet and making a good home for her *hijito*; he has been as indifferent to a grandson as he was to a daughter. Now, suddenly, there are two generations standing at the foot of his cross. He "beholds" them both.

In the final paragraph Valdez Quade offers us two quite different reactions to this Passion story. The first is heartfelt and deeply empathic. Witnessing her father's suffering, Angel assumes the iconic pose of the women in the Gospels who "stuck" with Jesus even as the disciples ran for cover: she "cries out and holds her hands aloft, offering them to him." (From the Spanglish that peppers the story, Valdez Quade alters her diction here with words like "aloft" and "offering." Now there are echoes of Scripture in her prose.)

It is also Angel's identification with Amadeo that brings the crucifixion home: "This is when the pain makes its searing flight down his arm and into his heart." It is as if daughter and father are at last united at heart as well as by DNA: pain courses through each of them at the same time. And so as Angel "cries out and holds her hands aloft," Amadeo "twists in agony on the cross." The two become "one flesh" in an extraordinary demonstration of what Valdez Quade has said matters most to her, in religion as well as in fiction: empathy.

But then there is the other response to this crucifixion, that of the assembled crowd who form the backdrop to the intense human drama of family wounds and love. As Angel and Amadeo both twist in agony, "the people applaud." They are only onlookers at a spectacle, not participants who have held our attention or have been reshaped by their experience. Valdez Quade gives the villagers' applause no adjective to describe its intensity or duration. We have only a bare fact: "the people applaud." With this phrase "The Five Wounds" gives its Passion play a last word—an ironic twist for a replay of Good Friday that over the course of the story has become much more than pious theatrics: "It's *not* a play—it's real. More real." More passionate is another way to put it. Or, to recall the other terms Valdez Quade has used to describe the mystery of the event, what we have witnessed is a "communion," a "transubstantiation." The people who linger momentarily at the foot of the cross remain on the outside of the experience, however, showing some appreciation for the show but no doubt ready to call it a day and go home.

With such an ending given over to the crowd, is the author also suggesting the kind of reader who turns pages and, after finishing this story—and appreciating its narrative skill—simply moves on to what's next in the collection? Or perhaps as at the end of the York Pinners' play, the discord between agony and "appreciation," screams and applause, is meant to be felt as discord, and to be troubling. Certainly, if one imagines "The Five Wounds" continuing to tell its tale, there is trouble in store for Amadeo, with his now ruined hands, unable to work, and for Angel (without imaginable prospects), and for the child only one month away from entry into a world that is not set up to receive him. And yet what we have encountered in the story is a transformation that may also have repercussions. There is a no-account narcissist who "all at once" can see someone other than himself, and a daughter, once discarded, who has now been acknowledged as essential. In the story, finally, "she's the *point!*"

In *Night at the Fiestas*, the heavens may not open up to choruses of Hallelujah, as occasionally they do in Flannery O'Connor. Nor is biblical reference as frequent a signpost to where the author wants her readers to go. Nonetheless, in "The Five Wounds," along with her ability to disarm a reader with humor and surprise, Kirstin Valdez Quade delivers revelations of her own. They are as disconcerting as Amadeo Padilla as Jesus, as incongruous as Angel reprising the Virgin Mary, and as bloody awful as a New Mexican Passion play that leaves disaster in its wake. They are full of unlikely grace.

10

Tobias Wolff

In *Matters of Life and Death*, his 1983 collection of what were then "new American short stories," Tobias Wolff identified the kind of writers to whom he is most drawn: "They write about fear of death, fear of life, the feelings that bring people together and force them apart, the costs of intimacy. They remind us that our house is built on sand. They are, every one of them, interested in what it means to be human."[1] This evocative description of others' work also describes the essential qualities of his own, which now includes two memoirs, two novels, a novella, and four books of stories. Wolff, like Raymond Carver and other so-called "dirty realists,"[2] addresses moral life as lived by people not likely to think about their experience in such high terms. They are, as he said of Carver's folk, "just hanging on day to day behind those sound-deflecting walls along the highway, waking up every morning not to an uplifting commercial but to a hard grind and the possibility of a pink slip."[3] Wolff's characters are hardscrabble as well, but perhaps not as desperately so: soldiers, teenagers, low-ranking teachers, men on a hunting trip, estranged couples, a priest turned Las Vegas night watchman. Carver's fiction may be, as Wolff described his friend's work, "deeply pessimistic . . . at the level of ordinary life";[4] his own brand of "dirty realism," on the other hand, is rueful and mitigated by affection, humor, and surprise.

*****

Throughout his writing, in fiction and memoir, Wolff has shown an abiding interest in liars, partly for autobiographical reasons (as he confesses in *This Boy's Life*), partly because the misrepresentation of reality can also be a way to imagine a world more generous and hospitable to our needs than the one that merely "is." Asked in an interview, "Why is lying so necessary to your characters?" Wolff replied with a question: "The world is not enough, maybe?"[5] This question may well be the springboard for fiction, for artful "misrepresentation," and for embroidered reality. The artist has much to learn from the accomplished liar. Both rely on the invention of a convincing narrative, which must be based on reality in order to do its work of persuading the listener or reader of its truth. "The truest poetry," says Shakespeare's Touchstone, "is the most feigning."[6]

But at what expense the deception? "Some of the lies are just destructive."[7] Many of Wolff's stories are about betrayal, the denial of another person, which he counts as "one of the original sins in the world."[8] In "Leviathan," a husband falls asleep when his wife is goaded into telling about the single moment in her life she is most proud of. In "Desert Breakdown, 1968," a young husband and father almost deserts his family for a fantasy of self-fulfillment, and then plans to return to them less as an act of loyalty than as a failure of nerve. Webster in "The Rich Brother" is simply a con man, a ludicrous mountebank—to use a word that suits his vocabulary—able to sell shares in a Peruvian gold mine to the hopelessly gullible.

On the other side of betrayal is generosity of spirit—the ability to overcome self-absorption, to take in the sheer fact of someone else. To this end, the short story can play a part. "Good stories slip past our defenses—we all want to know what happens next—and then slow time down, and compel our interest and our belief in other lives than our own, so that we feel ourselves in another presence. It's a kind of awakening, a deliverance, it cracks our shell and opens us to the truth and singularity of others—to their very being."[9]

*****

Perhaps because Wolff is a practicing Roman Catholic, and numbered among the literary faithful by the likes of Paul Elie and Geoffrey Wolfe,[10] he is often asked to comment on his relationship to Flannery O'Connor. He is happy to claim one. Like her, there are recurring patterns in his work, so that while certain subjects call out to him ("I feel like my feet are on the ground when I'm writing about them"), others do not: "I take comfort in the way, say, that Flannery O'Connor would tend to revisit the same situations without losing much in the way of her power or variety. You know, you have the surly daughter who is driven nuts by her mother's cheer and simplistic piety and common sense, and a shiftless handyman around somewhere."[11] Also like hers, his stories have to do with moral choices "between good and evil"[12] as well as with the sudden appearance of grace. His grace-filled moments, however, are less overtly theological and dramatic than O'Connor's. Instead, they reveal "a certain courage and verve and even a sense of play in facing things as they are."[13] Rather than going out with a bang, his stories favor the gentle anti-climax.

And then there is his discomfort with the forthrightness of O'Connor's religious beliefs, the explicitness of her convictions— overtly in her nonfiction prose but by no means possible to miss in her novels and stories. "I'm a great admirer of Flannery O'Connor, but even there I feel myself bridling a little sometimes at the discernible purposefulness of her work, seeing her thumb on the scales."[14] He is discomforted by the "too-evident orthodoxy [which] gives some of her work a forced, predetermined quality."[15] In O'Connor's "The Temple of the Holy Ghost," for instance, he takes issue with a standoff between country-boy Evangelicals and convent-bred girls, the one group singing "The Old Rugged Cross" and the other "Tantum ergo Sacramentum" (241): "That kind of thing doesn't interest me much. It isn't about the writer's argument with God, it's about persuading the reader to a particular orthodoxy. When we see a salesman coming, we brace."[16] Although O'Connor and Wolff share a faith and a church, in other words, they neither hold nor express their religion in the same way. He is neither a defender of the faith nor party to the "one flock, one shepherd" disposition that O'Connor confessed as her own: "If my fiction has a religious element, it simply rises from my view of life, not from any particular theology I'm pushing. What faith I have inheres in the way I see things, and of course the way I see things is expressed in my writing, but not polemically."[17]

Apart from questions of confessional forthrightness—of having the thumb on the scales versus keeping more hands-off—there is also a difference in how each understands the nature of a moral choice between good and evil, and consequently in how to portray such choices in the life of a character. "I think of my stories as leading up to such a point. The difference is, the choice O'Connor's characters are faced with—or have forced upon them—is an irrevocable one, a choice between salvation and damnation. That doesn't happen in such an obvious way in my stories." [18]

The "obvious way" is no doubt an allusion to O'Connor's penchant for shock and awe. Although Wolff's work certainly also includes violence, enacted or imagined, his fiction on the whole is not inclined to catastrophe. [19] He favors the more mundane; his characters' gestures are tentative, provisional, and often ambiguous. There may be lyrical flights of fancy when the imagination soars and the story's rhetoric follows, but the sky never opens and we never leave the earth: "I guess my sense of what saves people has as much to do with the ordinary responsibilities of family, adulthood, and work as it does with these violent eruptions from heaven, which one might look for in vain. I mean, that's the nature of grace. It doesn't come bidden, it comes unbidden. And so I have a different sense of what saves people than O'Connor." [20]

*****

Wolff also has ways of deploying the Bible that, if sometimes recalling O'Connor's ease with biblical reference, also highlight yet another contrast between them. For both, Scripture is embedded in our English language and its history, a familiar linguistic world that is readily, perhaps unconsciously, at hand. For O'Connor, as we have seen, the scriptural resonance of her work is meant to be caught. It is purposeful, invariably pointing to a subtext not only to be noticed but also to be interpreted. Indeed, her stories depend on our recognizing the "added dimension" the Bible provides, to the extent that in *A Circle in the Fire*, for instance, missing the biblical subtext of Daniel 3 brought forward in the closing line means missing her intentions for the entire story. Wolff's relationship to Scripture, by contrast, is seldom as immediately evident or programmatic. The Bible is carried in an inner pocket rather than worn on a sleeve.

Take Wolff's introductory remarks to *Matters of Life and Death*, when he refers to the writers he has selected (along with Carver, Ann Beattie, Richard Ford, and Richard Yates) because they "remind us that our house is built on sand." This metaphor is able to stand on its own as a commonplace expression of human vulnerability and thoughtlessness. (Who in his or her right mind builds on so infirm a foundation? Why do we keep on doing this?) The relevance of the phrase is especially apt when considering the contemporary fiction Wolf celebrates and which indeed he writes. Just think of dirty realism's cast of characters, their pipedreams, screwups, and inevitably foiled escape plans. The observant writer knows that "building on sand" in such a fictional world means visualizing a disaster in the making—forecasting a fall. It could have been avoided, but it will not be. The house is doomed.

And yet, for those who have ears that hear and eyes that see, this particular metaphor has a biblical origin and context. In Matthew's Sermon on the Mount, Jesus draws a contrast between the wise and the foolish, that is, between those who heed his words and those who do not. To make this point he resorts to parabolic speech about homebuilding, in which a familiar opposition ("there-are-two-kinds-of-people-in-the-world") comes down in this case to the importance of choosing a proper construction site.

> Therefore whosoever heareth these sayings of mine, and doeth them, I will liken him unto a wise man, which built his house upon a rock:
> And the rain descended, and the floods came, and the winds blew, and beat upon that house; and it fell not: for it was founded upon a rock.
> And every one that heareth these sayings of mine, and doeth them not, shall be likened unto a foolish man, which built his house upon the sand:
> And the rain descended, and the floods came, and the winds blew, and beat upon that house; and it fell: and great was the fall of it. (Matt. 7:24–27)

Wolff lauds the fact that even in his sermonizing, Jesus chose parable and allegory, revealing "an impatience with the discourse of argument, logic, precept, logic-chopping abstraction, high thought nobly phrased."[21]

Had O'Connor spoken about a "house built on sand," chances are that she would have meant us to consider Jesus's "sayings" in the Sermon, their intended impact on the listener, the necessity of making a choice about how to live in the face of them and the severity of the consequences of that choice in the face of the inevitable death-dealing flood. On the one hand, rock, on the other, sand; on the one hand, the house stands secure, on the other, "great was the fall of it." The drama of the Either/Or in matters of life and death is stark in Scripture, and as old as the Old Testament. When Moses, poised between Sinai and Mount Nemo, stands before his gathered people, he charges them in radical terms to declare who they most deeply are: "This day I call the heavens and the earth as witnesses against you that I have set before you life and death, blessings and curses. Now choose life" (Deut. 30:19). So too in the Revelation to John that closes the Christian canon: an angel tells the church at Laodicea, "I know thy works, that thou art neither cold nor hot: I would thou wert cold or hot. So then because thou art lukewarm, and neither cold nor hot, I will spue thee out of my mouth" (Rev. 3:15–16).

This kind of dramatic stance was congenial to O'Connor both as a religious person and as a writer. One thinks of the Misfit's ultimatum—"If He did what he said, then it's nothing for you to do but throw away everything and follow Him." (132)—or of any number of the pronouncements in her essays or letters: "Either one is serious about salvation or one is not."[22] Drawing a line in the sand is not, however, Wolff's custom any more than it is for the writers he most admires, from Chekhov to Carver. Those who remind us that our house is built on sand need not have the canon in mind. With the Bible perhaps only faintly in the background, a genuine warning against weak foundations does not have to be a prophetic Word of the Lord. It may well be enough to call out complacency, to alert the reader to what is already trembling underfoot—to say our hard knowledge is riddled with fantasy, our confidence founded on shaky evidence, and our places of security no more steadily grounded than on a shape-shifting dune.

*****

In Wolff's own case, however, it is likely that he knew where the house built on sand reference came from. And yet unlike O'Connor, with her lifetime of daily Mass going and developed interest in biblical scholarship, his exposure to Scripture is far more haphazard and circuitous. It is also more contentious. Commending Sean O'Faolain's line that all good writing is in the end the writer's argument with God, Wolff finds a scriptural precedent for doing so: "It's like the Psalmists who are complaining: They're pulling my beard and spitting in my face—where are you, God? And why do you allow things like this, why do the wicked prosper? It isn't being down on your knees, piously offering it up. It's Why are things like this, damn it? What's going on here?"[23]

Wolff was raised by a divorced Roman Catholic mother who "had a Bible, but it stayed on the shelf," his earliest religious education came not from church attendance but from a farm family who often minded him on weekends when his mother was at work. They took him to revival meetings that came straight out of O'Connor's fervent South rather than from Concrete, Washington, in the cool, secular Pacific Northwest where he grew up. In his recent contribution to Andrew Blauner's *The Good Book* (2015), Wolff recollects this borrowed evangelical upbringing as if it were yesterday: the big tent set up in a field ("It was hot and close under the canvas"), the bare wood folding chairs that "got harder and stickier as the hours—and I mean *hours*—went by," the red-faced crowds, the hymn singing broadcast live for a gospel radio program ("Our Catholic hymnal has nothing to compare").[24] What made the greatest impression on him, however, was the preaching:

> No dry bromides droned from a pulpit; this was theater. The preacher paced the stage, brandishing his big black Bible. He acted out the stories and the parables, speaking in the voices of Moses, of Job and his comforters, of Martha, the Good Samaritan, the woman at the well, Pilate, the Lord God Himself. I saw Abraham raise the knife over his son, heard the demons shriek as the Gadarene swine carried them over the cliff. (211)

These biblical stories, enacted with great passion, were all news to him. But if they grabbed his attention, they also disturbed him. There was the innocent Job, a good man bereft of everything because Satan wanted to put him to the test; there was the "lad" Isaac prepared for sacrifice at the hand of his own father ("How did a little kid deserve that?"). And apart from these individual plights, there was the rank injustice upheld in some of the parables, which Wolff must have felt keenly during those weekend revival meetings when his mother was at the local Dairy Queen earning their living: "The laborers in the vineyard—shouldn't the ones who worked all day get paid more than those who showed up right at the end?"

And yet, it is this troublesome aspect of Bible stories—of the Bible itself—that may well account for Scripture's abiding appeal to Wolff. Take, for instance, "A White Bible," one of the "New Stories" included in Wolff's 2009 selection of his work, *Our Story Begins*.[25] Set at the tail end of a cold, windy evening, it centers on a confrontation between a high school teacher and a feckless student's immigrant father. In another writer's hands, this meeting might well culminate in an assault or even a murder. Wolff actually prepares us for this kind of showdown when we are made privy to Maureen Casey's deliberations about what to do with this angry stranger who has forced his way into her car. Should she summon up what she can recall from a self-defense class and "go on the attack, kick the bastard in the balls, scream and kick and hit and bite and fight to the very death" (290)? Wolff does not take the story in that direction. Instead of bloodshed, we get a painful conversation that turns into a debate. Her antagonist is an immigrant Muslim who has lost his profession and his wife and finds himself at sea in an alien America. He threatens her with unspecified repercussions should his son, a flagrant cheater and n'er-do-well she has tolerated too long, be expelled from school because of her report. He wields neither knife nor gun, only a pious Muslim's outrage at "the great lady teacher" who uses alcohol ("A *drink*? You stink of it"), who emerges unsteadily from happy hour at Harrigans ("a discotheque!"), and who takes the Lord's name in vain ("Don't curse!"). He is outraged that she would presume to sit in judgment on Hassan and foil a father's (totally unrealistic) expectations of a career for the boy in medicine.

Although Maureen—"Mrs Maureen Casey," as he disdains to call her—is an ancestral Catholic who teaches under Father Crespi at the St. Ignatius School ("With your Jesus on the cross behind your desk"), she has none of the religious fervor that fuels her opponent. Quite the contrary, "I've had it with clueless men passing on orders from God," she tells him. To which he responds, "Without God, there is no foundation . . . Without God, we stand on nothing" (296). God, for him, is a matter of life and death.

This altercation takes place entirely in Maureen's car, with her in the front behind the steering wheel and him behind her in the back seat. Positioned in tandem, it is as if the two were in the confessional box at St. Ignatius Church. When the father's importuning finally comes to nothing, she asks the man why he would ever have believed her if she, in the pressure of the moment, had acquiesced to his demands: "Whatever made you think I'd keep my word?" What follows seems almost to come out of nowhere.

> He reached into the breast pocket of his coat and took out a white Bible, a girl's Bible bound in imitation leather with gilt lettering on the cover. "You would swear," he said, "Like in court, to the judge."
>
> Maureen opened it, rifled the thin, filmy pages. "Where did you get this?"
>
> "Goodwill."
>
> "Oh dear," she said. "You really thought you could save him."
>
> He pushed the door open. "I am sorry, Mrs Casey."
>
> "Here." Maureen held out the Bible, but he put up the palms of his hands and backed out of the car. (299)

The story ends as Maureen forgets her would-be assailant and focuses instead on the book he has summarily left in her hands—not the Qur'an, but her own sacred text. It transfixes her: "She got caught up leafing through the Bible. Her father had given her one just like it after her confirmation. She still kept it by her bedside" (299). The book acts as a Proustian madeleine that brings her into contact with her own past: her father, her confirmation, and a treasured gift once placed in her youthful hands. But more than that, it connects her to the completely unknown girl to whom the white Bible had once been given. Inside the cover, Maureen discovers her name, "Clara Gutierrez," along with a now undecipherable Spanish inscription and a legible date, "Pascua 1980." Lost for the moment in the imagined reality of a complete stranger, the boundaries blur between Maureen

Casey and Clara Guttierez, between Easter and "Pascua," as she brings the details of her own past to bear on what she imagines to be the girl's:

> Where was she now, this Clara? What had become of her? This ardent hopeful girl in her white dress, surrounded by family, godparents, that the Bible should end up in a Goodwill bin? Even if she no longer read it, or believed it, she wouldn't have thrown it away. Had something happened? Ah, girl, where are you? (300)

As these concluding questions come in quick succession, we realize that Maureen is asking them of herself as well as of Clara Guttierez. Earlier in the story we learned of her contentious relationships with her "old bird" of a disapproving mother, with her estranged daughter Katie ("Since when, Maureen wanted to know, had a few home truths become unforgivable?") and with the husband she divorced. We also know that by her bedside she keeps the same kind of white Bible as the one that is now in her hand—a traditional rite-of-passage token given by her Catholic father at a time when she had been a "hopeful girl in her white dress, surrounded by family, godparents." Given the accumulated scar tissue of her middle age, what—who—was Maureen Casey back then?

This question might have been posed in any number of ways; the one that Wolff chose, however, focuses our attention on the Bible and what it means. "What had become of her?" she asks of Clara. Clara remains a mystery—is she even alive as Maureen holds the book in her hands?—but so too does "the great lady teacher" herself who, after her ordeal with a hostile stranger, must wonder who *she* is and what has become of her. How much has she lost?

Or, for that matter, what has become of the Bible in her world? For Maureen it may no longer be read or believed in, but by no means should it be thrown away. Its retrieval from the dumping ground of a Goodwill genuinely shocks her. She may open its white leatherette cover only for clues, to see what someone may have written inside, entirely mindless of the text printed on its "thin, flimsy pages." Nonetheless, the book has staying power. She is mindful about where such "gift edition" Bibles end up, whether on a bedside table (no doubt untouched, tucked deep in a drawer) or, shamefully, in the jumble of a Goodwill pile. But ironically, it is her Muslim interlocutor who has the Scriptures at his disposal and who seems to have gone beyond the cover to take on the words inside.

It is he, after all, who introduces the Bible to the story a mere page from its ending. He introduces it, moreover, as a guarantor of truth telling: "'You would swear,' he said, 'Like in court, to the judge.'" Every time Maureen offhandedly takes the name of the Lord in vain, it is he who invokes the fourth commandment (Exod. 20:70): "Don't curse! No more cursing!" (294). On one occasion he pleads with her, "'Have some care,' he said. 'God is not mocked'" (296). Here, improbably, we have a Muslim citing not only Torah but Saint Paul in the Epistle to the Galatians: "Be not deceived; God is not mocked: for whatsoever a man soweth, that shall he also reap" (6:7). After Maureen repeatedly corrects him for referring to the St. Ignatius School principal "Father Crespi" as "Mr. Crespi," he offers her nothing less than a Gospel retort: "I call no man father but one" (296). He echoes Jesus's own words in Matthew 23:9, "And call no man your father upon the earth: for one is your Father, which is in heaven."

The place of the Bible in this story is uncertain. It is an object at once treasured and tossed aside, perhaps no longer read or believed in by those who allegedly hold it to be sacred but brought into view by someone of another faith. Although tucked in the drawer of a bedside table or left unattended on a high shelf, it nonetheless disturbs the peace just as surely as would a gun or a bolt of lightning. It makes a Tobias Wolff story.

*****

The Bible also makes an eleventh-hour appearance in the title story of Wolff's first volume, *In the Garden of the North American Martyrs* (1981).[26] Its academic setting is one well known to him after years of teaching at Syracuse University and (since 1997) at Stanford. The story's protagonist, Mary, is a familiar academic type: self-conscious, wary, someone intent never to rock the boat. She is a careful historian whose one scholarly monograph opens with words that effectively sum up everything about her: "It is generally believed that. . . ." We are told that Mary always writes out her lectures in full, using the arguments and words of other "approved" writers so as never to raise suspicion or step out of line. When she is forced to get a hearing aid, she suspects that her deafness is the result of always trying to catch what everyone else has said. "Her own thoughts she kept to herself, and the words for them grew faint as time went on; without quite disappearing they shrank to remote, nervous points, like birds flying away" (3).

Alongside Mary's personal decline is the downhill course of her career, with one job going belly-up when a college declares bankruptcy and another at a waterlogged standstill at an experimental college in Oregon. The possibility of deliverance comes out of nowhere when Louise, a former colleague, invites her to interview for a tenured position at a "famous college" in upstate New York. Full of hope, Mary travels to New York which is a region she learns through advance research was the ancestral home of the Iroquois. The college is quaintly beautiful; the prospect of living and teaching in its picture-perfect environs seems like a dream come true until shortly upon arrival she is told that, as part of her interview process, she must give a formal lecture later in the day. She has none prepared, and panics at the notion of doing what Louise suggests: "Just pick a subject and wing it."[27] Louise then comes to the rescue with an offer: "Last year I wrote an article on the Marshall Plan that I got bored with and never published. You can read that" (8). At first Mary has scruples, but then reflects that in one way or another she had been impersonating others' work for years. This was not the time to chart a different course.

One revelation leads to another. In the course of a campus tour Mary learns from a student guide that the college has a statute that requires that "they have to interview at least one woman for each opening" (11). After her meeting with the hiring committee proves absurdly perfunctory, she realizes that she has been brought to campus merely to satisfy a rule. When this is corroborated by Louise, Mary is led off to her certain humiliation in a suitably Gothic lecture hall as students spill across the aisles and professors sit cross legged in the front row. They await her meaningless show.

Louise then announces the subject of the Marshall Plan lecture. Suddenly, however, Mary changes her mind. Rather than read another person's cast-off lecture, she "wings it" after all. "'I wonder how many of you know,' she began, 'that we are in the Long House, the ancient domain of the Five Nations of the Iroquois.'" (13). Hearing this, the professoriate eye one another in confusion, and then grow steadily more appalled as Mary goes on to describe in gruesome detail—the fruit of her diligent preparatory research—the pitiless cruelty of the Iroquois toward their enemies: "They took scalps and practiced cannibalism and slavery." The generalized horror of her account gets even worse as she describes the step-by-step torture of two Jesuit missionaries, the martyrs of the story's title. Jean de Brébeuf has a burning iron thrust down his throat, red-hot hatchets draped around his neck, boiling water poured over his head, and his chest cut open. When it seems as if her narrative cannot get any worse, she tops herself. "Later, their chief tore out Brébeuf's heart and ate it, but just before he did this Brébeuf spoke to them one last time. He said—"

With that em-dash, the story moves quickly to its end:

"That's enough!" yelled Dr. Howells, jumping to his feet. Louise stopped shaking her head. Her eyes were perfectly round. Mary had come to the end of her facts. She did not know what Brébeuf had said. Silence rose up around her; just when she thought she would go under and be lost in it she heard someone whistling in the hallway outside, trilling the notes like a bird, like many birds. "Mend your lives," she said. "You have deceived yourselves in the pride of your hearts, and the strength of your arms. Though you soar aloft like the eagle, though your nest is set among the stars, thence I will bring you down, says the Lord. Turn from power to love. Be kind. Do justice. Walk humbly." Louise was waving her arms. "Mary!" she shouted. But Mary had more to say, much more; she waved back at Louise, then turned off her hearing aid so that she would not be distracted again. (14)

It is easy to see much of what Tobias Wolff is doing here. He knows his collegiate setting well: the debilitating caution of some academics (as well as the arrogance of others); the terror of being forced, unprepared, to "wing it"; the hunger and thirst for gainful employment. With Wolff we savor the sweetness of revenge as Mary, with no thought for the morrow, scandalizes the crowd. Nor are we baffled by Wolff's play with magical realism. When a faux Gothic lecture hall filled with the smoke of professorial pipes morphs into the smoky Iroquois Long House—or when Mary, standing in a stained glass "circle of red light," becomes one with the Jesuits on their funeral pyre—we understand the method of the author's madness.

But what are we to make of all this "winging"? Is it the result of a hearing aid gone haywire? Are we witnessing a mad woman hearing "voices"? Or are we watching someone who went deaf after listening too intently to other people now discovering the audacious sound of her own voice, and refusing for once to be distracted by the sound of any others? These are all interpretive possibilities, but none of them take into account what follows upon Dr. Howell's "That's enough!" For what Mary actually says when her facts run out is a torrent of Scripture, a pastiche of sayings drawn from the Hebrew prophets and recalled here in the sonorous tones of the KJV. Her judgment against those who "soar aloft like the eagle" and make their nests "among the stars"; her injunction to amend lives, do justice, and walk humbly—everything that she says, in fact, is derived from Amos and Hosea, Obadiah and Jeremiah, and most especially from the prophet Micah: "[The Lord] hath shewed thee, O man, what is good; and what doth the Lord require of thee, but to do justly, and to love mercy, and to walk humbly with thy God?" (Mic. 6:8).[28]

While Mary's "text" is not some boring lecture on the Marshall Plan once written and then discarded by Louise, it is also not her own speech. Wolff keeps her in character, much as O'Connor does Mrs. Turpin at the end of "Revelation." Mary begins "winging it" by referencing Francis Parkman's *The Jesuits in North America* (1900) for her martyrology; but when she is at the end of her facts, it is Scripture that takes her over. Telling her college audience to "Mend your lives," she becomes Micah denouncing the corruption of a proud Jerusalem. Or she becomes—who knows?—Jean de Brébeuf speaking one last time to the Iroquois chief who is about to eat him alive. In an example of grace under pressure (or in the nothing-left-to-lose spirit of "What the Hell?") the former parrot becomes an apostle, the anxious copycat a prophet going for broke.

Wolff's tone in this story is satirical and tricky, which makes it difficult to speak with confidence about the role that Scripture plays here. A witty revenge comedy sits uneasily with a prophet's jeremiad, as does a woman on the verge of a nervous breakdown—or hilarious personal breakthrough—with someone meant to be taken seriously as delivering the Word of the Lord. But uneasiness may always be the point about prophets, a feature of their mission, just as it is inevitably for the storyteller devoted to matters of life and death. "In the Garden of the North American Martyrs" gives Tobias Wolff a way to speak truth to power, and Micah a new context in which to proclaim his ancient challenge. Wolff gains the moral weight that modern speech seems by and large to have lost, while the Hebrew prophets get a chance once more to disturb those who are at ease in Zion. Mary's biblical fireworks are at once very funny and totally serious, with the result that Wolff gives earnest sacred texts a second coming in a fresh and comic context. As birds twitter—or is it someone whistling in the hallway outside?—a bizarre woman waving from the podium tells the crowd, "Turn from power to love. Be kind. Do justice. Walk humbly." These are ancient words but, disarmingly, the story delivers them as if they were brand new.

*****

Wolff gives us another revival of Scripture in "The Rich Brother," a story that concludes the 1985 collection *Back in the World*.[29] It engages themes found elsewhere in his work, especially the tension that exists between siblings, but deals with them in ways that reveal close and obvious ties to the Bible. One reviewer called it "a small classic about family life in America, what's left of it."[30] Wolff himself said that it is "as close to a fable as I have written."[31] Rather than "fable," he might well have described it as a parable, because in so many ways it is a reworking of the elder-younger contrast presented so powerfully in Luke 15:11–32. The comparison begins with the opening line, as Luke's "A certain man had two sons" (15:11) becomes "There were two brothers, Pete and Donald." Wolff eliminates the all-important father of the parable: parents are relegated to the story's background and play no significant role. As a result, there is no one to mediate between brothers or to deliver the parable's "point": "For this thy brother was dead, and is alive again; and was lost, and is found" (15:32).

Instead, Wolff heightens the contrast between the brothers. The elder, Pete, is stout and cynical, a family man who is successful in business. He is someone who owns a boat and drives a new car with a leather interior, who both resents and enjoys throwing around money. Donald comes from the antipodes: wraithlike, clad in a hoodie and "Try God" T-short worn inside out, he is a disciple of one spiritual master after another, improvident, impoverished, and perpetually on his brother's dole.

Donald is also haunted by what Pete dismisses as "Kid stuff . . . ancient history"—the violence inflicted by Pete when Donald was a boy recovering from surgery:

> If I was on my stomach you'd roll me over. Then you would lift up my pajama top and start hitting me on my stitches. As hard as you could, over and over. I was afraid you'd get mad if you knew I was awake. Is that strange or what? I was afraid you'd get mad if you found out that I knew you were trying to kill me. (81)

At first Pete will have none of this, but as Donald persists he makes some concession to the truth: "It may have happened once or twice. Kids do these things. I can't get all excited about something I maybe did twenty-five years ago." He even confesses to having a recent dream about his brother, in which the two were alone and, in a reversal of daytime reality, Donald was taking care of him. "Pete left it at that. He didn't tell Donald that in this dream he was blind" (81).

Tension between the two grows over the course of a car trip as Pete brings Donald to his home after his brother has once again self-destructed. Although not in Pete's dream life, he is in fact the one who rescues, and Donald the one who needs to be picked up and bailed out. The story reaches a breaking point when the gullible and empty-handed Donald "invests" the hundred dollars Pete has just given him for food to buy a share in a phony Peruvian gold mine from the patently bogus hitchhiker Webster, a cartoon shyster from Wolff's storehouse of liars. This dumb giveaway of Pete's hard-earned money is the last straw, a sign that he, the responsible nobody's-fool elder, has once again been taken advantage of by his prodigal younger brother—an immature squanderer who stands in stark contrast to himself, a mature man "who has finished his work and settled his debts, done all things meet and due" (90). At the end of the story he seems totally within his rights to say, like Dr. Howells at Mary's lecture, "That's enough!" He will drive away from the millstone around his neck who is his brother, teach him a lesson, and let him fend for himself.

And yet, smiling to himself in his new car, nodding to the Pachelbel Canon playing in his music system,

> He went down another mile or two and pretended that he was not already slowing down, that he wouldn't turn back, that he would be able to drive on like this, alone, and have the right answer when his wife stood before him in the doorway of his hope and asked, *Where is he? Where is your brother?* (90)

For the reader who recognizes that this question is none other than the one God poses to Cain after his slaying of Abel—"And the Lord said unto Cain, Where is Abel thy brother? And he said, I know not: Am I my brother's keeper?" (Gen. 4:9)—the story assumes greater significance than "a small classic about American life." It becomes a biblical probing of tensions as old as Genesis, as venerable as the struggle not only between Cain and Abel but also between Esau and Jacob, Ishmael and Isaac, Joseph (and David) and their brothers, or, to move from brothers to sisters, between Leah and Rachel. Furthermore, just as in the Hebrew Bible, where God favors the traditionally disadvantaged younger over the elder, so too "The Rich Brother" raises questions about who is first and who last, who is wise and who foolish. Or as Pete wonders to himself, suddenly insecure about whether or not he has won the game by playing by the sensible rules ("done all things meet and right"),

> [It] would be just like this unfair life for Donald to come out ahead in the end, by believing in some outrageous promise that turned out to be true and that he, Pete, rejected out of hand because he was too wised up to listen to anybody's pitch any more, except for laughs. What a joke if there really was a blessing to be had, and the blessing didn't come to the one who deserved it, the one who did all the work, but to the other. (89)

Pondering this "joke," one recalls the injustice not only of God's constant preference for the underdog in the Hebrew Bible but also for the "unfairness" of those parables of Jesus that so disturbed the young Wolff—"fables" where the last become first, or the vineyard latecomers are paid the same as those who toiled all day, or "a selfish wastrel" has a big fuss made over him by an indulgent father. Wolff does not force a conversion on his version of the prodigal son's elder brother. There is no explicit epiphany, no explicit moment when Pete's "head cleared for a minute" (as it does for the dizzy Grandmother in "A Good Man is Hard to Find"), nor does any "a visionary light" settle in his eyes (as it does for Ruby Turpin in "Revelation"). And yet, as the story draws to its close, we note that Pete's car is slowing down, getting ready for the inevitable U-turn that will take him back to a skinny man wearing his "Try God" T-shirt turned inside out.

Is this turnaround the result of an "intervention" of grace? Wolff allowed that it was, in a way, albeit without any "violent eruptions from heaven." Pete is going back for Donald because he can suddenly imagine his wife standing there and asking the question God asks Cain: "Where is your brother?" When it comes down to it, he *is* his brother's keeper. The realization—soft-pedaled, only implicit—may well be full of grace. "But it's also a natural psychological event in his life. She's going to ask him a question if he goes up to the door without his brother. And he's not going to be able to answer. He's got to go back for him."[32]

Sharing his recently published "Thoughts on the Prodigal Son" in Andrew Blauner's *The Good Book*, Wolff charts the changing course of his relationship to this particular biblical story, which has had so long a hold on him. In youth he identified with the resentful elder brother; at seventy, it is the parable's father who catches his attention—the father who looks far down the road hoping to catch sight of his son's return, until eventually, against the odds, he comes into sight:

And I know that this is true, because I am a father, and when my children are away I pine for them, and my greatest joy is having them under my roof. Nothing they can do, nothing will ever lessen the love I have for them. Even in their absence my love abides. And if I, weak and fickle as I am, can be so constant in this thing, how can I doubt the constancy, the abiding love, of the father who yearns for me? We are all a little lost, are we not? Trying, this way and that, to find our way home. The way is eased, at least for me, by this assurance—that I will be welcomed with a kiss.[33]

"Welcomed with a kiss": What we see in the work of Tobias Wolff is how powerfully a particular biblical story can enter so deeply into a writer's imagination that it enables him both to live his personal life in its light and to generate new fiction. The story begets stories: there is always a newer testament. We have no more idea at the end of "Rich Brother" what, if anything, will come of Pete's turnaround than we have from Jesus's parable whether the elder will reconcile with the younger or the father prove wise in his generosity to each. In both cases, however, a question is posed rather than answered. It is the reader who has work to do.

11

Bernard Malamud

Twentieth-century Jewish American literature is dominated by the triumvirate of Saul Bellow, Bernard Malamud, and Philip Roth—three male writers whose works were widely read and widely acclaimed, garnering tremendous critical attention from scholars of American literature and Jewish American literature alike. The trio tends to elicit strong opinions from both readers and critics—which often comprise pronouncements on who is the superior writer. When Boris Fishman put forth *The Fixer* as his contribution to *Tablet* magazine's list of the "100 Greatest Jewish Books," he proclaimed: "Keep your Rothian heat, your Bellovian prolixity and self-scratching cerebralism, and give me the wilted flesh (and blood), the bone-rattling cold, the granite-like prose of a Malamud novel. Roth and Bellow are mortal; Malamud is the Bible."[1]

It's not entirely clear what Fishman might mean by Malamud's *being* the Bible. As many have noted, Malamud is not only "the heir to rich Jewish traditions, and worthy heir that he is, he remakes them his way and reinvigorates them"[2] but also the heir to and reinvigorator of American, British, and European literary traditions.[3] Among the many texts to which he returns[4] only one is the Bible—sometimes explicitly, sometimes obliquely. His last novel, *God's Grace*, opens with a dialogue between God and man, and features characters named Esau, Luke, Saul of Tarsus, and one Mary "Madelyn." The *New York Times* described the book, an account of God's creating anew in the aftermath of nuclear war and a divine-induced flood, as "Malamud's new bible"—"nothing less than a retelling of the Old and

New Testaments, complete with the author's views on man's (and God's) nature, good and evil, cause and effect, fall from grace."[5] Some critics find the Bible evoked in his other works as well. One is even of the view that "the first and main key to understanding Bernard Malamud's fiction"[6] is the Akedah, the story of the binding of Isaac in Genesis 22.[7] But when Fishman says that "Malamud is the Bible," he is characterizing his style, not his influences. We see something of what Fishman is getting at when we hear Malamud's treatment of suffering—a particularly prevalent theme in his work[8]—described in biblical terms: Malamud "follows in the ancient Jewish tradition of the prophets, Amos, Jeremiah, the Second Isaiah, who announce suffering to be the Jew's special destiny, evidence of his unique covenant with God, proof of God's concern in that only those who are loved are chastised."[9] But of course Fishman has insisted that Malamud is not *like* the Bible: he *is* the Bible. It is an assertion as bold as the one Flannery O'Connor made of Malamud: "I have discovered a short-story writer who is better than any of them, including myself."

As Fishman illustrates, Malamud is often read alongside Bellow and Roth, but at least one critic—Bonnie Lyons—has argued that he is best understood in light of O'Connor herself. Both writers "considered their fiction as having serious moral purpose and sought to affect their readers' consciousness."[10] Virtually no one has written about Malamud without emphasizing the moral quality in his work. One commentator noted drily, "With the prevailing consensus thus in favor of Malamud's mission of moral improvement, readers might well wonder whether it would not be more direct to bypass him altogether and proceed directly to the synagogue for the original teachings."[11] Indeed, Malamud is frequently described as a fabulist. Sometimes the word indicates he writes Jewish fables, stories that exhibit "the old Jewish habit of turning history into myth."[12] More often, it means his stories are moral fables; sometimes they are even described as parables.

And yet despite their shared sense of morality, their writing "out of and against what they conceived as a pervasive nihilism,"[13] Malamud and O'Connor probably couldn't be more different in their approaches to both their readers and their characters. According to Lyons, O'Connor's "basic attitude toward humanity is an overwhelming sense of human depravity, of basic worthlessness, which is of course, the foundation of their total need for Jesus, for divine grace."[14] For O'Connor, humans are tainted by their "blinding, almost impossibly deep, egotism";[15] for Malamud, they are marred by their situational failures—notably the failure to love, to treat others well, or to recognize others' basic humanity. O'Connor's central drama is "man's recognition of his own worthlessness and his reliance on God, the breakthrough to grace,"[16] while for Malamud it is "the human aspiration to become humane and more human."[17] Lyons notes that the essential difference between the two is signaled in the pessimism and optimism evident in the titles of their best-known stories: "A Good Man is Hard to Find" and "The Magic Barrel."

Malamud's much-anthologized "The Magic Barrel," originally published in a collection of the same name, likely needs little introduction. Like "The First Seven Years," the initial story in the volume, it is about a matchmaking.[18] Leo Finkle, a rabbinical student about to complete his studies at New York's Yeshiva University, has "been advised by an acquaintance that he might find it easier to win himself a congregation if he were married." He enlists the services of Pinye Salzman, a *shadchan* (marriage broker), "whose two-line advertisement he had read in the Forward." At their first meeting, Salzman removes six profiles from a "thin packet of much-handled cards"—according to Salzman a small selection of the many in his care, so numerous that the "drawers are already filled to the top, so I keep them now in a barrel"—six profiles. Finkle wants photographs, but Salzman has established his own system: "First comes family, amount of dowry, also what kind of promises. After comes pictures, rabbi." He presents Finkle with a 24-year-old widow. A 32-year-old high school teacher. The 19-year-old daughter of a stomach specialist—in perfect health, Salzman says, "breathing a little heavily. 'Of course, she is a little lame in her right foot from an auto accident that it happened to her when she was twelve years, but nobody notices on account she is so brilliant and also beautiful.'" After only these three cards, Leo dismisses Salzman.

Leo finds himself "in low spirits the next day. He explained it as rising from Salzman's failure to produce a suitable bride for him," and determines he might not "care for the matchmaking institution." And yet he is not at peace with this realization. "By nightfall, however, he had regained sufficient calm to sink his nose into a book and there found peace from his thoughts." Then, "almost at once there [is] a knock on the door. Before Leo could say enter Salzman, commercial cupid, [is] standing in the room." Salzman persuades Finkle to meet the teacher Lily Hirschorn, whose age has apparently reduced from thirty-two to twenty-nine (a bookkeeping error, Salzman claims), for a walk on Riverside Drive.

The walk goes poorly: Lily is far too interested in Finkle's spiritual life, a dimension of himself he seems altogether to have neglected, despite his vocation. She asks, nervously, "How was it that you came to your calling? I mean was it a sudden passionate inspiration?" and Finkle for a time cannot construct an answer. Finally he admits to a long-standing interest in the Law, which prompts her to probe further, "You saw revealed in it the presence of the Highest?" He nods and changes the subject, but she is soon back at it. "'When,' she ask[s] in a trembly voice, 'did you become enamored of God?'"

Finkle is taken aback. He stares at her. He becomes aware that Lily has some conception of him, an image "of a total stranger, some mystical figure, perhaps even passionate prophet that Salzman had dreamed up for her." He is ashamed by the portrait of him that Salzman—"the trickster"—has painted. "'I am not,' he said gravely, 'a talented religious person.' And in seeking words to go on, found himself possessed by shame and fear. 'I think,' he said in a strained manner, 'that I came to God not because I love Him, but because I did not.'"

The candid response throws Lily off—she wilts—but has an even more profound effect on Finkle: he sees "a profusion of loaves of bread go flying like ducks high over his head, not unlike the winged loaves by which he had counted himself to sleep last night. Mercifully, then, it snowed." He returns home infuriated, ready to "throw [Salzman] out of the room the minute he reappeared," but the man does not reappear. Finkle falls out of anger and into despair. He comes to realize that he had enlisted Salzman to find him a bride "because he was incapable of doing it himself." Indeed, he seems to have been incapable of anything connected to love. Lily's questions had caused him to reveal "to himself more than her—the true nature of his relationship to God, and from that it had come upon him, with shocking force, that apart from his parents, he had never loved anyone. Or perhaps it went the other way, that he did not love God so well as he might, because he had not loved man." Leo has seen "himself for the first time as he truly was—unloved and loveless." The revelation, this newfound self-knowledge, sends Finkle into a spiral. He ceases to eat and to care for himself. He thinks of abandoning the rabbinate. He is irritable with those around him, then abjectly apologetic. Throughout this, he understands that he is a Jew and, yes, a Jew must suffer.

And then he begins to think that with this new knowledge he might be able to find a bride: "Perhaps love would now come to him and a bride to that love." At first he resolves to look without the aid of Salzman. Naturally, "the marriage broker, a skeleton with haunted eyes, returned that very night," to inquire after Finkle's walk with Lily Hirschorn. Finkle berates the matchmaker: "She had in mind a totally different person, a sort of semi-mystical Wonder Rabbi." Salzman barely bothers to defend himself—"All I said, you was a religious man"—before allowing that "This is my weakness that I have. . . . My wife says to me I shouldn't be a salesman, but when I have two fine people that they would be wonderful to be married, I am so happy that I talk too much." The admission mollifies Finkle for a moment, although he insists that he will not retain Salzman any longer and will search for his bride on his own. The exchange—a riff on an old Jewish story—is among the most cited and commented upon passages in the story:

"You don't want any more a bride?"

"I do," said Leo, "but I have decided to seek her in a different way. I am no longer interested in an arranged marriage. To be frank, I now admit the necessity of premarital love. That is, I want to be in love with the one I marry."

"Love?" said Salzman, astounded. After a moment he remarked "For us, our love is our life, not for the ladies. In the ghetto they—"

"I know, I know," said Leo. "I've thought of it often. Love, I have said to myself, should be a byproduct of living and worship rather than its own end. Yet for myself I find it necessary to establish the level of my need and fulfill it."

Salzman shrugged but answered, "Listen, rabbi, if you want love, this I can find for you also. I have such beautiful clients that you will love them the minute your eyes will see them."

Uninterested in this pitch, Leo sends Salzman away then follows immediately after intending to return an envelope of pictures, but Salzman is gone—it was "as if on the wings of the wind, Salzman had disappeared." The envelope sits on the table gathering dust until one day, "with a sudden relentless gesture [Finkle] tore it open." In it he finds photographs of six women, each of whom seems to him to be a variant of Lily Hirschorn. They are "all past their prime, all starved behind bright smiles, not a true personality in the lot. Life, despite their frantic yoohooings, had passed them by; they were pictures in a briefcase that stank of fish." He looks them over and returns them to the envelope where he finds another, different than the others, taken in a photo booth. The face in the photo "deeply moved him" and "he knew he must go urgently to find her."

When Finkle arrives at Salzman's apartment to inquire after the woman in the packet that Salzman left behind, he is met by Salzman's wife—a familiar woman Finkle could swear he has seen before—who tells him that Salzman is not in. He asks where his office is, and his wife replies, "In the air." "You mean he has no office?" Leo clarifies, and the wife answers only, "In his socks." Finkle peers past her into the apartment, but "there was no sign of Salzman or his magic barrel, probably also a figment of his imagination." There is, however, the "odor of frying fish." The wife tells Finkle, "Go home, he will find you"—and indeed he does. He arrives home to find Salzman "breathless, waiting at his door." He tells Salzman, "Here is the one I want," but Salzman is insistent that this woman he absolutely cannot have:

> "She is not for you. She is a wild one—wild, without shame. This is not a bride for a rabbi."
> "What do you mean wild?"
> "Like an animal. Like a dog. For her to be poor was a sin. This is why to me she is dead now."
> "In God's name, what do you mean?"
> "Her I can't introduce to you," Salzman cried.
> "Why are you so excited?"
> "Why, he asks," Salzman said, bursting into tear. "This is my baby, my Stella, she should burn in hell."

Finkle retreats upstairs, hides under the covers. Neither sleep nor prayers help him shake the image of the woman. Tormented, "he endlessly struggled not to love her" but has no success. "He then concluded to convert her to goodness, himself to God. The idea alternately nauseated and exalted him."

In a Broadway cafeteria he encounters Salzman, "haggard and to the point of vanishing." He tells him he has found love. Salzman rejoins, "If you can love her, then you can love anybody." But Finkle desires only her: "Just her I want," he murmurs. He asks to be put in touch with her, that he might, he says humbly, "be of service." Salzman stops eating his fish. Saying nothing, he has agreed.

They will meet on "a certain corner." It is a physical location as vague and concrete as "not long ago," the temporal location that begins the story. The season has turned and Leo appears, "carrying a small bouquet of violets and rosebuds." It is the type of arrangement favored by Chagall,[19] and indeed the whole scene evokes one of the artist's romantic paintings. Stella is standing under a lamppost, wearing "a white dress with red shoes, which fitted his expectations, although in a troubled moment he had imagined the dress red, and only the shoes white." She is uneasy, shy. He can see that "her eyes—clearly her father's—were filled with desperate innocence. He pictured, in her, his own redemption. Violins and lit candles revolved in the sky. Leo ran forward with flowers out-thrust." The words (white and the red, the undercurrent of transgression and the suggestion of innocence) all evoke the prophet Isaiah—"though your sins be as scarlet they shall be as white as snow; though they be red like crimson, they shall be as wool" (Isa. 1:18). The image is all Chagall.[20]

It is not the story's final note, however. The scene seems not to be observed by Salzman, despite his apparent omnipresence. He is "around the corner, leaning against a wall, chant[ing] prayers for the dead."[21]

Like so many Malamud stories, "The Magic Barrel" manages to evoke the *shtetl* in the twentieth-century American metropolis. Malamud's New York City is a landscape of dingy rooms in tenement houses, apartment buildings on the brink of being condemned, forlorn urban cafeterias, Old World stores that patrons have all but abandoned for more modern establishments. Finkle lives off a "dark fourth-floor hallway [in a] graystone rooming house" in "a small, almost meager room" lined with "shelves upon shelves of books" and crowded with others, not on shelves, that seem to cover everything but a table by the window—even the one-burner gas stove. The setting is not entirely suffused in desolation, however. Salzman looks around his claustrophobic surroundings and "let[s] out a soft, contented sigh." The dark of the building and the weight of the books are counterbalanced by light: the window "overlooks the lamp-lit city." Looking out, Finkle noticed—"for the first time in years"—signs that winter was coming to an end; he "observed the round white moon, moving high in the sky through a cloud menagerie, and watched with half-opened mouth as it penetrate[d] a huge hen, and drop[ped] out of her like an egg laying itself." In this same late winter sky, Finkle later sees the profusion of flying loaves of bread on his walk with Lily. Here we see typical Malamud at work: the world he creates is concrete, tangible, realistic—until suddenly it is not. A cloud becomes a celestial hen, the moon a self-laying egg. The story ends on a New York street corner where "violins and lit candles revolve in the sky."

Much like the story itself, Pinye Salzman "seems both absolutely realistic and concrete and partly fantastic, magical, allegorical."[22] Salzman is a marriage broker, not a fishmonger, but "he smelled frankly of fish, which he loved to eat." He carries everywhere with him the quintessential scents of the appetizing shops and delicatessens of the Lower East Side. Within his briefcase is "an oily paper bag, from which he extracted a hard, seeded roll and a small, smoked white fish" and the photographs of the women for whom he seeks matches are tainted by the fact—if not by the smell—of their being stored in that "briefcase that stank of fish." His apartment is sunless and dingy and filled with an odor of frying fish that makes his visitor "weak to the knees." When Finkle encounters him for the final time, it is in a Broadway cafeteria, where Salzman sits "alone at a rear table, sucking the bony remains of a fish." He appears "haggard and to the point of vanishing." The descriptions are so concrete, so vivid, the reader can not only picture Salzman, but also practically smell him. And yet what do we make of this association with fish? And why, when Finkle "encounters" him in the cafeteria, is the marriage broker so reduced?

There is something unnatural, or supernatural, about Salzman. Once Finkle first contacts him, the *shadchan* "appeared one night out of the dark fourth-floor hallway." Subsequent appearances are equally unexpected: "almost at once there was a knock on the door. Before Leo could say enter, Salzman, commercial cupid, was standing in the room"; inexplicably, Salzman later beats Finkle home—Finkle finds him "breathless, waiting at his door." He vanishes as readily as he materializes: "as if on the wings of the wind, Salzman had disappeared." He seems to be both strangely absent—his office is "in the air," also, possibly, "in his socks"—and present in his absence: Finkle "senses [him] to be somewhere around, hiding perhaps high in a tree along the street." Finkle believes him to have the ability to control events: after Lily's dismay at his sudden confession about not loving God, "it snowed, which [Finkle] would not put past Salzman's machinations." When Finkle finally meets Salzman's daughter Stella, he is "afflicted by a tormenting suspicion that Salzman had planned it all to happen this way."[23]

Salzman is thought by some critics to be an angel, like Alexander Levine in another story in the collection. In "Angel Levine," as in "The Magic Barrel," the lot of the heavenly figure seems tethered to that of the main character: when Angel Levine seems not to be succeeding in his earthly mission, he deteriorates in appearance.[24] Similarly, after Finkle renounces Salzman, the older man becomes "gray and meager," looking "as if he would expire on his feet"—though he regains his strength and spirits once he has eaten his fish sandwich and has reengaged Finkle in the prospect of finding a match.

One might wonder how the references to fish play into the idea that Salzman is an angel. Here David Robertson makes an intriguing biblical connection. He points Malamud's reader to the Book of Tobit, an ancient Jewish story preserved in the Catholic Bible but not in the Jewish or Protestant Scriptures. The canonicity of the book does not trouble Robertson, however, who quotes Malamud as having said, "I'm influenced by the Bible, both Testaments."[25] The apocryphal book is about Tobit, a devout Israelite carried captive to Nineveh who maintains his piety away from Jerusalem by eating only kosher food, giving alms to the poor, and providing proper burials for Israelites killed by the Assyrian king Sennacherib. Tobit is blinded one night when bird droppings land in his eyes. He falls into poverty, and is so afflicted that he prays he might die. At the very same time, in Media, a woman named Sarah offers a similar prayer. She has been married seven times and on each of her wedding nights her new husband was slain by the demon Asmodeus before the marriage was consummated. God hears both prayers. Tobit suddenly recalls having placed some money in trust in Media. He sends his son Tobias to collect it: the son gains as a traveling companion the angel Raphael disguised as an Israelite named Azariah. En route to Media, Tobias catches a fish in the Tigris and his companion instructs him to keep the gall, heart, and liver. When Tobias meets Sarah—as orchestrated by Raphael—and desires to marry her, Raphael instructs him to burn the liver and heart of the fish in the bridal chamber. The smell drives away Asmodeus, and the couple consummate their marriage. The two return with Raphael to Nineveh, and the angel again instructs Tobias to use the fish innards. This time, he spreads the gall on Tobit's eyes and restores his sight. Raphael reveals himself to Tobit and his family, explaining that it was he who had delivered their prayers to God, who had made Tobit blind as a test of his faithfulness. After great praises, the angel ascends to heaven and the humans go on to live well. The book closes with an account of the death and burial of each of the main characters.

Robertson catalogs the strong intertextual connections between the Book of Tobit and "The Magic Barrel." A matchmaking angel who is associated with fish. A devout Jew who experiences blindness (with Tobit it is physiological; Finkle, spiritual). Pious men who do not love well (Tobit insults his wife, Anna; "apart from his parents, [Finkle] had never loved anyone"). A troubled woman who might well be more innocent than her reputation suggests (Milton calls Sarah "the seven-times-wedded maid"[26]). The restoration of sight—both literally and metaphorically (Finkle gains "inner vision—'he had lived without knowledge of himself, and never in the Five Books and all the Commentaries—mea culpa—had the truth been revealed to him'"— but comes to "new knowledge of himself"). Prayers and burials for the dead as the final note of the book.

There are also more ephemeral allusions. Finkle rejects a woman in Salzman's stack of cards because she is a widow, to which Salzman counters, "Am I responsible that the world is full of widows?"—a question that Raphael through his own redemptive action answers in the affirmative. Yes, it is the job of the angel to find love for the widow. In Tobit, Raphael reveals himself to be a seraph (12:15), a type of angel that Isaiah describes as having six wings (Isa. 6:1–3). In a curious passage, Finkle realizes—"with an emptiness that seized him with six hands—that he had called in the broker to find him a bride because he was incapable of doing it himself." The six hands of Salzman, the six wings of Raphael. In the Catholic tradition, the angel Raphael is the patron saint of both healers and matchmakers.

Not everyone reads Salzman as an angel. Stephen Bluestone has argued that the matchmaker is none other than God himself and that Finkle is Adam, and "The Magic Barrel" is a rewriting of the garden story. His reading reflects the notion that Malamud was the heir to and invigorator of both Jewish and English literary traditions: it uses a combination of Genesis 2–3, Milton's *Paradise Lost*, and two midrashim (rabbinic tales mentioned in our discussion of Allegra Goodman) to make sense of the story. The first midrash imagines a conversation between a Roman matron and a renowned second-century Jewish sage. She asks what God has been doing since he created the world in six days, and he replies that "He has been making matches: (Miss) So-and-So to (Mr.) So-and-So."[27] The second is a rabbinic tale that seeks to reconcile the textual incongruity of woman seeming to have been created simultaneously with man in Genesis 1 and then well after his creation in Genesis 2. Rather than synchronize the accounts, the rabbis imagined that two distinct women were created. The first, Lilith, a carnal being, refuses to submit to Adam because she was created alongside him. God banishes her for her defiance. (In Jewish lore, in her exile she becomes a lustful night demon who preys on sleeping men; in the Middle Ages, she gets cast as the wife of the demon king Asmodeus—yes, *that* Asmodeus—and they propagate a race of demons who kill sleeping infants.) God begins anew with Eve, created out of Adam's side as—to use the language of the KJV—a fitting "help meet."

In Bluestone's reading, Salzman is the divine matchmaker, making a match for his creation, Adam. The match is Lily, a total inversion of the Lilith figure: pure, innocent, utterly appropriate, the ideal *rebbetzin.* Indeed, in his attempts to persuade Finkle of the rightness of the match, Salzman alludes to the garden: "Also her father guarantees further twelve thousand [dollars]. Also she has a new car, wonderful clothes, talks on all subjects, and she will give you a first-class home and children. How near do we come in our life to paradise?"

But this Adam refuses—he, not God, banishes the first woman and seeks his own match. Here is where Bluestone turns to Milton. Adam's desires the fallen Eve: "In refusing Salzman's well-intentioned and rational matches, Finkle-Adam rejects the insufficient first version of creation, the lonely abyss of self, the loveless Eden set, as it were, in time and place."[28] Enabled by the very free will God has granted him, Finkle-Adam seeks his own Eve, not the Madonna but the whore. Bluestone reads this as a broader commentary: "In such a magical midrash it would follow that Finkle's chosen future will become the American future—the new course of assimilation, the cultural break with the Old World. In this brilliant recasting of the American myth of the New Eden, Malamud's New World, with its revitalized covenant also becomes—or remains (the ambiguity is central)—the familiar Fallen World."

If Bluestone's reading seems far-fetched, there are more reliable ways to root "The Magic Barrel" in the Adam and Eve story. As he casts Eve from Eden, God declares that Eve's desire shall be to her husband, and he will rule over her (Gen. 3:16). The fall alienates woman from man, inscribes a relational inequality. But Malamud's Eden story reinstills reciprocity between man and woman. When Finkle comes upon the image of Stella, "her face deeply moved him." He perceives her as "having been used to the bone"; he sees in her something "hauntingly familiar, yet absolutely strange."[29] Are these echoes of Adam's recognition of the rightness of Eve, after God has first presented him with the other animals? "This at last is bone of my bone, flesh of my flesh" (Gen. 2:23), he exclaims. Finkle "had a vivid impression that he had met her before, but try as he might he could not place her although he could almost recall her name, as he had read it in her own handwriting"—he, like Adam, seeks to find a name for his wife (3:20). Finkle is consumed by the picture—"she lapsed forth to this heart." She "lapsed"; later, he is "afflicted." Malamud's language becomes notably more biblical, but never more so than when Finkle concludes, "Her he desired." The diction is Salzman's Yiddish, the sentiment the lover's in the Song of Songs. The inequality of desire in Genesis is briefly rectified. *His desire is to her.*

The recalibration is uncertain—an instant later Finkle's "head ached and eyes narrowed with the intensity of his gazing . . . he experienced fear of her and was aware that he had received an impression, somehow, of evil." Stella is no longer the Eve, but Lilith. Stella-Lilith is the woman who sent Finkle under his covers to think his life through. The woman he prays to have exorcised from his mind. The woman who consumed his nights. The woman associated with demons.

But maybe she is something other entirely. Richard Reynolds reaches across the Testaments for his biblical woman: he describes Stella as "the prodigal daughter"—"she has dared, sinned, suffered."[30] His characterization resonates with Lionel Trilling's assessment of Stella: "We see her not as Sin but as what William Blake called Experience, by which he meant the moral state of those who have known the passions and have been marked, and beautified, by the pain which that knowledge inflicts."[31]

There is another biblical possibility still, one more closely tethered to the story itself. Finkle is not Adam, but Hosea, the Old Testament prophet whom God commanded to marry a prostitute that he might understand what it is for God to love the wayward people Israel. It is a story Malamud knows well: while in prison, Yakov Bok, protagonist of *The Fixer*, "turned often to pages of Hosea and read with fascination the story of this man God had commanded to marry a harlot. The harlot, he had heard it said, was Israel, but the jealousy and anguish Hosea felt was that of a man whose wife had left his bed and board and gone whoring after strangers." The description of Bok reading the prophet is followed in the novel by the complete text of Hosea 2:4–9—God's appeal to Israel to put away her harlotries, her attachments to the rulers of other nations and their gods, lest he take away what he has provided her and she be naked and ashamed.

So too is it a story that Finkle would have known. Each morning, he would have recited a passage from Hosea as he wound the *tefillin* strap around his middle finger: "I will betroth you to myself forever; I will betroth you to myself in righteousness and in justice, in kindness and in mercy. I will betroth you to myself in faithfulness, and you shall know the Lord" (Hos. 2:21–22). Daily, he would have spoken aloud words that reflect both God's commitment to Israel (and his forgiveness of her worship of Baal) and Hosea's commitment to his wayward wife, Gomer. And yet, despite the repeated ritual action, despite the regular recitation, Finkle never internalized God's fidelity—nor human's: "he did not love God so well as he might, because he had not loved man." Hosea's love for his flawed wife was a manifestation of his love for God. When Finkle realizes "that apart from his parents, he had never loved anyone," he begins to understand the fullness of what he had said to Lily: "I think I came to God not because I loved Him, but because I did not." Sanford Pinsker notes that Lily Hirschorn had "expected an Old Testament prophet, a man 'enamored with God,' and instead she got a man incapable of passion in either the physical or spiritual sense of the word."[32] Finkle is no Hosea, but his story is shot through with the prophet's.[33]

The equivalences between the tales are manifold and fluctuating. In one sense, Finkle could be Hosea, a prophet whose "striking figures of speech" have led commentators to suggest that he "was associated with the priesthood and the sanctuaries, had a strongly developed sex instinct which he vigorously repressed"[34]—qualities we might see in Finkle, the rabbinical student who finds himself excited by the pictures of women in Salzman's envelope, who in seeking love finds "it necessary to establish the level of [his] need and fulfill it." As Hosea to Gomer, Finkle binds himself to Stella the prostitute. His aim is "to convert her to goodness, himself to God." Of course, as Abraham Heschel reminds us, "Gomer was not at first unfaithful and not thereafter merely a harlot. She had fallen away, rather, into the promiscuity of idolatry."[35] So too might we resist the characterization of Stella as harlot. Reynolds notes, "Whether Stella is the fallen woman Salzman has suggested and Leo has visualized, is uncertain. She plays the part, standing by the lamppost smoking. But she waits for Leo 'uneasily' and 'shyly.'"[36] And Trilling reminds us, "The reader, of course, is not under the necessity of believing that Stella is what her father makes her out to be."[37] We have been allowed to perceive the "desperate innocence" that Finkle saw in her eyes.

Stella may be the prostitute Gomer, but Finkle too is a version of the straying wife. Through his rabbinical study, he enters into a marriage of sorts with God, only to find he does not love him. Bonnie Lyons notes the theme of t'shuva[38]—repentance—throughout Malamud's works. The word means return. The story is about Finkle's return to God, Israel's return to the Lord—his desire of course is "to convert [Stella] to goodness," but as important is his rededication of "himself to God."

In some senses, Salzman is a personification of God. It is hard not to notice the use of diction in "The Magic Barrel." It is not enough that Salzman has an Old World profession, he speaks in an Old World English, heavily inflected with Yiddish. When Finkle wonders what might be wrong with a potential match, Salzman says, "Who says there is wrong?" Finkle doesn't understand why a young American woman would use a marriage broker. Salzman responds, "So for the same reason you went, she comes." Finkle's English, by contrast, is refined—he asks questions like "Do you keep photographs of your clients on file?" and makes statements like "I detest stomach specialists." His speech accords with his "distinguished face," his "long, severe scholar's nose, brown eyes heavy with learning, sensitive yet ascetic lips," his brisk and erect walk, his dress. The narrator moves easily between a "rough-and-ready New York immigrant's richly Yiddish-flavored dialect and an elegantly polished king's English"[39] that he even occasionally sprinkles with French. His language bridges the two characters' worlds, as does Finkle's when he begins his return to Salzman and to God. Throughout the story, Finkle uses language that distances himself from Salzman, until he begins to realize what he is missing—love of God, love of man. As he begins the process of transformation, his speech changes: he draws nearer linguistically to Salzman. He sees the image of Stella and knows, "Just her I want." Ultimately, this drawing near becomes physical as well, as he binds himself to Stella, whose face is familiar because it reminds him of Salzman's, whose eyes are her father's.

But Salzman is also possibly a revision of Hosea, if we understand him as Heschel casts him. God tells Hosea to marry Gomer, "whom he loved. For a time they were happy in their mutual affection. . . . Subsequently, however, he discovers that Gomer had been unfaithful and had given herself to many lovers. . . . She then left him, or was sent away by him. That was the legal way: to expel the woman who became an adulteress."[40] In plot, this is a refraction of the story of Salzman and Stella. A loving father casts out "[his] baby, [his] Stella" because she is wild, "like an animal. Like a dog." Like Gomer's, Stella's transgression seems clearly to be sexual, and—like Gomer's—it instigates the end of a relationship. Gomer is expelled; Stella, "she should burn in hell," "is dead to [Salzman] now." But God commands, "Bring Gomer back to your home, renew your love for her, even as the Lord loves the people of Israel, though they turn to other gods" (Hos. 3:1); obedient, Hosea renews their marriage. Similarly, we might read Salzman as metaphorically bringing Stella back to his home when he arranges for her to meet Finkle. Hosea's reunion with his former, unfaithful wife serves as a symbol for the love of God for Israel despite her faithlessness. Salzman's resumed relationship with the faithless rabbinical student becomes a symbol of his love for Stella despite *her* faithlessness. Salzman is God; Salzman is Hosea.

And if God in the Book of Hosea "is conceived, not as the self-detached Ruler, but as the sensitive Consort to Whom deception comes and Who nevertheless goes on pleading for loyalty, uttering a longing for reunion, a passionate desire for reconciliation,"[41] then there is something of God in Finkle too. He cannot seem to shake his need for Salzman, despite his trickery and deception;[42] he is desperate for union with Stella, despite her being "a wild one—wild, without shame." To the prophet Hosea, "marriage is the image for the relationship of God and Israel."[43] So too, it seems, for Finkle as Hosea. Lucky for him, then, that God is in the business of matchmaking.

12

Nathan Englander

The announcement of new work by Nathan Englander is unfailingly hailed as a literary event. Englander was selected as one of "20 Writers for the 21st Century" by the *New Yorker*, has received a Guggenheim Fellowship, a PEN/Malamud Award, the Bard Fiction Prize, and the Sue Kaufman Prize from the American Academy of Arts & Letters, despite having published only two collections of short stories and one novel. His work has garnered almost universal praise.[1] His debut collection, *For the Relief of Unbearable Urges* (1999), prompted critics to liken Englander to coreligionists Kafka, Malamud, Roth, and Singer, as well as to Cheever. They described him as having a "genius for telling a tale" and took solace in the perceived shortcomings of the book's final story, as "sustained perfection in such an emerging talent, wise beyond his years, would have been unbearable in its own right."[2] Published thirteen years later (2012), Englander's follow-up collection *What We Talk About When We Talk About Anne Frank* (*pace* Raymond Carver) drew comparisons to Babel, Gogol, Singer—and of course, Carver. It was nearly universally well received: as the critic for *The Guardian* put it, "the new book (which comes garlanded with praise from just about every A-list author in America) turns out to be a remarkable collection."[3] The *Seattle Times* described Englander's novel *The Ministry of Special Cases* as a "tour-de-force" and the *New York Times* critic was left wondering, "Who is this Nathan Englander, so young in novelist years, but already possessed of an old master's voice? . . . One reads this novel in awe of Englander's talent." Even the Passover Haggadah Englander created with fellow literary darling Jonathan Safran Foer met with critical acclaim.

Englander is one of the primary exemplars of the new wave of Jewish American literature, with its turn toward religion. *For the Relief of Unbearable Urges* was notable for its depictions of the Orthodox world in which Englander was raised. In his rendering of it, the Talmud takes precedence over the Tanakh, and Jewish law shapes the fictional landscape more than Jewish narrative. Here, Englander's Jews navigate various possible relationships to *halakhah* and to tradition. They are far less concerned with negotiating an American identity (which had been the preoccupation of the prior generation of Jewish American writers) than with negotiating a Jewish one.

Jewish identity is a theme that also pervades *What We Talk About When We Talk About Anne Frank.* The setup of the titular story mimics Carver's "What We Talk About When We Talk About Love": four characters sit in discussion around a table. In a *New Yorker* interview with Englander, Cressida Leyshon noted,

> Carver's characters argue about love. Your story is about love, too, but your characters are debating notions of Jewish identity. The narrator and his wife have a secular life in Florida, whereas his wife's old friend from yeshiva, who lives in Israel, has shifted from an Orthodox to an ultra-Orthodox existence with her husband Mark—or Yerucham, as he is now known. Mark argues that Judaism is a religion, not a culture, attacking what he sees as an American obsession with the Holocaust and claiming that Judaism cannot be built "only on the foundation of one terrible crime."[4]

Despite fictional Mark/Yerucham's rejection of the Holocaust as a defining element of contemporary Jewish identity, the *Shoah* looms large in the very collection in which his character is contained. Four of the eight stories in *What We Talk About When We Talk About Anne Frank* deal with the Holocaust or anti-Semitism, and one with the Arab-Israeli conflict. The question of Jewish identity, explored in *For the Relief of Unbearable Urges* primarily in terms of religious observance, is here pegged to the Holocaust and, to a lesser extent, to the State of Israel. In this respect, as one reviewer has noted, the second collection is more political than the first.[5]

If, as some suggest, religion, the State of Israel, and the Holocaust are the three central concerns of this generation of American Jewish writers, Israel seems to occupy Englander the least. That said, *For the Relief of Unbearable Urges* contains one "political" story that is set in Israel and reflects a particular religious sensibility. "In This Way We Are Wise," the collection's closing piece, records the thoughts of Natan, an American living in Israel, during and in the aftermath of a series of bombings in Jerusalem. It is a shock to the expatriate to feel so acutely the political reality of the modern state, until this moment more emblem than actuality: "A biblical Israel, crowded with warriors and prophets, fallen kings and common men conscripted to do God's will. An American boy's Israel. A child raised up on causality and symbol. Holocaust as wrath of God. Israel the Phoenix rising up from the ashes."[6] Orienting himself after the bombings, Natan seems unable to reconcile the city in which he lives with the Jerusalem of the Jewish imagination. He muses, "I was raised on tradition. Pictures of a hallowed Jerusalem nestled away like Eden. A Jerusalem so precious God spared it when he flooded the world. I can guide you to the valley where David slew Goliath. Recite by heart the love songs written by Solomon, his son."[7] Less a resident of a contemporary city in a modern state than the inheritor of an ancient nation at once temporally distant but psychically near, Natan processes his harrowing experience "through the biblical models,"[8] anchoring himself with symbols.

The most surprising of these, given Natan's evident Jewishness, is his metaphor about the work of the *Chevra Kadisha*, the burial society: Orthodox Jews dispatched following an accident or a bombing to gather every trace of human flesh and blood for proper burial. Coming out of the café in which he had sat during the attacks, mere steps from the "wounded weeping and the dead unmoving," Natan thinks, "The Hasidim will soon come to collect scattered bits, partial Christs. Parts of victims nailed up, screwed in, driven to stone and metal. Hand pierced with rusted nail and hung on the base of a tree."[9] The dead are not merely casualties but sufferers in the flesh, like Christ himself, whose body was pierced by his enemies. Here—as in Jesus's time—the political is religious and the religious political.

In "The Gilgul of Park Avenue," the first of Englander's four short stories to have been included in *Best American Short Stories* anthologies, religion is framed not in political terms but in aesthetic and ritual ones. Even Robert Alter approved, calling it "Another quite touching story . . . distinctly reminiscent of Malamud." Charles Luger, an affluent Upper East Side WASP, experiences a sudden awareness in the back of a New York taxi cab on his way home from work: He "understood he was the bearer of a Jewish soul. *Ping!* Like that it came. Like a knife against a glass."[10] The way Charles understands it, he is not merely a proselyte: he is a *gilgul*, a reincarnated Jewish soul. He is eager to share his news, and knocks on the cab's glass divider. "The driver looked into his rearview mirror. 'Jewish,' Charles said. 'Jewish, here in the back.'"[11]

Not surprisingly, the driver's response—"No problem here. Meter ticks the same for all creeds"—is far more tempered than that of Charles's wife. An "art director at a glossy magazine" who has decorated the house in "all in chintz fabric, an overwhelming amount of flora and fauna patterns," Sue is a model of WASP gentility. "Mortified by a white purse after Labor Day," she is—naturally—nearly undone by Charles's instant adoption of a brand-new religion. "I've heard of wolf men and people being possessed," she rants. "I've even seen modern vampires on TV. Real people who drink blood. But this beats all."[12]

It is especially galling to her that in his transformation from a "Christian nonbeliever to Orthodox Jew," Charles has taken on the yoke of the commandments. As one would expect of a Protestant, it seems she might have sanctioned an onslaught of private belief. Even, perhaps, have tolerated Charles becoming "a West Side Jew," more like "the Browns in [apartment] six-K [whose] kid goes to Haverford."[13] But no, Charles's religion has a material dimension. Judaism's rituals might at the best of times be at odds with Sue's genteel sensibilities, but in her neophyte husband's iteration they are utterly anathema. She is repelled by the kosher food he insists on buying, infuriated by his insistence on using paper dishware rather than their fine but unkosher china. She is mortified to discover Charles has pried the mezuzah from the lintel of a neighboring apartment because he does not know where to purchase one. She derides him for riding "the elevator up and down like an idiot waiting for someone to press our floor, like a retarded child. He gets in the elevator and keeps explaining it to everyone, 'Can't press the button on my Sabbath, ha ha.'"[14] Worst of all, however, is his choice of spiritual guide.

The day after discovering "there was a Yiddishe neshama functioning inside" him,[15] Charles searches for a rabbi in the Yellow Pages. He finds one in Royal Hills, a fictionalized but recognizable Crown Heights. Like so many residents of the neighborhood, Charles's rabbi is Hasidic, but—surprisingly—not Jewish. Or at least, not halakhically Jewish. A *gilgul* himself, R. Zalman Meintz had been "miserable in Bolinas, addicted to sorrow and drugs, . . . on the brink when he discovered his Jewish soul."[16]

Charles's own cultural stereotypes drive his attraction to Zalman: he looks like a real Jew. When Zalman comes to meet Charles at his office, a coworker asks, "Who's the fiddler on the roof?"[17] The overt display of a retrograde Judaism evoking profound embarrassment is a trope explored by Philip Roth in "Eli, The Fanatic." In that story, Eli Peck, a Jewish lawyer living in a neighborhood where he and his fellow Jews have sought to be assimilated into the Protestant landscape,[18] is called to represent an Orthodox rabbi and his yeshiva, whose religious aesthetic is at odds with the gentility of the neighbors. Rather than persuade the Old World Jews to leave town, Eli finds himself entering their world—ultimately donning their garb. There is a naturalness to his transition that we don't see with Charles, who awkwardly dons phylacteries: Eli, by contrast "felt those black clothes as if they were the skin of his skin."[19]

Eli Peck's wife believes he is having a breakdown and tries to direct him to his psychiatrist; so too does Sue process Charles's radical reorientation in psychological terms. "What you're really trying to tell me is: Honey, I'm having a nervous breakdown," she says when Charles informs her that he's Jewish.[20] Sue would far rather Charles seek counsel—spiritual or otherwise—from his Jewish therapist, Dr. Birnbaum, whom Charles has stopped seeing. In an attempt at an intervention, Sue invites Birnbaum to dinner with Zalman. The one arrives "sporting a yellow sweater" and the other in a black suit. During dinner at a table bedecked in plastic dishware and laden with kosher food, Sue "just stares. A man with a beard, a long black beard and sidelocks, was sitting in her house. Charles wanted to tell her she was staring but stopped himself with, 'Sue.'"[21] The man is so foreign to her that her response is to become foreign to herself: she utterly abandons her WASP civility. When Charles calls her on her lack of manners in embarrassing a guest, she replies, "He, Charley, is not even Jewish. And neither are you, One need not be polite to the insane. As long as you don't hose them down, all is in good taste."[22] Naturally, the four cannot find common ground: Charles will not be talked out of his Judaism. The dinner conversation devolves to the point that both Zalman and Birnbaum depart.

After they leave, Sue and Charles find themselves together in the study. He has seen her from the doorway, picking at the wax drippings that have fallen from the Shabbat candles onto the windowsill. He crosses over to her and "look[s] around at the study, at the lamp and the bookcase, then out to the buildings and the sky. He had not read that far into the Bible and still thought God might orchestrate his rescue."[23] He takes her hands, hoping she will "understand that there had indeed been a chance of magnitude, but that the mark it left was not great. The real difference was contained in his soul, after all." The story ends in this frozen pose. In this moment, Charles wants Sue to perceive him, "to observe him with the profound clarity he had only so recently come to know. . . He struggled to stand without judgment, to be only for Sue, to be wholly seen, wanting her to love him changed."[24]

The story has been read as an allegory of the return to Judaism seen in recent Jewish American fiction. Indeed, Adam Meyer sees the character of Charles Luger as a metaphor for Jewish American literature itself:

> In his WASP incarnation, he represents second-generation Jewish American writers who moved away from their Judaism, even their Jewishness, in aligning themselves with some aspect of the larger culture. Dr. Birnbaum is the obvious second-generation Jew in the story, having turned away from the torah in favor of Freud . . . Rabbi Zalman Meintz, on the other hand, represents a transitional figure between this second generation and the third generation, where Charles will find himself after his revelatory experience. In this sense he is like Cynthia Ozick or Chaim Potok.[25]

While certainly this is one way to read the story, and one that weaves Englander into the discussion of religion in Jewish American literature undertaken in Chapter 5, there are certainly other entries into it. Ours, naturally, is through the Bible.

Englander himself provides a cue for thinking about biblical (rather than merely rabbinic) dimensions in his work: Natan of "In This Way We Are Wise"—whom most critics describe as a more obviously autobiographical depiction than other Englander characters— eloquently described the place of the Bible in the imagination of the traditional Jew. It shapes his expectations of—and confounds his ability fully to understand—Israel, a place that in his mind is populated by biblical figures not suicide bombers.

The biblical story to which we appeal here, however, is not part of Englander's canon. It is the New Testament story of Saul's conversion on the road to Damascus. It is clear from his reference to Christ in "In This Way We Are Wise" that Englander is familiar with images from the Jesus story. Indeed, it is probably reasonable to assume that most educated American Jews are. But the direction of our reading, the story of Saint Paul, is far less well known to Jews than the story of Jesus, which has seeped out of the gospels into the broader American cultural consciousness.

In recounting the sudden conversion of a Protestant New Yorker to Judaism, Englander is again inviting his reader to think about Judaism in Christian terms—something he also does with his story "Reb Kringle," about an Orthodox Jew with the perfect Santa beard. We cannot know, however, that Englander is familiar with Acts, which means that our drawing the biblical analogy is cross-textual reading.

In an essay on Genesis 1–3 in light of ancient Chinese creation myths, Yan Lin explains the method:

> Cross-textual reading is a method that juxtaposes two different texts by looking at them together, so that text A is read in the light of text B, and vice versa. We can understand text A more profoundly in the light of text B, and then reread text B using this deeper knowledge. The crossovers from text A to text B happen many times during the reading process, not only once. Of course, comparison/analogy is part of this process, but is not the final purpose. After the bidirectional cross-overs, what we want to achieve is that both the cultural text and the biblical text seriously interact with each other in a creative and meaningful way so that both can be mutually enriched, transformed, integrated, and updated.[26]

We read "The Gilgul of Park Avenue" alongside (against?) the story of the conversion of Saul (later Paul), so that we might deepen and even transform our understanding not only of the short story in question but perhaps also of the biblical episode(s) as well.

Saul, a passionately observant Jew from Tarsus (Turkey), had dedicated himself to "breathing threats and murder against the disciples of the Lord" (Acts 9:1, NRSV). He was relentless in his persecution of Jesus's followers: He "ravaged the church by entering house after house; dragging off both men and women, he committed them to prison" (8:3). In his zeal, he travels toward Damascus to round up Christians and bring them back—bound— to Jerusalem. On the road, "suddenly a light from heaven flashed around him. He fell to the ground and heard a voice saying to him, 'Saul, Saul, why do you persecute me?' He asked, "Who are you, Lord?" The reply came, 'I am Jesus, whom you are persecuting'" (9:3–5). Jesus directs him to get up and enter the city. He rises and opens his eyes, but finds he cannot see. For three days, he is blind and neither does he eat nor drink. Jesus dispatches his disciple Ananias to lay his hands on the afflicted Saul. When he does, "immediately something like scales fell from his eyes, and his sight was restored. Then he got up and was baptized, and after taking some food, he regained his strength" (9:18–19). The conversion is total and immediate. Saul spends a few days among the disciples in Damascus, and "immediately he began to proclaim Jesus in the synagogues, saying, 'He is the Son of God.' All who heard him were amazed and said, 'Is not this the man who made havoc in Jerusalem among those who invoked this name? And has he not come here for the purpose of bringing them bound before the chief priests?'" (9:20–21) In his preaching, Paul is met with recognition and disbelief, but the conversion is radical and complete.

Charles's conversion likewise occurs in transit. He is in the back of a New York taxi when "*Ping!* Like that it came. Like a knife against glass."[27] Like Paul, who recounts his conversion experience in Galatians, Charles feels "obligated to share." So he knocks on the glass in the cab and tells his driver. There are two markers of his conversion here: Charles is "not one to engage taxicab drivers in conversation," but he sheds this WASP self-containment to share his own good news. After all, "was not this a rebirth in itself? It was something, he was sure."[28] The framing of his experience is as a rebirth that signals the beginning of the transformation.

A central part of Saul's conversion experience is his being struck blind. Here we have an intriguing counterpart in Charles, who is also struck blind, although not literally: what he simply cannot see (and foresee) is the full effect of his conversion on his wife. He cannot see why she resists his change, why she cannot embrace his happiness. A second dimension of Saul's conversion is that he does not eat or drink following it. In an additional inversion of the imagery from Acts, Charles eats immediately after his transformative experience, but is keenly aware that he ought not to. The maid has prepared creamed chicken and he suspects—but is not certain—that this is not permissible by Jewish dietary law: "Half an hour Jewish, and already he felt obliged." Because he does not know, and does not have a counselor to whom to turn (he is like the fourth child at the seder, who does not know how to ask), "Charles ate his chicken like a gentile—all the while a Jew in his heart."[29] Significantly, the heart is not generally thought of as the seat of Judaism (consider how radical was Paul's shifting the locus of circumcision to the heart).

Whereas Saul had persecuted Christians before his conversion, Charles merely stereotyped Jews. Newly Jewish, he takes in Park Avenue through the window of the cab, "already searching for someone with a beanie, a landsman who might look his way, wink, confirm what he already knew."[30] He lacks the vocabulary for *yarmulke* or *kippah*; he conceives of Jews as a brotherhood, insiders who recognize one another at a glance. When—like Saul who kept company with the disciples immediately following his conversion—he seeks a rabbi to help him enact his Judaism, Charles finds a suitable one in the Yellow Pages. Rabbi Zalman "looks, to Charles, like a real Jew: long black beard, black suit, black hat at his side, and a nice big charicaturish nose, like Fagin's, but friendlier."[31] Charles's image of the authentic Jew is the fodder of anti-Semitic propaganda.

This is maybe not surprising, given that Charles had "moved to New York from Idaho so many years before."[32] He comes from the Protestant hinterland to the Upper East Side, the epicenter of wealthy WASP culture. In this biography too, there are echoes of Paul. Born in the provinces, Paul came to Jerusalem and—as he explains—"was brought up in this city at the feet of Gamaliel, educated strictly according to our ancestral law, being zealous for God, just as all of you are today" (Acts 22:3). Charles strives to be a latter-day student of Gamaliel, taking on the yoke of *kashrut*, Sabbath observance, daily prayer. This is all too much for Sue, who prefers Jews to be intellectual and secular, like Birnbaum and the Browns in 6K—in short, as *goyische* as possible. "'Why,' she said closing her eyes and pressing two fingers to her temple, 'why do people who find religion always have to be so goddamn extreme?'"[33]

Charles is stringent in his new observance, except in one key respect: he does not undergo a formal conversion. Neither, it seems did Zalman, who also simply recognized himself to be a Jewish soul. "'And you never needed a formal conversion?' Charles asked, astounded. 'No,' Zalman said. 'Such things are for others, for the litigious and stiff minded . . . [not] for those who are called by their souls.'"[34] Zalman suspects that although Charles has no known Jewish blood, his soul may have been at Sinai. He was "maybe an Egyptian slave that came along. But once the soul witnessed the miracles at Sinai, accepted there the word, well it became a Jewish soul."[35] Here Zalman sounds more Christian than Orthodox, with Christianity's shift of emphasis from the letter of the law to its spirit, from the body to the heart. Jesus abrogated kosher law, indicating that "it is not what goes into the mouth that defiles a person, but it is what comes out of the mouth that defiles" (Matt. 15:11). In Paul's articulation of Christianity, Gentile followers of Jesus no longer needed to come to him through Judaism: as noted, circumcision of the heart could replace circumcision of the body (Rom. 2:29). Despite his insistence on eating only kosher food, Zalman downplays Charles's concern that his soul must once have occupied a Jewish body, "No, no. That's exactly the point. Jew, non-Jew, doesn't matter. The body doesn't matter. It is the soul itself that is Jewish."[36] Zalman is also a Paul figure: at once Jew and non-Jew, simultaneously an upholder of the law and trumpeter of the spirit. Indeed, Zalman's lack of concern with bloodlines and embodiment recall Paul's declaration that "there is neither Jew nor Greek, there is neither bond nor free, there is neither male nor female: for ye are all one in Christ Jesus. And if ye be Christ's, then are ye Abraham's seed, and heirs according to the promise" (Gal. 3:28–29).

The penultimate scene in the story pits Birnbaum and Zalman against one another, wrestling over who better understands Charles's situation. Here we have a scene familiar from the New Testament, such as between Jesus and the Pharisees, or between Pharisees and Saducees: an interreligious debate among Jews over who is the correct—and authoritative—interpreter of Judaism. Similarly, the final scene—Charles and Sue alone in the study—is also redolent with New Testament imagery. The scene is fraught, and Charles thinks, looking out at the sky, that "God might orchestrate his rescue." That God does not swoop in and save Charles in his moment of trial by and alienation from Sue further sets him as a Paul, a figure who is "heroic for being a human being unaided by miraculous advantage."[37] Indeed, in this closing scene, Charles is fully and only human, and desperately wants Sue "to observe him with the profound clarity he had only so recently come to know. . . . He struggled to stand without judgment, to be only for Sue, to be wholly seen, wanting her to love him changed."[38] The desperate desire not to be judged recalls Jesus's teaching in Matthew: "Do not judge, so that you may not be judged" (7:1); the yearning to be loved unconditionally, the teaching in Leviticus (19:9) reinscribed by Mark (12:31) and Matthew (22:39) to love your neighbor as yourself. For all the sharp distinctions drawn between Judaism and Christianity, both traditions distill themselves to two commandments: Love your God and love your neighbor.

Charles's conversion strikes him as radical because it comes to him from nowhere in the back of a taxicab. Ping! Like a knife on glass. It strikes Sue as radical because it demands he change his outward behavior—the domain with which she, as an image- and status-conscious woman of a certain class, is most concerned. To the reader who takes it in light of Scripture—both the Old Testament law and the New Testament conversion of Paul—the story strikes us not so much as radical but as extraordinary in the way that so much of the Bible is extraordinary. It is a story very much embedded in a biblical framework, a story of God and Israel (admittedly focused more on the human than the divine), of body and soul, of law and spirit. These dichotomies are not at odds in Charles's experience, rather they are parts of a whole—a whole that has changed him. It is a whole he desperately wants Sue to perceive, without judgment, but it is something that Sue can only yet perceive (as Paul would have it) "through a glass, darkly" (1 Cor. 13:12).

Notes

Preface

1 Adam Gopnik, "Introduction," in *The Good Book: Writers Reflect on Favorite Bible Passages*, ed. Andrew Blauner (New York: Simon & Schuster, 2015), x.
2 Gopnik, "Introduction," x.
3 In this series, Magdalena Maczynska has written *The Gospel According to the Novelist* (2015) and Adam S. Miller, *The Gospel According to David Foster Wallace* (2016). Jordan Cofer's *The Gospel According to Flannery O'Connor* looks at the short story but in the work of a single author and as well as her short fiction.
4 T. S. Eliot, "The Dry Salvages" V, *The Complete Poems and Plays 1909-1950* (New York: Harcourt, Brace & World, Inc. 1962), 136.
5 Charles E. May, "The Nature of Knowledge in Short Fiction," *The New Short Story Theories* (Athens, Ohio: Ohio University Press, 1994), 131–43, 142.
6 Lesleigh Cushing Stahlberg, *Sustaining Fictions: Intertextuality, Midrash, Translation, and the Literary Afterlife of the Bible* (New York: T&T Clark, 2008), xi.
7 Paul Elie, "Has Fiction Lost its Faith?," *New York Times*, December 19, 2012, www.nytimes.com/2012/12/23/books/review/has-fiction-lost-its-faith.html?_r=0.
8 James Wood, "Joy Williams' Refractory Brilliance," *The New Yorker* (accessed August 22, 2016), http://www.newyorker.com/magazine/2016/08/22/joy-williams-refractory-brilliance (accessed August 26, 2016). Denis Johnson, *Jesus' Son: Stories* (New York: Farrar, Straus and Giroux, 1992), George Saunders, "Winky," *Pastoralia* (New York: Riverhead Books, 2000).

Chapter 1

1 Melanie Wright, *Moses in America: The Cultural Uses of Biblical Narrative* (Oxford: Oxford University Press, 2003), 10.

2 David Lyle Jeffrey, "The Bible and Literature," in *The Encyclopedia of Protestantism*, vol. 1, ed. Hans J. Hillerbrand (London and New York: Routledge, 2004), 375.

3 David Norton, *A History of the English Bible as Literature* (Cambridge: Cambridge University Press, 2011), 312.

4 Jesper Rosenmeier, "'With my owne eyes': William Bradford's *of Plymouth Plantation*," in *The American Puritan Imagination*, ed. Sacvan Bercovitch (Cambridge: Cambridge University Press, 1974), 79.

5 William Bradford in *The American Tradition in Literature*, vol. 1, 10th edn, eds. George Perkins and Barbara Perkins (New York: McGraw-Hill Education, 2002), 47–48.

6 Nicholas Street, "The American States Acting over the Part of the Children of Israel in the Wilderness and Thereby Impeding Their Entrance into Canaan's Rest," in *God's New Israel: Religious Interpretations of America's Destiny*, ed. Conrad Cherry (Englewood Cliffs, NJ: Prentice Hall, 1971), 83.

7 David W. Kling, *The Bible in History: How the Texts Have Shaped the Times* (New York: Oxford University Press, 2004), 207.

8 Scott M. Langston, *Exodus through the Centuries* (Malden, MA: Blackwell, 2006), 7.

9 Langston, *Exodus through the Centuries*, 7.

10 Mark Noll, "The Image of the United States as a Biblical Nation, 1776–1865," in *The Bible in America: Essays in Cultural History*, eds. Nathan O. Hatch and Mark Noll (New York: Oxford, 1982), 44.

11 Gail E. Husch, *Something Coming: Apocalyptic Expectation and Mid-Nineteenth-Century Painting* (Hanover, NH and London: University Press of New England, 2000), 93.

12 Mark A. Noll, "The Bible and Slavery," in *Religion and the American Civil War*, ed. Randall M. Miller (New York and Oxford: Oxford University Press, 1998), 74–88.

13 Scott Langston, "The Exodus in American History and Culture," *Teaching the Bible*, Society of Biblical Literature, January 2010, www.sbl-site.org/assets/pdfs/TB6_Exodus_SL.pdf.

14 John Filson, *The Discovery, Settlement, and Present State of Kentucky* (Whitefish, MT: Kessinger Publishing, 2005), 129.

15 David Jasper and Stephen Prickett, "General Introduction," in *The Bible and Literature: A Reader*, eds. David Jasper and Stephen Prickett (Oxford: Blackwell, 1999), 4.

16 Tresa Grauer, "Identity Matters: Contemporary Jewish American Writing," in *The Cambridge Companion to Jewish American*

Literature, eds. Michael P. Kramer and Hana Wirth-Nesher
(Cambridge: Cambridge University Press, 2003), 277.

17 Susannah Heschel, "Imagining Judaism in America," in Kramer and
Wirth-Nesher, eds., *Cambridge Companion to Jewish American
Literature*, 31.

18 L. Tom Perry, "The Tradition of Light and Testimony," *Ensign*,
December 2012, 29.

19 Kim Warren, "Seeking the Promised Land: African American
Migrations to Kansas," www.kclibrary.org/sites/default/files/Seeking_
the_Promised_Land_African_American_Migrations_to_Kansas.pdf.

20 Nicholas Lemann, *The Promised Land: The Great Black Migration
and How It Changed America* (New York: Vintage, 1992).

21 Daniel T. Rodgers, *The Work Ethic in Industrial America 1850–1920*,
2nd edn. (Chicago: University of Chicago Press, 2014), 4.

22 Louis Owens, "The American Joads," in *Bloom's Modern Critical
Interpretations: The Grapes of Wrath*, ed. Harold Bloom (New York:
Chelsea House, 2007), 71.

23 Thomas Paine, "Appendix to Common Sense," in *The Writings of
Thomas Paine*, vol. 1: *1774–1779*, ed. Moncure Daniel Conway
(New York: G. P. Putnam's Sons, 1894), 118–19.

24 http://xroads.virginia.edu/~hyper/hns/garden/rengarden.html.

25 Claudia Setzer and David A. Shefferman, eds., *The Bible and
American Culture*, (Abingdon and New York: Routledge, 2011), 4.

26 http://americanart.si.edu/exhibitions/archive/2012/art_civil_war/.

27 www.cosmopolis.ch/english/cosmo12/americanlandscape.htm.

28 Ibid.

29 Harry Stout, "Word and Order in Colonial New England," in *The Bible
in America: Essays in Cultural History* (New York: Oxford, 1982), 19.

30 Noll, "Image of the United States," 46.

31 "Articles of the Constitution of Connecticut," in Setzer and
Shefferman, eds., *The Bible and American Culture*, 63.

32 For example, Exod. 20:1–17, Deut. 30:19, Ps. 119:142–52, Jn 10:10,
Rom. 2:15, Heb. 13:8. See www.faithfacts.org/christ-and-the-culture/
the-bible-and-government.

33 WDLeeper, "The Constitution, the Bible, and America," *Red State*,
August 30, 2010, www.redstate.com/diary/wdleeper/2010/08/30/the-
constitution-the-bible-and-america/.

34 See, for example, www.blowthetrumpet.org/JamesMadison.htm.

35 Deacon John Paine's Journal, April 28, 1704, *The Mayflower
Descendant*, 1906. http://www.americanantiquarian.org/Exhibitions/
Reading/colonial.htm

36 David L. Barr and Nicholas Piediscalzi, "Introduction," in *The Bible in
American Education: From Sourcebook to Textbook*, eds. David L.
Barr and Nicholas Piediscalzi (Philadelphia: Fortress Press; Society of
Biblical Literature Centennial Publications, 1982), 1.

37 Barr and Piediscalzi, "Introduction," 1.

38 www.americanantiquarian.org/Exhibitions/Reading/colonial.htm.

39 Allene Stuart Phy, "The Bible as Literature for American Children," in *The Bible and American Popular Culture*, ed. Allene S. Phy (Philadelphia: Fortress Press, 1985), 167.

40 David Norton, *A History of the English Bible as Literature* (Cambridge: Cambridge University Press, 2000), 363.

41 Asa Rhoads, *The New Instructor: Being the Second Part of the American Spelling-Book Designed for the Use of Our Common Schools* (Stanford: Daniel Lawrence, 1803).

42 Norton, *History of the English Bible*, 364.

43 Ibid.

44 Ibid.

45 Phy, "The Bible as Literature," 170.

46 See, for instance, Steven K. Green, *The Bible, the School and the Constitution: The Clash that Shaped Modern Church-State Doctrine* (Oxford: Oxford University Press, 2012).

47 Randall Stewart, *American Literature and Christian Doctrine* (Baton Rouge: Louisiana State University Press, 1958), 3.

48 Carlos Baker, "The Place of the Bible in American Fiction," in *Religious Perspectives in American Culture*, eds. James Ward and A. Leland Jamison (Princeton: Princeton University Press, 1961), 247.

49 Giles Gunn, *The Bible and American Arts and Letters* (Philadelphia: Fortress Press, 1983), xx.

50 Herman Melville, *Redburn, His First Voyage; White-Jacket, or the World in a Man-O-War, Moby Dick or the Whale* (New York: Library of America, 1983), 506.

51 David Lyle Jeffrey, "Literature and the Bible," in *The Oxford Companion to the Bible*, eds. Bruce M. Metzger and Michael David Coogan (Oxford: Oxford University Press, 1993), 457.

52 Randall Stephens, "American Literature and the King James Bible: An Interview with Robert Alter," *Religion in American History*, March 23, 2012, http://usreligion.blogspot.com/2012/03/american-literature-and-king-james.html.

53 Thomas Kiernan, *The Intricate Music* (Boston and Toronto: Little, Brown & Co, 1979), 4.

54 Owens, "The American Joads," 70.

55 Jeffrey, "Literature and the Bible," 457.

56 Ibid.

57 Mark Twain, "Letter to Mrs. Whitmore," 1907, www.pbs.org/marktwain/scrapbook/06_connecticut_yankee/page2.html.

58 Jason Dobbins, "What's in a Name," www.politicsinvivo.com/2011/07/whats-in-a-name/.

59 David Lyle Jeffrey and C. Stephen Evans, "Introduction," in *The Bible and the University*, eds. David Lyle Jeffrey and C. Stephen Evans (Grand Rapids, IL: Zondervan, 2009), 13.

60 For more on the lectionary tracks, see, for instance, http://episcopaldigitalnetwork.com/lessons/revised-common-lectionary/.

61 This statistic is somewhat surprising, given the tendency of evangelical churches to favor the New International Version (NIV), first published in 1978 by Zondervan, a conservative evangelical press. About one-fifth of both individual respondents and congregations either use or encourage the use of the NIV. Among congregations, approximately 40 percent report using the KJV in worship and 10 percent the New Revised Standard Version.

62 Philip Goff, Arthur E. Farnsley II, and Peter J. Thuesen, "The Bible in American Life: A National Study by the Center for the Study in Religion and American Culture, Indiana University-Purdue University Indianapolis," March 6, 2016. http://www.raac.iupui.edu/research-projects/bible-american-life/bible-american-life-report/.

63 http://unlockingthebible.org/bible-verses-on-tim-tebow-eye-black/.

64 www.washingtonpost.com/news/the-fix/wp/2014/12/10/is-president-obamas-glass-houses-scripture-reference-in-the-bible-not-exactly/.

65 www.christianheadlines.com/blog/obama-and-bush-rely-on-scripture-in-dallas-interfaith-speeches.html.

66 Jeffrey and Evans, "Introduction," 13.

67 Stephens, "American Literature and the King James Bible."

68 Ibid.

69 Ibid.

70 Ibid.

Chapter 2

1 There are exceptions to this rule in the subgenre of "short-short stories" that can be as brief as a sentence. One thinks of the work of Lydia Davis and Joy Williams (and in the context of this volume most especially of the latter's *Ninety-Nine Stories of God* (Portland, OR: Tin House Books, 2016)). See also *Sudden Fiction: American Short-Short Stories*, eds. Robert Shapard and James Thomas (Layton, UT: Gibbs M. Smith, 1986). On the other, lengthier, side of the genre is the work collected by Richard Ford in *Granta Book of American Long Stories* (London: Granta Books, 2003).

2 Edgar Allen Poe, "Review of *Twice-Told Tales*" (1842), in *New Short Story Theories*, ed. Charles E. May (Athens: Ohio University Press, 1994), 59–64, 61.

3 Poe, "Review of *Twice-Told Tales*," 65.

4 Raymond Carver, "On Writing" (1981), in May, ed., *New Short Story Theories*, 273–77, 273.

5 John Updike, "Introduction," in *Best American Short Stories*, ed. John Updike with Shannon Ravenel (Boston: Houghton Mifflin, 1984), xvii.

6 *Selected Letters of William Faulkner*, ed. Joseph Blotner (New York: Random House, 1977), 345, cited by James Ferguson, *Faulkner's Short Fiction* (Knoxville: University of Tennessee Press, 1991), 9.

7 William Faulkner, *Faulkner in the University*, eds. Frederick L. Gwyan and Joseph L. Blottner (Charlottesville: University of Virginia Press, 1977), 207, cited by Ferguson, *Faulkner's Short Fiction*, 8.

8 Francine Prose, "What Makes a Short Story," in *On Writing Short Stories*, ed. Tom Bailey (New York: Oxford University, 2010), 3–12, 6.

9 R. C. Feddersen, *A Reader's Guide to the Short Story in English*, eds. Erin Fallon, R. C. Feddersen, James Kurtzleben, Maurice A. Lee, and Susan Rochette-Crawley, under the auspices of the Society for the Study of the Short Story (Westport, CT: Greenwood Press, 2001), xx.

10 Joyce Carol Oates, *The Oxford Book of American Short Stories*, ed. Joyce Carol Oates (Oxford and New York: Oxford University Press, 1992), 7–8: "To read stories as disparate as Katherine Anne Porter's 'He,' Paul Bowles's 'A Distant Episode,' Ray Bradbury's 'There Will Come Soft Rains,' Raymond Carver's 'Are These actual Miles?' and Tobias Wolff's 'Hunters in the Snow' . . . is to read stories so structured as to provide the reader, and not the characters themselves, with insight."

11 Carver, "On Writing," May, ed., *New Short Story Theories*, 275.

12 Günter Leypoldt, "Raymond Carver's 'Epiphanic Moments,'" *Style* 35, no. 3 (2001): 531–47, 535.

13 See storyteller definitions of the genre collected in Charles May, "Twenty-five Random Facts about the Short Story," *Reading the Short Story*, February 17, 2009, http://may-on-the-short-story. blogspot.com/2009/02/twenty-five-random-facts-about-short.html.

14 Jamie Quatro, "Asking Directions," *New Oxford Review*, Summer 2015, May 27, 2015, www.oxfordamerican.org/magazine/item/592-asking-for-directions.

15 Steven Millhauser, "The Ambition of the Short Story," *New York Times*, October 3, 2008, www.nytimes.com/2008/10/05/books/review/Millhauser-t.html?_r=0.

16 Our focus is American, but the Canadian Alice Munro was recognized as the "master of the contemporary short story" by the Nobel Prize for Literature committee in 2007. For other Canadian authors, see the collections: Margaret Atwood and Robert Weaver, eds., *New Oxford Book of Canadian Short Stories* (Oxford: Oxford University Press, 1997), and Russell Brown and Donna Bennett, eds., *Canadian Short Stories* (Toronto: Penguin Canada, 2007), as well as Kerry Clare, "The State of the Canadian Short Story in 2015," *49th Shelf*, February 16, 2015, http://49thshelf.com/Blog/2015/02/16/The-State-of-the-Canadian-Short-Story-in-2015.

17 Frank O'Connor, *The Lonely Voice: A Study of the Short Story* (Hoboken, NJ: Melville House Publishing, 2004), 39. O'Connor knew the American scene well, having taught at Stanford University throughout the 1950s and appearing frequently in the *New Yorker*. He published thirteen collections, and one of his stories, "Guests of the Nation," inspired Neil Jordan's 1992 film *The Crying Game*. In 2000, a short-story festival was established in his honor in Cork, Ireland, together with a lucrative 35,000-euro prize awarded to the best short fiction collection published in English anywhere in the world in the year preceding the festival.

18 See Philip Hensher, "The Long Tale of the British Short Story," *The Guardian*, November 6, 2015, www.theguardian.com/books/2015/nov/06/british-short-story-philip-hensher-anthology, as well as his two-volume *Penguin Book of the British Short Story* (Harmondsworth, UK: Penguin, 2015). Hensher's broadly historical collection, beginning with Daniel Defoe, was preceded by Malcolm Bradbury's contemporary focus in *Penguin Book of Modern British Short Stories* (Harmondsworth, UK: Penguin, 1987).

19 A good deal of attention is being paid to the Irish short story in the twenty-first century. See David Malcolm and Cheryl Alexander, eds., *A Companion to the British and Irish Short Story* (Malden, MA: Wiley-Blackwell, 2008); Anne Enright, ed., *Granta Book of the Irish Short Story* (London: Granta Books, 2010); Heather Ingman, ed., *A History of the Irish Short Story* (Cambridge: Cambridge University Press, 2011); Elke d'hoker and Stephanie Eggermont, eds., *The Irish Short Story: Traditions and Trends* (Bern, Switz.: Peter Lang, 2015).

20 William Boyd, "Brief Encounters," *The Guardian*, October 1, 2004, www.theguardian.com/books/2004/oct/02/featuresreviews.guardianreview38. See also Boyd's "A Short History of the Short Story," in *Prospect: The Leading Magazine of Ideas*, July 10, 2006, www.prospectmagazine.co.uk/arts-and-books/william-boyd-short-history-of-the-short-story.

21 An excellent survey of the national tradition is offered by Martin Scofield, *The Cambridge Introduction to the American Short Story* (Cambridge: Cambridge University Press, 2006). Another good overview, with coverage of decade-by-decade trends, is Lorrie Moore and Heidi Pitlor, eds., *100 Years of the Best American Short Stories* (Boston: Houghton Mifflin Harcourt, 2015).

22 Boyd, "Short History of the Short Story," 1.

23 Scofield, *Cambridge Introduction to the American Short Story*, 6.

24 Both quotes are from Poe's letters from ca. 1837, cited by Andrew Levy, *The Culture and Commerce of the American Short Story* (Cambridge: Cambridge University Press, 1993), 11, 17.

25 Alexis de Tocqueville, *Democracy in America*, vol. 2 (London: Collins, 1968), 608–9, cited by Scofield, *American Short Story*, 7.

26 Boyd, "Brief Encounters."

27 Updike, "Introduction," *Best American Short Stories,* 1984, xiv. He continues his lament: "The popular market for fiction has shriveled while the academic importance of 'creative writing' has swelled; academic quarterlies, operating under one form of subsidy or another, absorb some of the excess. The suspicion persists that short fiction, like poetry since Kipling and Bridges, has gone from being a popular to a fine art, an art preserved in a kind of floating museum made up of little superfluous magazines" (xv).

28 For a list of American and Canadian magazines publishing short fiction, see Tom Bailey, ed., *On Writing Short Stories* (Oxford: Oxford University Press, 2010), 317–32. A number of these publications are connected to universities with creative writing MFA programs. Although it is customary to lament the demise of magazines that pay their contributors and have a decent distribution, there remain exceptions to that rule. In addition to the *New Yorker* (unique in offering a weekly story), the best known are the *Atlantic Monthly, Vanity Fair, Esquire, Granta,* the *Kenyon Review,* the *Sewanee Review, Harper's,* and *McSweeney's.*

29 "Selected Shorts," *NPR,* www.google.com/webhp?sourceid=chrome-instant&ion=1&espv=2&ie=UTF-8#q=selected+shorts+npr (accessed August 27, 2016).

Chapter 3

1 The English word Bible comes from the Latin *biblia,* a singular noun that means "the book" and that itself comes from the Greek *ta biblia*—the books. Originally a collection of scrolls, then codices that could be arranged and read in any order, the many "books" of the Bible came to be bound in a single volume and the library came to be understood as a singularity.

2 Hermann Gunkel, *The Legends of Genesis: The Biblical Saga and History,* trans. W. H. Carruth (New York: Schocken Books, 1964), 45.

3 Gunkel, *Legends of Genesis,* 46.

4 Ibid., 47.

5 Ibid.

6 Stephen Prickett, *Origins of Narrative: The Romantic Appropriation of the Bible* (Cambridge: Cambridge University Press, 1996).

7 D. H. Lawrence, "Why the Novel Matters," in *The Cambridge Edition of the Works of D. H. Lawrence: Study of Thomas Hardy and Other Essays,* ed. Bruce Steele (Cambridge: Cambridge University Press, 1985), 196. Lawrence defines the novel as "the book of life," and continues, "In this sense, the Bible is a great confused novel. You may say, it is about God. But it is really about man alive" (195).

8 Robert Alter, "Introduction," in *The Literary Guide to the Bible*, eds. Robert Alter and Frank Kermode (Cambridge, MA: Belknap; Harvard, 1987), 23.

9 Alter, "Introduction," 22.

10 On this point, see Alter, "Introduction," and Tod Linafelt, "Narrative and Poetic Art in the Book of Ruth," *Interpretation* 64, no. 2 (2010): 117–29.

11 Deut. 25:5-6.

12 In the genealogy that opens Matthew's Gospel, Ruth and David are both ancestors of Jesus.

13 Allen, *Short Story in English*, 3.

14 Prose, "What Makes a Short Story?," 3.

15 Ibid., 4.

16 Ibid., 11.

17 Ibid., 5.

18 Ibid., 4.

19 Ibid., 7.

20 For a fuller discussion of these character types, see Adele Berlin, *Poetics and Interpretation of Biblical Narrative* (Sheffield: Almond Press, 1983).

21 Haim Chertok, "The Book of Ruth: Complexities within Simplicity," *Judaism* 35, no. 3 (1986): 294.

22 Prose, "What Makes a Short Story?," 7.

23 For a fuller articulation of this point, see David M. Gunn and Danna Nolan Fewell, *Narrative in the Hebrew Bible* (Oxford and New York: Oxford University Press, 1993), 83–85.

24 Gunn and Fewell, *Narrative in the Hebrew Bible*, 83.

25 Prose, "What Makes a Short Story?," 11.

26 Ibid.

27 See Peter Hawkins' earlier consideration of the parable, "'A Man Had Two Sons': The Question of Forgiveness," in *Ancient Forgiveness: Classical, Judaic, and Christian*, eds. Charles L. Griswold and David Konstan (Cambridge: Cambridge University Press, 2012), 158–94.

28 See James Tackach, "The Biblical Foundation of James Baldwin's 'Sonny's Blues,'" *Renascence: Essays on Values in Literature* 59, no. 2 (2007): 109–18. In addition to the relevance of biblical siblings, Tackach discusses the story's reference to "the cup of trembling" in Isa. 51:17-23.

Chapter 4

1 Flannery O'Connor, *The Habit of Being: Letters Edited and with an Introduction by Sally Fitzgerald* (New York: Farrar, Straus & Giroux, 1979). Abbreviated in the text as HB.

2 Letter to Ben Griffith: "What I had in mind to suggest with the
artificial nigger [sic] was the redemptive quality of the Negro's
suffering for us all. You may be right that Nelson's reaction to the
colored woman is too pronounced, but I meant for her in an almost
physical way to suggest the mystery of existence to him—he not
only has never seen a nigger [sic] but he didn't know any women
and I felt that such a black mountain of maternity would give him
the required shock to start those black forms moving up from his
subconscious. I wrote that story a good many times, having a lot
of trouble with the end. I frequently send my stories to Mrs. Tate
[Caroline Gordon] and she is always telling me that the endings
are too flat and that at the end I must gain some altitude and get a
larger view. Well the end of 'The Artificial Nigger' was a very definite
attempt to do that and in those last paragraphs I have practically
gone from the Garden of Eden to the Gates of Paradise. I am not
sure if it is successful but I mean to keep trying with other things."

3 In a letter to Betty Hester ("A" in HB), O'Connor addresses "the
embarrassing subject of what I have not read and been influenced
by" (HB 98). The list is long: "all the Catholics novelists" (Mauriac,
Bernanos, Bloy, Greene, Waugh); "the best Southern writers";
"the Russians, not so much Tolstoy but Dostoevsky, Turgenev,
Chekhov and Gogol." She goes on to name Hawthorne, Flaubert,
Balzac, Kafka, and then The Master: "I've read almost all of Henry
James—from a sense of High Duty and because when I read James
I feel something is happening to me, in slow motion but happening
nevertheless." She ends with another American who comes as
no surprise: "But always the largest thing that looms up is The
Humerous [sic] Tales of Edgar Allen Poe" (98–99).

4 John Updike speaks of the "main charge" he gets out of writing as
describing precisely "a certain moment of experience, whether it's a
dress, a chair, or how a person's face looks"; "any act of description is,
to some extent, an act of praise." Conversations with John Updike, ed.
James Path (Jackson: University Press of Mississippi, 1994), 210, 253.

5 O'Connor's interest in Hawthorne is revealed in her letters,
especially one to the novelist John Hawkes: "I think I would admit
to writing what Hawthorne called 'romances,' but I don't think that
has anything to do with the romantic mentality. Hawthorne interests
me considerably. I feel more of a kinship with him than any other
American, though some of what he wrote I can't make myself read
through to the end" (HB 457). Hawthorne also figures prominently
in A Memoir of Mary Ann (MM 213–34).

6 Flannery O'Connor: The Cartoons, ed. Kelly Gerald, with an
introduction by Barry Moser (Seattle, WA: Fantagraphics Books, 2012).

7 Robert H. Brinkmeyer Jr., "A Closer Walk with Thee: Flannery
O'Connor and Southern Fundamentalists," Southern Literary Journal
18, no. 2 (1986): 3–4.

8 On O'Connor's delivering shock on behalf of the kingdom of heaven, see James Parker, "The Passion of Flannery O'Connor," *The Atlantic,* November 2013, www.theatlantic.com/magazine/archive/2013/11/ the-passion-of-flannery-oconnor/309532/. "Where the Word was operational, for O'Connor, it was always disruptive: in its presence, one's head was *supposed* to explode. Her short stories, especially, reengineered the Joycean epiphany, the quiet moment of transcendence, as a kind of blunt-force baptismal intervention: her characters are KO'd, dismantled, with a violence that would be absurdist, if the universe were absurd. But the universe is not absurd."

9 All quotations of the fiction are from *The Complete Stories of Flannery O'Connor* (New York: Farrar, Straus & Giroux, 2001).

10 I offer a reading of the story's climactic moment in *The Language of Grace: Flannery O'Connor, Walker Percy, and Iris Murdoch* (New York: Seabury Classics, 2004), 39–49. Charles Baxter, "Counterpointed Characterization," in *Burning Down the House: Essays on Fiction* (Minneapolis: Graywolf Press, 1997), 123–25, studies the story's juxtaposition of its two main characters and makes the following judgment: "Without the Misfit we have a mild satire on colorful Southern characters. With him, the story turns into a fiction in which one feels the breathing of a living metaphysical disorder" (125).

11 All citations of the Scripture are from the Douay–Rheims version O'Connor relied on. *The Holy Bible Translated from the Latin Vulgate* (Rockford, IL: Tan Books, 1971).

12 Arthur F. Kinney, *Flannery O'Connor's Library. Resources of Being* (Athens: University of Georgia Press, 2008).

13 For a collection of O'Connor's book reviews from 1956 to 1964, see *The Presence of Grace and Other Book Reviews,* compiled by Leo J. Zuber, ed., with introduction by Carter W. Martin (Athens: University of Georgia Press, 1983).

14 For O'Connor on country living, see, for instance, a letter to Robert and Sally Fitzgerald (HB 473).

15 The source here is Ralph C. Wood, *Flannery O'Connor and the Christ-Haunted South* (Grand Rapids, MI: William B. Eerdmans, 2004), 30: "When once asked what kind of Christian she would become if she were not a Roman Catholic, she replied, far from jestingly, that she would join a Pentecostal Holiness church" (30). To Thomas Mabry she wrote on March 1, 1955, that she was a Catholic "not like someone else would be a Baptist or Methodist, but some like someone else would be an atheist," *Flannery O'Connor Collected Works* (New York: Library of America, 1988), 930.

16 Brinkmeyer, with reservations, compares O'Connor as a writer to no-middle-ground-for-belief Fundamentalists. Her fictional style may

be much less explicit than altar-call preachers, yet "her underlying strategies of shock and distortion are very similar to the evangelist's in terms of technique and intention," Brinkmeyer, "A Closer Walk with Thee," 7.

17 Sam Fentress, *Bible Road: Signs of Faith in the American Landscape*, photographs by Sam Fentress, foreword by Paul Elie (Cincinnati, OH: D&C, 2007).

18 "Letter to Can Grande della Scala," Princeton Dante Project, http://etcweb.princeton.edu/dante/index.xhtml.

19 In a letter to Betty Hester O'Connor wrote, "For my money Dante is about as great as you can get" (HB 116). Elsewhere, she noted all that separated him from her: "I am often told that the model of balance for the novelist should be Dante, who divided his territory up pretty evenly between hell, purgatory, and paradise. There can be no objection to this, but there also can be no reason to assume that the result of doing it in these times will give us the balanced picture that it gave in Dante's. Dante lived in the thirteenth century, when that balance that was achieved in the faith of his age. We live now in an age which doubts both fact and value, which is swept this way and that by momentary convictions. Instead of reflecting a balance from the world around him, the novelist now has to achieve one from a felt balance inside himself" (MM 49).

20 Jordan Cofer, *The Gospel According to Flannery O'Connor: Examining the Role of the Bible in Flannery O'Connor's Fiction* (New York and London: Bloomsbury, 2014), offers a book-length of this relationship. Looking at the two novels as well as many of the stories, he highlights O'Connor's "recapitulation or retelling of biblical stories so that their power can once again be felt; demonstrating the redemptive power of violence through her prophetic figures (grounded in the Bible); and, finally, [her] allowing the reader to feel the full power of the Bible's reversing vision" (5).

21 O'Connor had in fact a traveling salesman in her life, although not of the Manley Pointer variety. See Brad Gooch, *Flannery: A Life of Flannery O'Connor* (New York: Little, Brown & Company, 2009), 254–58.

22 Cofer suggests that what Ruby Turpin sees is inflected by Jacob's dream ladder in Genesis 28:12 ("a ladder was set on the earth with its top reaching to heaven"), as well as by the apocalyptic vision of the Revelation to John, which presents heaven as a place where "the nations shall walk in the light" and "they shall bring the glory and the honor of the nations into it" (Apoc. 21:24, 26–27).

23 See Prov. 20:12, Isa. 6:10, Jer. 5:21, Ezek. 12:2, Matt. 13:15, Mark 8:18, Acts 28:27, Rom. 11:8.

24 In the Vulgate's Daniel 3, O'Connor's Scripture in the Douay–Rheims translation, the Hebrew Bible's account of the three Jews has appended to it the prayer of Azariah (verses 25–100).

Chapter 5

1 Irving Howe, "Introduction," in *Jewish American Stories*, ed. Irving Howe (New York: New American Library and Penguin, 1977), 16.

2 Leslie Fiedler, *Waiting for the End* (New York: Stein & Day, 1964), 64.

3 Marcus Lee Hansen, "The Problem of the Third Generation Immigrant," in *American Immigrants and Their Generations: Studies and Commentaries on the Hansen Thesis after Fifty Years*, eds. Peter Kivisto and Dag Blanck (Urbana: University of Illinois Press, 1990), 195.

4 Ezra Cappell, "Appendix: An Interview with Rebecca Goldstein," in *American Talmud: The Cultural Work of Jewish American Fiction* (Albany, State University of New York Press, 2007), Kindle edition, locations 2471–2472.

5 Cappell, *American Talmud*, Kindle, locations 100–103.

6 Melvin Jules Bukiet, "The Golden Calf and the Red Heifer" in *While the Messiah Tarries* (Syracuse, NY: Syracuse University Press, 1997).

7 See Andrew Furman's chapter on Bukiet in his *Contemporary Jewish American Writers and the Multicultural Dilemma: The Return of the Exiled* (Syracuse: Syracuse University Press, 2000).

8 Melvin Jules Bukiet, "The Golden Calf and the Red Heifer," in *While the Messiah Tarries: Stories* (Syracuse: Syracuse University Press, 1997).

9 Max Apple, "The Eighth Day," in *Jewish American Literature*, ed. Jules Chametzky et al.

10 Apple, "The Eighth Day," 1080.

11 Ibid.

12 Lev Raphael, "Dancing on Tisha B'Av" in *Secret Anniversaries of the Heart: New and Selected Stories* (New York: Leapfrog, 2006), 204.

13 Bloom, Foreword to *Zakhor*, xxiii.

14 Yaacov Shavit, Mordechai Eran, and Chaya Naor, *The Hebrew Bible Reborn: From Holy Scripture to the Book of Books: A History of Biblical Culture and the Battles over the Bible in Modern Judaism* (Berlin: DeGruyter, 2007), 501.

15 Grace Paley, "Zagrowsky Tells," in *The Collected Stories: Grace Paley* (New York: Farrar Strauss and Giroux, 2007).

16 Grace Paley, "Samuel," in *The Collected Stories: Grace Paley* (New York: Farrar Strauss and Giroux, 2007), 198.

17 Gloria L. Cronin, "Immersions in the Postmodern: The Fiction of Allegra Goodman," in *Daughters of Valor: Contemporary Jewish American Women Writers*, eds. Jay L. Halio and Ben Siegel (Newark: University of Delaware Press, 1997), 248.

18 Allegra Goodman, "Writing Jewish Fiction in and out of the Mulicultural Context," in *Daughters of Valor*, eds. Halio and Siegel, 273.

19 Raanen Omer-Sherman, "Tradition and Desire" *MELUS* 29, no. 2 (Summer, 2004): 265–289, 266.

20 Goodman, "Writing Jewish Fiction," 273.

21 Cronin, "Immersions in the Postmodern," 247.

22 This aspect of her work is not much discussed by critics, who are more interested in the religious dimensions of her fiction. A notable exception is Gustavo Sanchez Canales's "'Creative Midrash Forces the Students to Read, So They Realize They Aren't the First to Feel, Think, or Write Anything Down': Biblical Archetypes in Allegra Goodman's *The Family Markowitz* and *Kaaterskill Falls*," *IUP Journal of American Literature* 3, no. 4 (2010): 51–73.

23 See Raanen Omer-Sherman, "Orthodox Community and Individuality" *Religion and Literature* 36, no. 2 (Summer 2004): 75–97.

24 Allegra Goodman, "The Story of Rachel," in *Genesis: As It Is Written: Contemporary Writers on Our First Stories*, ed. David Rosenberg (New York: HarperCollins, 1996), 174.

25 Allegra Goodman, "Four Stories" in *The Family Markowitz* (New York: Farrar Strauss and Giroux, 1996), 188.

26 Goodman, *The Family Markowitz*, 193.

27 Ibid., 198.

28 Cappell, *American Talmud*, locations 1598–1600.

29 Victoria Aarons, "The Covenant Unraveling: The Pathos of Cultural Loss in Allegra Goodman's Fiction," *Shofar* 22, no. 3 (2004): 15.

30 Goodman, *The Family Markowitz*, 207.

31 Ibid., 209.

32 Bloom, Foreword to *Zakhor*, xxiii

33 Goodman, "Sarah" *The Family Markowitz*, 219.

34 Goodman, *The Family Markowitz*, 219–20.

35 Cappell, *American Talmud*, location 71.

36 Cappell, *American Talmud*, locations 375–76.

Chapter 6

1 For Updike's long engagement with the *New Yorker*, see "The Short Story and I," *Odd Jobs: Essays and Criticism* (New York: Alfred A. Knopf, 1991), 762–66. For his impact on the magazine, see Adam

Gopnik's eulogy, "John Updike," February 9, 2009, www.newyorker.
com/magazine/2009/02/john-updike.

2 John Updike, "John Cheever I," in *Odd Jobs*, 109. Although Updike
  was aware of Cheever's religious observance—"he was for the
  most part of his adult life a regular, indeed compulsive, communicant
  at Episcopal morning High Mass"—he discounted its depth:
  "Though of a religious disposition, Cheever had no theology in which
  to frame and shelter his frailty; he had only inflamed, otherworldly
  sensations of debasement and exaltation," John Updike, "Basically
  Decent: A Big Biography of John Cheever," *New Yorker*, March 9,
  2009, www.newyorker.com/magazine/2009/03/09/basically-decent,
  and "John Updike Beautifully Explains How Difficult It Was to Read
  John Cheever's Tortured Journals," *New Republic*, December 2,
  1991, https://newrepublic.com/article/77068/john-updike-explains-
  john-cheevers-life-novels. For another assessment, see my "John
  Cheever," in *Listening for God: Contemporary Literature and the
  Life of Faith*, eds. Paula J Carlson and Peter S. Hawkins, vol. 3
  (Minneapolis: Augsburg Fortress, 2000), 9–11, and Ralph C. Wood,
  "The Modest and Charitable Humanism of John Cheever" (1982),
  Religion-Online, www.religion-online.org/showarticle.asp?title=1353.
  Although the Bible is largely only of casual and cultural reference in
  Cheever's short fiction, Job 28:12, 14, 22 plays a provocative role in
  one of his most celebrated stories, "The Five Forty-Eight."

3 John Updike, *Self-Consciousness: Memoirs* (New York: Random
  House, 1989), 228–31.

4 John Updike, "Foreword to *Love Factories*," in *Odd Jobs*, 770.

5 The secular literati were not the only ones who found Updike unusual
  in this regard. His practice of religion, like his patriotism, represented
  qualities that set him apart from his peers, expressing for Adam
  Gopnik, for instance, "a sympathy of feeling that connected him to
  his own lower-middle-class roots." Intimates were also dismayed.
  According to Updike, "My consorts through the years have, I believe,
  found my going off to church, usually alone, an annoying affectation
  and not, as I felt it, a gallant donning of the armor in which a good
  citizen sallies forth: 'Since we belong to the day,' Paul wrote to the
  Thessalonians, 'let us be sober, and put on the breastplate of faith
  and love, and for a helmet the hope of salvation,'" "The Future of
  Faith," first published in the *New Yorker*, November 29, 1999, 84–91,
  and then in a slightly revised form in *Due Considerations: Essays and
  Criticism* (New York: Alfred A. Knopf, 2007), 27–41, 35.

6 Interview with Terry Gross (1988), *Conversations with John Updike*,
  ed. James Plath (Jackson: University Press of Mississippi, 1994), 208.

7 Updike, *Self-Consciousness*, 234.

8 Ian McEwan, "On John Updike," *New York Review of Books*, March
  22, 2009, www.nybooks.com/articles/2009/03/12/on-john-updike/
  printpage=true.

9 Updike, "The Future of Faith" (rpt. 2000), 31.

10 Updike's own thoughts on his need for God, in plentiful evidence throughout his essays and interviews, is expressed in his novel *Roger's Version* (New York: Alfred A. Knopf, 1986) through the character Dale Kohler as understood by the protagonist, Harvard Divinity professor Roger Lambert: "What was this desolation in Dale's heart, I thought, but the longing for God—that longing which is, when all is said and done, our only evidence of His existence? Why do we feel such loss, but that there was Something to lose?" (67); "Without it—faith, I mean—there's this big hole, and what's strange, the hole is a certain shape, that it just exactly fits. That He just exactly fills" (203). On a similar if more restrained note Updike concludes "The Future of Faith" with a reference to *The Varieties of Religious Experience*: "The yearning, the insistence that there be, to quote Williams James, 'something more,' will persist. Our concepts of at and virtue and purpose are so tied up with the supernatural that it is hard to foresee doing altogether without it" (2000 rpt., 41). On the religious trajectory of Updike's life through his lyric poetry, moving from the ringing affirmation of "Seven Stanzas at Easter" (1960) to the greater reticence of "Fine Point 12/22/08," see David E. Anderson, "On Easter and Updike," *R&E: Religion and Ethics Newsweekly*, April 7, 2009, www.pbs.org/wnet/religionandethics/2009/04/07/april-7-2009-on-easter-and-updike/2618/.

11 For Updike on Kierkegaard, Barth, and Tillich, see the interviews with Jeff Campbell (1976), Katherine Stephen (1986), and Jan Nunley (1993) in Plath, ed., *Conversations with John Updike*. Two book reviews from the early sixties, the period of Updike's crisis of faith, can be found in *Assorted Prose* (New York: Alfred A. Knopf, 1965), both a glowing appreciation of Karl Barth (273–82) and the opposite evaluation of Paul Tillich (282–83). See also these stanzas from Updike's long autobiographical poem "Midpoint" (1969), cited in Anderson, "On Easter and Updike": "An easy Humanism plagues the land; / I choose to take an otherworldly stand . . . Praise Kierkegaard, who splintered Hegel's creed / Upon the rock of Existential need; / Praise Barth, who told how saving Faith can flow / From Terror's oscillating Yes and No." On Barth's understanding of "Yes and No," see Updike's "To Wolfgang Amadeus Mozart, *by Karl Barth*," in *Odd Jobs*, 247–50.

12 John Updike, "Religion and Literature," in *More Matter: Essays and Criticism* (New York: Random House, 2014), 59; see also his "Remarks on Religion and Contemporary Literature" and "Remarks upon Receiving the Campion Medal," 848–52. See also *John Updike and Religion: The Sense of the Sacred and the Motions of Grace*, ed. James Yerkes (Grand Rapids, MI: Wm. B. Eerdmans, 1999).

13 Updike, *Self-Consciousness*, 53.

14 John Updike, "The Gospel according to Matthew," in *Incarnation: Contemporary Writers on the New Testament*, ed. Alfred Corn (New York: Viking, 1990), 1–11, and reprinted in Updike's *Odd Jobs*, 231–39, 239. This passage in Updike's essay lingered in mind when Adam Gopnik wrote his *New Yorker* "post script" cum eulogy shortly after the author's death: "Who can forget his description of the Parable of the Talents, and how he could feel the damp earth of the boy who buried them?"

15 John Updike, "The Great I AM," *New Yorker*, November 1, 2004, reprinted in *Due Considerations*, 187–96, 191.

16 For Updike's use of epigraphs, theological as well as biblical, see Jeff Campbell's interview in Plath, ed., *Conversations*, 84–89, and especially the discussion (88–89) around his choice of Ps 45:1 as the first epigraph in *A Month of Sundays*.

17 According to Jack de Bellis, *The John Updike Encyclopedia* (Westport, CT: Greenwood, 2000), 401–2, the "young minister" in *Of the Farm* who preaches on the creation of Eve by relying heavily on Karl Barth's *Church Dogmatics* is actually delivering verbatim John Updike: "Updike had originally written this sermon for publication in *Ladies' Home Journal* in 1964. When it was not published, Updike explained, 'I used the novels as a mounting for it.'" John McTavish, *Myth and Gospel in the Fiction of John Updike* (Eugene, OR: Cascade, 2016), 32, claims that the rejecting journal was the *New Yorker*. He considers the *Of the Farm* sermon at some length; see 32–35.

18 "The Lifeguard," in *Updike: Collected Early Stories*, ed. Christopher Carduff (New York: Library of America, 2013), 332.

19 John Updike, "Introduction to *Self-Selected Stories of John Updike*," in *Odd Jobs*, 767–70, 768.

20 "Made in Heaven" (1994) appears in *Updike: Collected Later Stories*, ed. Christopher Carduff (New York: Library of America, 2013).

21 For a discussion of Updike's theology, in addition to *John Updike and Religion*, ed. Yerkes, see Robert K. Johnston, "John Updike's Theological World," (1977), *Religion-Online*, www.religion-online.org/showarticle.asp?title=1195; Peter J. Bailey, *Rabbit (Un)Redeemed. The Drama of Belief in John Updike's Fiction* (Madison, NJ: Fairleigh Dickinson University Press, 2006), 13–26.

22 "The Full Glass," Updike's last published *New Yorker* story, appeared in the issue of May 26, 2008. It completes *Updike: Collected Later Stories*, ed. Carduff.

23 *Updike: Collected Later Stories*, ed. Carduff, 418.

24 Interview with Jan Nunley, in *Conversations*, ed. Plath, 249, 253.

Chapter 7

1 Jamie Quatro, "The Pleasure of Suddenness," interview with Brian Blanchfield, *New Oxford American*, June 23, 2016, www.oxfordamerican.org/item/891-the-pleasure-of-suddenness.

2 Quatro, "The Pleasure of Suddenness."

3 Jullianne Ballou, "Act of Faith: A Conversation with Jamie Quatro," March 1, 2013, www.oxfordamerican.org/item/511-act-of-faith.

4 "I find truth and spiritual meaning equally in the works of those who aren't necessarily writing out of a religious tradition. Barthelme, for one. Kafka, Camus. And Beckett, his pulsing absent God(ot) filling every inch of reality—the song of our experience of His absence (who among us has not doubted?) just as true and necessary as the song of His presence. I do think there are works of utter despair, that communicate a nihilism. Though the chronicling of a loss of faith can also lift the gaze, remind one of the gift of the imagination. O'Connor says that loss of faith is precisely that: a failure, first, of the imagination." Nick Ripatrazone, Interview of Jamie Quatro, *The Fine Delight: Book and Interview Series: Contemporary Catholic Literature*, September 16, 2013, http://catholiclit.blogspot.com/2013/09/jamie-quatro.html.

5 "Sherwood Anderson, Barry Hannah, Denis Johnson, Gordon Lish, David Means, Steven Millhauser, Alice Munro, Tim O'Brien, Grace Paley, Mary Robinson, Christine Schutt, and Eudora Welty" (206).

6 Ripatrazone, Interview of Jamie Quatro.

7 Jamie Quatro, "God Texts the Ten Commandments," *Timothy McSweeney's Internet Tendency*, June 3, 2009, www.mcsweeneys.net/articles/god-texts-the-ten-commandments.

8 "The KJV Store is proud to carry the Rainbow Bible, the only entirely color-coded Bible in the world." "Rainbow Bible," *The KJV Store*, www.thekjvstore.com/articles/rainbow-bible.

9 James Wood, "Broken Vows: Jamie Quatro's Stories," *New Yorker*, March 11, 2013, www.newyorker.com/magazine/2013/03/11/broken-vows.

10 Jill McCorkle, *I Want to Show You More*, book-jacket copy. It begins, "Fasten your seat belt: Jamie Quatro is a writer of great talent who knows how to take a dark turn without ever tapping the brakes and then bring you back into daylight with breathtaking precision." For other summary reviews, see www.buffalolib.org/vufind/Record/1886237/Reviews.

11 A rare exception to Quatro's positive reception is one review offered anonymously, "Jamie Quatro's I WANT TO SHOW YOU MORE: Pardon My Skepticism," *Brokerages & Day Trading*, www.

brokeragesdaytrading.com/article/923089272/jamie-quatro-s-i-want-to-show-you-more-pardon-my-skepticism/. The reviewer does not take a conservative Christian stance in his disapproval, such as the ones Quatro references more generally in her interviews.

12 Ripatrazone, Interview of Jamie Quatro.

13 Ibid.

14 In "Holy Ground" there is another citation of the Song, this time in transliterated Hebrew (that came to Quatro from Joyce's *Ulysses*). An African American man says to the fleeing narrator, "*Schorach ani wenowach, benoith Hierushaloim*" (190), "I am black but comely, O ye daughters of Jerusalem" (1:5).

15 Ibid.

16 "Jamie Quatro, interviewed by Dawn Raffel," *Center for Fiction*, http://centerforfiction.org/jamie-quatro-interviewed-by-dawn-raffel.

17 "Jamie Quatro, interviewed by Dawn Raffel."

18 Jamie Quatro, "A Plain Kiss (Letters to Allison, 2006)," *Forty Stories: New Writing from Harper Perennials* (New York: Harper Collins, 2012), https://glose.com/book/forty-stories/35-a-plain-kiss-letters-to-allison-2-6-by-jamie-quatro#7089

19 Ripatrazone, Interview of Jamie Quatro.

20 *The Collected Poems of W. B. Yeats* (New York: Macmillan, 1964), 185, 212.

21 Quatro's interest in this material will preoccupy a forthcoming book of stories: "I've got another collection in the works, a linked series of stories about characters waiting for the 'rapture.' Ballou, "Act of Faith."

22 For the cinematic version of these "Rapture" accounts, see "Late Great Planet Earth: the Film" (1979), "Left Behind: the Movie" (2005); also "FINAL" (2013).

23 In "Caught up," Quatro might also have had in mind another one of Saint Paul's visionary moments, where the Apostle refers to the experience of a "man in Christ" who is clearly himself (2 Cor. 12:2–4).

24 Wood ("Broken Vows") asks in reference to one aspect of Quatro's biblical frame of reference, "Who needs the New Testament?" The point is that she needs both the Old and the New, the hard sayings and those that are "softer." For Kelsey Joseph, Quatro's women cannot escape "the ringing of that relentless commandment: *thou shalt not commit adultery. . . .* The idea is pure Old Testament: God exists through his laws, his holy unions. Follow the commandments; faith will come," Kelsey Joseph, "God in Wayward Form: Jamie Quatro's Salvation-Seeking Adulteresses," *Los Angeles Review of Books*, June 18, 2013, https://lareviewofbooks.org/article/god-in-wayward-forms-jamie-quatros-salvation-seeking-adulteresses/.

Chapter 8

1 Steven Millhauser, "The Ambition of the Short Story," *New York Times*, October 3, 2008, www.nytimes.com/2008/10/05/books/review/Millhauser-t.html?_r=0.

2 Millhauser, "Ambition of the Short Story."

3 Alejandro Herrero-Olaizola, "Writing Lives, Writing Lies: The Pursuit of Apocryphal Biographies," *Mosaic* 35, no. 3 (2002): 73.

4 "Up Front," *New York Times*, October 5, 2008, www.nytimes.com/2008/10/05/books/review/Upfront-t.html.

5 Millhauser, "Ambition of the Short Story."

6 Josh Lambert, "Identity Recruitment and the 'American Writer': Steven Millhauser, *Edwin Mullhouse*, and Biographical Criticism," *Contemporary Literature* 54, no. 1 (2013), 23–48, quotation on p. 27.

7 Lambert, "Identity Recruitment," 41.

8 "Up Front."

9 Danielle Alexander, Pedro Ponce, Alicita Rodriguez "Steven Millhauser" *The Review of Contemporary Fiction* 26, no. 1 (Spring 2004), 1.

10 Steven Millhauser, "The Fascination of the Miniature," *Grand Street* 2, no. 4 (1983), 128–35, p. 135.

11 Millhauser, "Fascination of the Miniature," 129.

12 Ibid., 135.

13 Arthur M. Saltzman, "In the Millhauser Archives," *Critique* 37, no. 2 (1996): 149–60.

14 Earl G. Ingersoll, *Understanding Steven Millhauser* (Columbia, University of South Caroline Press, 2014), 81.

15 D. T. Max, "The Illusionist," review of *Dangerous Laughter* by Steven Millhauser, *New York Times*, February 24, 2008, www.nytimes.com/2008/02/24/books/review/Max-t.html.

16 Ingersoll, *Understanding Steven Millhauser*, 139, n. 6.

17 Millhauser's heading for the middle four stories of *Dangerous Laughter* (New York: Vintage Contemporaries, 2008).

18 Ingersoll, *Understanding Steven Millhauser*, 121.

19 Millhauser, "The Tower" in *Dangerous Laughter*, 152.

20 Etienne Fevrier, "An Interview with Steven Millhauser," *Transatlantica: Revue d'etudes americaines* 2011, no. 1, https://transatlantica.revues.org/5302.

21 Millhauser, "The Tower," 154.

22 Ibid.

23 Ibid.

24 Ibid., 156.

25 Ibid., 158.

26 Millhauser, "The Tower," 158.

27 Keir Graff, review of *We Others: New and Selected Stories* by Steven Millhauser, August 2011, http://booklistonline.com/We-Others-New-and-Selected-Stories-Steven-Millhauser/pid=4878006.

28 Anna-Claire Stineberg, "We Others—Steven Millauser," book review, *Full Stop*, October 5, 2011, www.full-stop.net/2011/10/05/reviews/anna-claire-stinebring/we-others-steven-millhauser/.

29 Zachary Houle, "Steven Millauser the Illusionist: We Others," book review, *PopMatters*, October 25, 2012, www.popmatters.com/review/164632-we-others-new-selected-stories-by-steven-millhauser/

30 Adam brings death into the world; Noah's generation prompts God to limit a human lifespan to 120 years; and Methuselah is the oldest man in the Bible, but does not make it to 1,000 years, a number thought by some to be metonymic with immortality.

31 Jim Shepard, "Steven Millhauser," *Bomb* 83 (Spring 2003), 76–80, p. 78.

32 Max Winter, "Finely Tuned Grand Illusions," review of *We Others: New and Selected Stories* by Steven Millhauser, *Boston Globe*, September 23, 2011, www.bostonglobe.com/arts/books/2011/09/23/finely-tuned-grand-illusions/U39VcCi92ALTQbmZRYwhvl/story.html.

33 Review of *We Others: New and Selected Stories* by Steven Millhauser, *Kirkus*, August 23, 2011, www.kirkusreviews.com/book-reviews/steven-millhauser/we-others/.

34 Ingersoll, *Understanding Steven Millhauser*, 131.

35 We see this especially in the description of the propagation of books, "each one reflecting the original tablets, but more and more faintly."

36 Mark Greenspan, "Talmud Torah: Mitzvah, Mission and Meaning" www.rabbinicalassembly.org/sites/default/files/public/resources-ideas/source-sheets/tol-parashot/naso.pdf.

37 Steven Millhauser, "A Voice in the Night," *New Yorker*, December 10, 2012, www.newyorker.com/magazine/2012/12/10/a-voice-in-the-night.

38 See the discussion of Auerbach in Part Two, "The Literariness of the Bible."

39 Michael Upchurch, "Millhauser's 'Voices in the Night': Short Stories by a Master," *Seattle Times*, May 3, 2015, www.seattletimes.com/entertainment/books/millhausers-voices-in-the-night-short-stories-by-a-master/.

40 Steven Millhauser, *Portrait of a Romantic* (New York: Knopf, 1977), 28.

Chapter 9

1 It is true that the Evangelists Matthew and Luke balance the end of Jesus's life with a glimpse of his beginning with birth narratives (the one with Wise Men, the other with shepherds); they also offer genealogies that put the newborn savior in his ancestral place. But neither Mark (chronologically the oldest Gospel) nor John (the youngest) finds it necessary to narrate a birth. Instead, all four Evangelists achieve their dramatic climax in the cross. Jesus's death in effect makes his life.

2 For Egeria's account of her pilgrimage to Jerusalem, see *Christian Classics Ethereal Library*, www.ccel.org/m/mcclure/etheria/etheria. htm.

3 On the English medieval mystery plays, see V. A. Kolve, *The Play Called Corpus Christi* (Stanford, CA: Stanford University Press, 196), David M. Bevington, *Medieval Drama* (Boston: Houghton Mifflin, 1975), and Sarah Beckwith, *Signifying God: Social Relations and Symbolic Act in York's Play of Corpus Christi* (Chicago: University of Chicago, 2001).

4 All citations of the Pinners' Play are from *York Mystery Plays: A Selection in Modern Spelling*, eds. Richard Beadle and Pamela M. King (Oxford: Oxford University Press, 1999), 212–21.

5 "Today is Friday," in *The Complete Short Stories of Ernest Hemingway*, Finca Vigia edition (New York: Simon & Shuster, 1987), 271–73.

6 On Hemingway's decision to present his text as drama, see Christopher Dick, "Drama as Metaphor in Ernest Hemingway's TODAY IS FRIDAY," *Explicator* 69, no. 4 (2011): 198–202.

7 George Plimpton, "Ernest Hemingway, The Art of Fiction No. 21," interview, *Paris Review* 18 (Spring 1958), www.theparisreview.org/ interviews/4825/the-art-of-fiction-no-21-ernest-hemingway.

8 Matthew C. Nickel, *Hemingway's Dark Night: Catholic Influences and Intertextualities in the Work of Ernest Hemingway* (Wickford, RI: New Street Publications, 2013), 86–93, explores the theological ramifications of the story. He discusses the two draft titles on 89-90.

9 Octavio Paz, *Labyrinth of Solitude: Life and Thought in Mexico*, trans. Lysander Kemp (New York: Grove Press, 1961), 23. "[One] of the most noble traits of the Mexican's character is his willingness to contemplate horror: he is even familiar and complacent in his dealings with it." His chapter "The Day of the Dead," 47–64, has a consideration of fiestas relevant to Valdez Quade's collection.

10 Daphne Sidor, review of *Night at the Fiestas* by Kirstin Valdez Quade, *Lambda Literary*, July 5, 2015, www.lambdaliterary.org/ reviews/07/05/night-at-the-fiestas-by-kirstin-valdez-quade/.

11 Willing Davidson, "This Week in Fiction: Kirstin Valdez Quade," *New Yorker*, October 13, 2014, www.newyorker.com/books/page-turner/fiction-this-week-kirstin-valdez-quade-2014-10-20.

12 Ann Hulbert, "Passion Plays: Kirstin Valdez Quade's Theatrical New Short-Story Collection," review of *Night at the Fiestas: Stories*, by Kirstin Valdez Quade, *Atlantic*, March 2015, www.theatlantic.com/ magazine/archive/2015/03/passion-plays/384979/.

13 Other writers of early importance to Valdez Quade include Tobias Wolff, Virginia Woolf, Raymond Carver, and Sandra Cisneros. "Each of these writers influenced me and made me think about the stories I wanted to tell," Daniel Ford, "Short Stories and String Cheese: Author Kirstin Valdez Quade on Her Debut Collection *Night at the Fiestas*," interview, *Writer's Bone*, May 5, 2015, http://writersbone. com/interviewsarchive/2015/5/5/short-stories-and-string-cheese-author-kirstin-valdez-quade-on-her-debut-novel-night-at-the-fiestas.

14 Dominic Preziosi, "Writing into Uncertainty," interview of Kirstin Valdez Quade, *Commonweal*, May 7, 2015, www. commonwealmagazine.org/interview-kirstin-valdez-quade.

15 "I have always been interested in religion and faith. As a child I always spent a lot of time with my older relatives and my extremely Catholic grandmother and great-grandmother. And yet my father is a geochemist so I have this other very scientific background as well. Certainly I think one of the reasons I'm interested in faith is that faith is so much about longing. It's about longing for transcendence, it's longing to be closer to the infinite and longing to connect with others; it's about empathy. And I think that's also the project of fiction. Fiction is about longing and empathy," "*Night at the Fiestas* Spins Stories of Faith and Family," interview of Kirstin Valdez Quade, *NPR*, March 8, 2015, www.npr. org/2015/03/28/395304257/night-at-the-fiestas-spins-stories-of-faith-and-family.

16 Preziosi, "Writing into Uncertainty." Elsewhere, Valdez Quade has said that *Night at the Fiestas* is held together by her characters' longing to "transcend their limitations": all of them "seek transformation and to resolve the messiness of their lives," Davidson, "This Week in Fiction."

17 Kyle Minor's rave review in the *New York Times* characterizes the story as "one of three legitimate masterpieces in Kirstin Valdez Quade's haunting and beautiful debut collection." He continues: "While reading, I often wondered whether a better title for the collection might have been 'Via Dolorosa,' or 'The Way of Suffering.' This is a book suffused with the desire to reclaim what has been lost, with longing for love misplaced, with the search for the 'astonishing' relief, as one character puts it, at being 'the kind of person who might meet another person's need,'" March 24, 2015, www.nytimes.com/2015/03/29/books/review/night-at-the-fiestas-by-kirstin-valdez-quade.html?_r=0 For additional readings of "The Five Wounds," see Peter Savaiano (March 11, 2013, https://iiereadingcircle.wordpress.com/author/petersavaiano/), and Charles May (blog, July 28, 2009, http://may-on-the-short-story.blogspot.com/2009/07/five-wounds-by-kirsten-valdez-quade.html).

18 At a later point in the story Angel regales Amadeo with facts she has learned in her parenting class, about fluid and brain stems and genitals. "Like did you know he had his toes before he even got his little dick?" Amadeo is horrified by her comments: 'this is his *daughter.*' But she is undeterred: 'Jesus, too,' she says, singsong. 'Jesus had his stuff in Mary.' She laughs. 'Couple of virgins. There's something for your research.' She settles back into the couch, pleased" (68).

Chapter 10

1 Tobias Wolff, *Matters of Life and Death: New American Stories* (Green Harbor, MA: Wampeter Press, 1983), xi. Wolff goes on to liken his preferred kind of writer to Ivan Ilyich's servant, Gerasim, who uniquely had "the willingness to say that unspeakable thing which everyone else in the house is too coy, or too frightened, or too polite to say."

2 Bill Buford, "*Granta* 8: Dirty Realism," *Granta: The Magazine of New Writing.* Summer 1983, http://granta.com/issues/granta-8-dirty-realism/, defines "dirty realism" as fiction, especially short stories, "devoted to the local details, the nuances, the little disturbances in language and gesture."

3 Jack Livings, "Tobias Wolff, The Art of Fiction No. 183," interview, *Paris Review*, Fall 2004, www.theparisreview.org/interviews/5391/the-art-of-fiction-no-183-tobias-wolff.

4 Livings, "Tobias Wolff."

5 Bonnie Lyons, Bill Oliver, and Tobias Wolff, "An Interview with Tobias Wolff," *Contemporary Literature* 31, no. 1 (1990): 1–16, 7.

6 William Shakespeare, *As You Like It* (New Haven: Yale University Press, 1954), act 3, scene 3.

7 Lyons, Oliver, and Wolff, "Interview with Tobias Wolff," 7.

8 Ibid., 15.

9 Livings, "Tobias Wolff."

10 Gregory Wolfe, "Cultural Anorexia: Doubting the Decline of Faith in Fiction," First Things, December 23, 2013, www.firstthings.com/web-exclusives/2013/12/cultural-anorexia-doubting-the-decline-of-faith-in-fiction. Wolfe's honor roll includes established fiction writers Ron Hansen, Alice McDermott, Cormac McCarthy, Tobias Wolff, Robert Clark, Stuart Dybek, Oscar Hijuelos, Louise Erdrich, David Plante, Ann Patchett, Mary Gordon, Robert Girardi, and the late Andre Dubus. There are also science-fiction and detective writers, such as Gene Wolfe, Dennis Lehane, Dean Koontz, and the late Tony Hillerman.

11 Livings, "Tobias Wolff."

12 Lyons, Oliver, and Wolff, "Interview with Tobias Wolff," 12.

13 Livings, "Tobias Wolff."

14 Quyen Nguyen, "An Interview with Tobias Wolff," *Boston Review*, August 25, 2014, http://bostonreview.net/books-ideas/quyen-nguyen-tobias-wolff-interview.

15 Livings, "Tobias Wolff."

16 Ibid.

17 Ibid.

18 Lyons, Oliver, and Wolff, "Interview with Tobias Wolff," 12.

19 "I've had some experience of violence. I've lived in fear of it, and I guess it would be strange if it didn't find its way into my work. I grew up on a world where violence was all too common—not deadly violence, so much, but beating, bullying, and threats—certainly in relations between boys, and between boys and men. I spent four years in the army, one of those in Viet Nam. You know, an army is basically an enormous threat of violence or it is violence in motion," Livings, "Tobias Wolff."

20 Lyons, Oliver, and Wolff, "Interview with Tobias Wolff," 12.

21 Tobias Wolff, foreword to *On Writing Short Stories*, ed. Tom Bailey (New York and Oxford: Oxford University Press, 2000), xii. Wolff goes on to say that spiritual leaders like Chuang Tzu and Jesus "spoke to their followers [as they did] not as a concession to their naivete but because only a story can express the most difficult, paradoxical, unparaphraseable truths of life as it is actually lived" (xii).

22 Flannery O'Connor, *Mystery and Manners: Occasional Prose Selected and Edited by Sally and Robert Fitzgerald*. (New York: Farrar, Straus & Giroux, 1974), 167.

23 Livings, "Tobias Wolff."

24 Tobias Wolff, "Long Road Home: Thoughts on the Prodigal Son," in *The Good Book: Writers Reflect on Favorite Bible Passages*, ed. Andrew Blauner (New York: Simon & Schuster, 2015), 210–14.

25 Tobias Wolff, "A White Bible," in *Our Story Begins: New and Selected Stories*, ed. Alfred Knopf (New York: Alfred A. Knopf, 2008), 287–300.

26 Tobias Wolff, *Our Story Begins*, 314. For Wolff on the Jesuit martyrs, see his short essay, "Second Thoughts on Certainty: Saint Jean de Brébeuf among the Hurons," in *A Tremor of Bliss: Contemporary Writers on the Saints*, ed. Paul Elie (New York: Riverhead Books, 1995), 177–85. I have given another consideration of this story in 'Lost and Found: The Bible and Its Literary Afterlife,' *Religion & Literature* 36, no. 1 (2004): 1–14. For a reading of this story, hear Jane Curtin in a "Selected Shorts" NPR recording, www.youtube.com/watch?v=8CFHwpha55A.

27 On this theme, see Martin Scofield, "Winging It: Realism and Invention in the Stories of Tobias Wolff," *Yearbook of English Studies*

31 (2001), 93–108. See also Lyons, Oliver, and Wolff, *Contemporary Literature*, 8–9.

28 "Mend your lives" (Jer. 7:3, 5; 35:15); "the pride of your hearts" (Jer. 48:29, 49:16, Ezek. 39:6, Obad. 1:3); "soar aloft like the eagle, though your nest is hid among the stars": (Obad. 1:4); "Turn from power to love" (Amos 5:14–15); "Be kind. Do justice. Walk humbly" (Mic. 6:8).

29 Tobias Wolff, *Our Story Begins*, 73–90. See Wolff's comments on the title of this collection, *Back in the World*, which is also the title of one of its stories and which has associations with the way soldiers spoke about the Vietnam War: "It wasn't just Vietnam. 'The world' is what people in religious orders—nuns and priests—call secular life. That's the way Jesus talks about it: The world's yoke is heavy, my yolk is light. So 'back in the world' is an expression which has many connotations . . . that caught the spirit of a lot of the stories," Lyons, Oliver, and Wolff, "Interview with Tobias Wolff," 9.

30 Russell Banks, "Aging Clay and the Prodigal Son," *New York Times*, October 20, 1985, www.nytimes.com/1985/10/20/books/aging-clay-and-the-prodigal-son.html. For insight into Wolff's own sibling history—"the economy of brotherhood, whose accounting practices defy and embarrass the world's" (146), see the matching essays by Tobias and Geoffrey Wolff in *Brothers: 26 Stories of Love and Rivalry*, ed. Andrew Blauner (San Francisco, CA: Jossey-Bass, 2009, 141–47 and 125–39 respectively.

31 Lyons, Oliver, and Wolff, "Interview with Tobias Wolff," 12.

32 Ibid.

33 Wolff, "Long Road Home," 214.

Chapter 11

1 Boris Fishman, "*The Fixer*, Bernard Malamud (1966)," *Tablet Magazine*, September 16, 2013, www.tabletmag.com/100-greatest-jewish-books/144379/fixer-bernard-malamud-1966.

2 Sheldon Grebstein, "Bernard Malamud and the Jewish Movement," in *Bernard Malamud: A Collection of Critical Essays*, eds. Leslie Field and Joyce Field (Englewood Cliffs, NJ: Prentice Hall, 1975), 27.

3 Laura Krugman Ray, "Dickens and 'The Magic Barrel'," in *Studies in American Jewish Literature*, 4 (1978): 35-40.

4 For the beginnings of a list, see Sam Bluefarb, "The Syncretism of Bernard Malamud," in *Bernard Malamud*, ed. Field and Field, 72–79.

5 Alan Lelchuk, "Malamud's Dark Fable," review of *God's Grace* by Bernard Malamud, *New York Times*, August 29, 1982, www.nytimes.com/1982/08/29/books/malamud-s-dark-fable.html?pagewanted=all.

6 Ita Sheres, "The Alienated Sufferer: Malamud's Novels from the Perspective of Old Testament and Jewish Mystical Thought," *Studies in American Jewish Literature* 4, no. 1 (1978): 68–76.

7 In "'Akedah' and Community in 'The Magic Barrel'" (*Studies in American Jewish Literature* 10, no. 2 [1991]: 188–96), Brian Adler uses this key to unlock "The Magic Barrel." He reads Finkle and Salzman as an Isaac and Abraham who bind themselves to one another and in so doing bind Finkle-Isaac to Jewish community.

8 In an interview with the *Paris Review*, Malamud was asked, "What about suffering? It's a subject much in your early work." To which he famously replied, "I'm against it, but when it occurs, why waste the experience?"

9 Grebstein, "Bernard Malamud and the Jewish Movement," 21.

10 Bonnie K. Lyons, "American-Jewish Fiction since 1945," in *Handbook of American-Jewish Literature*, ed. Lewis Fried (New York: Greenwood Press, 1988), 79.

11 Mark Shechner, *Conversion of the Jews and Other Essays* (New York: St. Martin's Press, 1990), 70.

12 Daniel Fuchs, *Writers and Thinkers: Selected Literary Criticism* (New York: Transaction Books, 2015), 230.

13 Lyons, "American-Jewish Fiction since 1945," 79.

14 Ibid.

15 Ibid.

16 Ibid., 80.

17 Lyons, "American-Jewish Fiction since 1945," 80.

18 Understanding the motley collection of thirteen stories as itself a "magic barrel," Goodhardt reads the two stories—which are the first and last of the volume—as "paired opposites." In his view, chapters 1 and 13, 2 and 12, 3 and 11, 4 and 10, etc. are paired, with story 7—"The Prison"—not merely standing alone but functioning structurally as the bottom of the barrel. In this reading, each of the opposing stories passes through this central one about theft and recovery: "The First Seven Years" is refracted through "The Prison" to emerge, significantly altered, as "The Magic Barrel."

19 Lionel Trilling, *Prefaces to the Experience of Literature* (New York: Harcourt, Brace, & Jovanovich, 1979), 171.

20 Possibly specifically Chagall. In "The Garden of Eden," an angel floats above Adam and Eve. Its white figure rests above two bright-red bouquets that seem to be as feet.

21 Critics make much of this enigmatic final image, but it is beyond the scope of this essay to deal with what Salzman's kaddish might mean.

22 Lyons, "American-Jewish Fiction since 1945," 69.

23 Gary Sloan reads Salzman as having intended all along for Finkle to fall in love with Stella; this he achieved through practical, not magical, means, playing the rabbinical student at every turn, "Malamud's Unmagic Barrel," *Studies in Short Fiction* 32, no. 1 (1995): 51–57.

24 Bernard Malamud, "Angel Levine," in *The Magic Barrel* (New York: Farrar Strauss & Giroux, 1958), 50.

25 David Robertson, "Fish and the Book of Tobit in Malamud's 'The Magic Barrel,'" *Studies in American Jewish Literature* 28 (2009): 75.

26 Robertson, "Fish and the Book of Tobit," 77.

27 Stephen Bluestone, "God as Matchmaker: A Reading of Malamud's 'The Magic Barrel,'" *Critique* 41, no. 4 (2000): 406.

28 Bluestone, "God as Matchmaker," 408.

29 Bonnie Lyons connects the familiarity of Stella's face to the familiarity of the Misfit's face in "A Good Man is Hard to Find": "In each story there is the motif of the climactic encounter with the familiar face. In 'The Magic Barrel' it is Stella's face which is 'hauntingly familiar, yet absolutely strange' (139). In 'A Good Man,' when the grandmother first sees The Misfit, 'His face was as familiar to her as if she had known him all her life but she could not recall who he was' (126). While the familiar face in 'The Magic Barrel' is the complex image of life, 'spring flowers yet age,' and the story moves toward Leo's loving embrace arms 'outthrust,' The Misfit is a mass murder. Malamud's and O'Connor's familiar faces are familiar indeed," Lyons, "American-Jewish Fiction since 1945," 83.

30 Richard Reynolds, "The Magic Barrel: Pinye Salzman's Kaddish," *Studies in Short Fiction* 10, no. 1 (1973): 100.

31 Trilling, *Prefaces to the Experience of Literature*, 173.

32 Sanford Pinsker, "Bernard Malamud's Ironic Heroes," in *Bernard Malamud*, ed. Field and Field, 48.

33 Mark Goldman makes the connection between "The Magic Barrel" and Hosea in "Bernard Malamud's Comic Vision and the Theme of Identity," *Critique* 7, no. 2 (1964): 92–109: "'The Magic Barrel' ends in fantasy, in a deliberately stagy scene under a lamppost, where Salzman's own daughter waits for the young rabbi—the fallen woman (in white, with red shoes, smoking a cigarette) finally chosen from the matchmaker's file, out of the depths of the denial of life and demand for penance and salvation that recalls the Biblical prophet and his God-sent wife and whore" (96–97).

34 Abraham J. Heschel, *The Prophets* (New York: Harper Perennial Classics, 2001), 47.

35 Haim Chertok, "The Book of Ruth—Complexities within Simplicity," *Judaism* 35, no. 3 (1986): 290–97, 293.

36 Reynolds, "The Magic Barrel," 101.

37 Trilling, *Prefaces to the Experience of Literature*, 173.

38 Lyons, "American-Jewish Fiction since 1945," 69.

39 Lawrence Dessner, "Malamud's Revisions to 'The Magic Barrel,'" *Critique* Summer 1989, 254.

40 Heschel, *The Prophets*, 64.

41 Ibid., 58.

42 In this permutation, Salzman is neither God nor Hosea but Gomer—a possibility that seems somewhat apt when we recall that one of Gomer's children is called "Lo-Ami," "not-my-people." The name is a parental disavowal of the child.

43 Heschel, *The Prophets*, 62.

Chapter 12

1 His most vocal and (it happens) most well-known detractor is Robert Alter, who began a review of *What We Talk About*, "The great mystery about the fiction of Nathan Englander is the rapturous response that it has elicited. . . . The jacket of *What We Talk About When We Talk About Anne Frank* comes with a full minyan of blurbs by highly visible, mostly younger, American novelists, printed in double columns like the King James Bible," Robert Alter, "Enough Already," review of *What We Talk About When We Talk About Anne Frank* by Nathan Englander, *New Republic*, March 15, 2012, https://newrepublic.com/article/101711/enough-already-anne-frank-englander.

2 James E. Young, "Men in Black," review of *For the Relief of Unbearable Urges* by Nathan Englander, *New York Times*, March 25, 1999, http://www.nytimes.com/1999/04/25/books/men-in-black.html?_r=0.

3 James Lasdun, "*What We Talk About When We Talk About Anne Frank* by Nathan Englander: A Review," *The Guardian*, February 1, 2012, www.theguardian.com/books/2012/feb/01/what-we-talk-anne-frank. Alter ("Enough Already") enumerates the Who's Who: "Among the blurbers are the three Jonathans—Franzen, Lethem, and Safran Foer; Dave Eggers; Richard Russo; and Michael Chabon."

4 Cressida Leyshon, "This Week in Fiction: Nathan Englander," *New Yorker*, December 5, 2011, www.newyorker.com/books/page-turner/this-week-in-fiction-nathan-englander-2.

5 James Lasdun ("*What We Talk About*") notes that *For the Relief of Unbearable Urges* "was a terrific book, but a notably apolitical one. History was present in the form of the Holocaust, but there was little interest in the wider contemporary context of Jewish life."

6 Nathan Englander, "In This Way We Are Wise" in *For the Relief of Unbearable Urges* (New York: Alfred A. Knopf, 1999), 199.

7 Englander, "In This Way We Are Wise," 203.

8 Ibid., 205.

9 Ibid., 197.

10 Englander, "The Gilgul of Park Avenue" in *For the Relief of Unbearable Urges*, 109.

11 Ibid.

12 Ibid., 123.

13 Ibid., 122.

14 Ibid., 131.

15 Ibid., 109.

16 Ibid., 116.

17 Ibid., 119.

18 Judith Paterson Jones and Guinevera A. Nance, *Philip Roth* (New York: Frederick Ungar, 1981), 31.

19 Philip Roth, "Eli the Fanatic," in *Goodbye, Columbus* (New York: Bantam, 1981), 212.

20 Englander, "Gilgul," 118.

21 Ibid., 129.

22 Ibid., 131.

23 Ibid., 137.

24 Ibid.

25 Adam Meyer, "Putting the 'Jewish' Back in 'Jewish American Fiction': A Look at Jewish American Fiction from 1977 to 2002 and an Allegorical Reading of Nathan Englander's 'The Gilgul of Park Avenue,'" *Shofar* 22, no. 3 (2004): 116.

26 Yan Lin, "Re-reading Genesis 1–3 in the Light of Ancient Chinese Creation Myths," in *Genesis*, eds. Athalya Brenner, Archie Lee, and Gale Yee (texts@contexts; Minneapolis: Fortress Press, 2010), 69.

27 Englander, "Gilgul," 109.

28 Ibid.

29 Ibid., 111.

30 Ibid., 109–10.

31 Ibid., 113.

32 Ibid., 112.

33 Ibid., 122.

34 Ibid., 116.

35 Ibid., 115.

36 Ibid.

37 Willis Barnstone, *The Restored New Testament* (New York: W.W. Norton, 2009), 616.

38 Englander, "Gilgul," 115.

Bibliography

Aarons, Victoria (2004), "The Covenant Unraveling: The Pathos of Cultural Loss in Allegra Goodman's Fiction," *Shofar* 22 (3): 12–25.

Adler, Brian (1991), "'Akedah' and Community in 'The Magic Barrel'," *Studies in American Jewish Literature* 10 (2): 188–96.

Alexander, Danielle, Pedro Ponce, and Alicita Rodriguez (2004), "Steven Millhauser," *The Review of Contemporary Fiction* Vol. XXVI (1).

Alter, Robert (2012), "Enough Already," review of *What We Talk About When We Talk About Anne Frank* by Nathan Englander, *New Republic*, https://newrepublic.com/article/101711/enough-already-anne-frank-englander.

Alter, Robert and Frank Kermode, eds. (1987), *The Literary Guide to the Bible*, Cambridge, MA: Belknap; Harvard.

Apple, Max (2000), "The Eighth Day," in Jules Chametzky et al. (eds.), *Jewish American Literature*, 1074–92, New York: W. W. Norton.

Baker, Carlos (1961), "The Place of the Bible in American Fiction," in James Ward and A. Leland Jamison (eds.), *Religious Perspectives in American Culture*, 243–72, Princeton: Princeton University Press.

Ballou, Jullianne (2013), "Act of Faith: A Conversation with Jamie Quatro," www.oxfordamerican.org/item/511-act-of-faith.

Banks, Russell (1985), 'Aging Clay and the Prodigal Son', *New York Times*, 20 October. Available online: www.nytimes.com/1985/10/20/books/aging-clay-and-the-prodigal-son.html.

Barnstone, Willis (2009), *The Restored New Testament*, New York: W. W. Norton.

Barr, David L. and Nicholas Piediscalzi, eds. (1982), *The Bible in American Education: From Sourcebook to Textbook*, Philadelphia: Fortress Press.

Baxter, Charles (1997), *Burning Down the House: Essays on Fiction*, Minneapolis: Graywolf Press.

Berlin, Adele (1983), *Poetics and Interpretation of Biblical Narrative*, Sheffield: Almond Press.

Bluefarb, Sam (1975), "The Syncretism of Bernard Malamud," in Leslie and Joyce Field (eds.), *Bernard Malamud*, 72–79, New York: New York University Press.

Bluestone, Stephen (2000), "God as Matchmaker: A Reading of Malamud's 'The Magic Barrel'," *Critique*, 41 (4): 403–10.

Boyd, William (2004), "Brief Encounters," *Guardian*, October 2. Available online: www.theguardian.com/books/2004/oct/02/featuresreviews. guardianreview38.

Brinkmeyer, Robert H. Jr. (1986), "A Closer Walk with Thee: Flannery O'Connor and Southern Fundamentalists," *Southern Literary Journal*, 18 (2): 3–13.

Buford, Bill (1983), "*Granta* 8: Dirty Realism," *Granta: The Magazine of New Writing*. (Summer). Available online: http://granta.com/issues/ granta-8-dirty-realism/.

Bukiet, Melvin Jules (1997), *While the Messiah Tarries*, Syracuse, NY: Syracuse University Press.

Canales, Gustavo Sanchez (2010), "'Creative Midrash Forces the Students to Read, So They Realize They Aren't the First to Feel, Think, or Write Anything Down': Biblical Archetypes in Allegra Goodman's *The Family Markowitz* and *Kaaterskill Falls*," *IUP Journal of American Literature*, 3 (4): 51–73.

Cappell, Ezra (2007), *American Talmud: The Cultural Work of Jewish American Fiction*, Albany: State University of New York Press.

Carver, Raymond (1994), "On Writing," in Charles May (ed.), *The New Short Story Theories*, 273–80, Athens, OH: Ohio University Press.

Chertok, Haim (1986), "The Book of Ruth: Complexities within Simplicity," *Judaism*, 35 (3): 290–7.

Cofer, Jordan (2014), *The Gospel according to Flannery O'Connor: Examining the Role of the Bible in Flannery O'Connor's Fiction*, New York and London: Bloomsbury.

Cronin, Gloria L. (1997), "Immersions in the Postmodern: The Fiction of Allegra Goodman," in Jay L. Halio and Ben Siegel (eds.), *Daughters of Valor: Contemporary Jewish American Women Writers*, 247–66, Newark: University of Delaware Press.

Davidson, Willing (2014), "This Week in Fiction: Kirstin Valdez Quade," *New Yorker*, 13 October. Available online: www.newyorker.com/ books/page-turner/fiction-this-week-kirstin-valdez-quade-2014-10-20.

Dessner, Lawrence (1989), "Malamud's Revisions to 'The Magic Barrel'," *Critique* (Summer): 252–60.

Eliot, T. S. (1962), *The Complete Poems and Plays 1909–1950*, New York: Harcourt, Brace & World.

Elie, Paul (2012), "Has Fiction Lost its Faith?," *New York Times*, December 19.

Englander, Nathan (1999), *For the Relief of Unbearable Urges*, New York: Alfred A. Knopf.

Fallon, Erin, R. C. Feddersen, James Kurtzleben, Maurice A. Lee, and Susan Rochette-Crawley eds. (2001), *A Reader's Guide to the Short Story in English*, Westport, CT: Greenwood Press.

Faulkner, William (1977), *Faulkner in the University*, edited by Frederick L. Gwyan and Joseph L. Blottner, Charlottesville: University of Virginia Press.

Faulkner, William (1977), *Selected Letters of William Faulkner*, edited by Joseph Blottner, New York: Random House.

Fentress, Sam (2007), *Bible Road: Signs of Faith in the American Landscape*, Cincinnati, OH: D&C.

Fiedler, Leslie (1964), *Waiting for the End*, New York: Stein & Day.

Filson, John (2005), *The Discovery, Settlement, and Present State of Kentucky*, Whitefish, MT: Kessinger Publishing.

Fishman, Boris (2013), "*The Fixer*, Bernard Malamud (1966)," *Tablet Magazine*. Available online: www.tabletmag.com/100-greatest-jewish-books/144379/fixer-bernard-malamud-1966.

Ford, Daniel (2015), "Short Stories and String Cheese: Author Kirstin Valdez Quade on Her Debut Collection *Night at the Fiestas*," *Writer's Bone* (May). Available online: http://www.writersbone.com/interviewsarchive/2015/5/5/short-stories-and-string-cheese-author-kirstin-valdez-quade-on-her-debut-novel-night-at-the-fiestas

Fuchs, Daniel (2015), *Writers and Thinkers: Selected Literary Criticism*, New York: Transaction Books.

Furman, Andrew (2000), *Contemporary Jewish American Writers and the Multicultural Dilemma: The Return of the Exiled*, Syracuse: Syracuse University Press.

Gerald, Kelly (2012), *Flannery O'Connor: The Cartoons*, Seattle, WA: Fantagraphics Books.

Goff, Philip, Arthur E. Farnsley II, and Peter J. Thuesen (2016), "The Bible in American Life: A National Study by the Center for the Study in Religion and American Culture, Indiana University-Purdue University Indianapolis." Available online: http://www.raac.iupui.edu/research-projects/bible-american-life/bible-american-life-report/

Goldman, Mark (1964), "Bernard Malamud's Comic Vision and the Theme of Identity," *Critique* 7 (2): 92–109.

Gooch, Brad (2009), *Flannery: A Life of Flannery O'Connor*, New York: Little, Brown & Company.

Goodman, Allegra (1996), *The Family Markowitz*, New York: Farrar Strauss and Giroux.

Goodman, Allegra (1996), "The Story of Rachel," in David Rosenberg (ed.), *Genesis: As It Is Written: Contemporary Writers on Our First Stories*, 169–76, New York: HarperCollins.

Goodman, Allegra (1997), "Writing Jewish Fiction in and out of the Multicultural Context," in Jay L. Halio and Ben Siegel (eds.), *Daughters of Valor: Contemporary Jewish American Woman Writers*, 269–89, Newark: University of Delaware Press.

Gopnik, Adam (2015), "Introduction," in Andrew Blauner (ed.), *The Good Book: Writers Reflect on Favorite Bible Passages*, New York: Simon & Schuster.

Grauer, Tresa (2003), "Identity Matters: Contemporary Jewish American Writing," in Michael P. Kramer and Hana Wirth-Nesher (eds.), *The Cambridge Companion to Jewish American Literature*, 269–84, Cambridge: Cambridge University Press.

Grebstein, Sheldon (1975), "Bernard Malamud and the Jewish Movement," in Leslie Field and Joyce Field (eds.), *Bernard Malamud: A Collection of Critical Essays*, 18–34, Englewood Cliffs, NJ: Prentice Hall.

Gunkel, Hermann (1964), *The Legends of Genesis: The Biblical Saga and History*, translated by W. H. Carruth, New York: Schocken Books.

Gunn, David M. and Danna Nolan Fewell (1993), *Narrative in the Hebrew Bible*, Oxford and New York: Oxford University Press.

Gunn, Giles (1983), *The Bible and American Arts and Letters*, Philadelphia: Fortress Press.

Hansen, Marcus Lee (1990), "The Problem of the Third Generation Immigrant," in Peter Kivisto and Dag Blanck (eds.), *American Immigrants and Their Generations: Studies and Commentaries on the Hansen Thesis after Fifty Years*, 191–203, Urbana: University of Illinois Press.

Hawkins, Peter S. (2000), "John Cheever," in Paula J Carlson and Peter S. Hawkins (eds.), *Listening for God: Contemporary Literature and the Life of Faith*, Vol. 3, Minneapolis: Augsburg Fortress.

Hawkins, Peter S. (2004), *The Language of Grace: Flannery O'Connor, Walker Percy, and Iris Murdoch*, New York: Seabury Classics.

Hawkins, Peter S. (2012), "'A Man Had Two Sons': The Question of Forgiveness," in Charles L. Griswold and David Konstan (eds.), *Ancient Forgiveness: Classical, Judaic, and Christian*, 158–74, Cambridge: Cambridge University Press.

Herrero-Olaizola, Alejandro (2002), "Writing Lives, Writing Lies: The Pursuit of Apocryphal Biographies," *Mosaic*, 35 (3): 73–88.

Heschel, Abraham J. (2001), *The Prophets*, New York: Harper Perennial Classics.

Heschel, Susannah (2003), "Imagining Judaism in America," in Michael P. Kramer and Hana Wirth-Nesher (eds.), *The Cambridge Companion to Jewish American Literature*, 31–49, Cambridge: Cambridge University Press.

Howe, Irving, ed. (1977), *Jewish American Stories*, New York: New American Library and Penguin.

Hulbert, Ann (2015), "Passion Plays: Kirstin Valdez Quade's Theatrical New Short-Story Collection," *Atlantic* (March), www.theatlantic.com/magazine/archive/2015/03/passion-plays/384979/.

Husch, Gail E. (2000), *Something Coming: Apocalyptic Expectation and Mid-Nineteenth Century Painting*, Hanover, NH and London: University Press of New England.

Ingersoll, Earl G. (2014), *Understanding Steven Millhauser*, Columbia: University of South Carolina Press.

Jasper, David and Stephen Prickett, eds. (1999), *The Bible and Literature: A Reader*, Oxford: Blackwell.

Jeffrey, David Lyle (1993), "Literature and the Bible," in Bruce M. Metzger and Michael David Coogan (eds.), *The Oxford Companion to the Bible*, 438–45, Oxford: Oxford University Press.

Jeffrey, David Lyle (2004), "The Bible and Literature," in Hans J. Hillerbrand (ed.), *The Encyclopedia of Protestantism*, vol. 1, London and New York: Routledge.

Jeffrey, David Lyle and C. Stephen Evans, eds. (2009), *The Bible and the University*, Grand Rapids, IL: Zondervan.

Johnson, Denis (1992), *Jesus' Son: Stories*, New York: Farrar, Straus and Giroux.

Jones, Judith Paterson and Guinevera A. Nance (1981), *Philip Roth*, New York: Frederick Ungar.

Joseph, Kelsey (2013), "God in Wayward Form: Jamie Quatro's Salvation-Seeking Adulteresses." Available online: *Los Angeles Review of Books*, https://lareviewofbooks.org/article/god-in-wayward-forms-jamie-quatros-salvation-seeking-adulteresses/.

Kiernan, Thomas (1979), *The Intricate Music*, Boston and Toronto: Little, Brown & Co.

Kinney, Arthur F. (2008), *Flannery O'Connor's Library. Resources of Being*, Athens: University of Georgia Press.

Kling, David W. (2004), *The Bible in History: How the Texts Have Shaped the Times*, New York: Oxford University Press.

Lambert, Josh (2013), "Identity Recruitment and the 'American Writer': Steven Millhauser, *Edwin Mullhouse*, and Biographical Criticism," *Contemporary Literature*, 54 (1): 23–48.

Langston, Scott (2006), *Exodus through the Centuries*, Malden, MA: Blackwell.

Langston, Scott (2010), "The Exodus in American History and Culture," *Teaching the Bible*, Society of Biblical Literature, www.sbl-site.org/assets/pdfs/TB6_Exodus_SL.pdf.

Lasdun, James (2012), "*What We Talk About When We Talk About Anne Frank* by Nathan Englander: A Review," *The Guardian*, February 1. Available online: www.theguardian.com/books/2012/feb/01/what-we-talk-anne-frank.

Lawrence, D. H. (1985), "Why the Novel Matters," in Bruce Steele (ed.), *The Cambridge Edition of the Works of D. H. Lawrence: Study of Thomas Hardy and Other Essays*, Cambridge: Cambridge University Press.

Lelchuk, Alan (1982), "Malamud's Dark Fable," review of *God's Grace* by Bernard Malamud, *New York Times*, August 29. Available online: www.nytimes.com/1982/08/29/books/malamud-s-dark-fable.html?pagewanted=all.

Lemann, Nicholas (1992), *The Promised Land: The Great Black Migration and How It Changed America*, New York: Vintage.

Levy, Andrew (1993), *The Culture and Commerce of the American Short Story*, Cambridge: Cambridge University Press.

Leypoldt, Günter (2001), "Raymond Carver's 'Epiphanic Moments'," *Style*, 35 (3): 531–46.

Leyshon, Cressida (2011), "This Week in Fiction: Nathan Englander," *New Yorker*, December 5. Available online: www.newyorker.com/books/page-turner/this-week-in-fiction-nathan-englander-2.

Lin, Yan (2010), "Re-reading Genesis 1–3 in the Light of Ancient Chinese Creation Myths," in Athalya Brenner, Archie Lee, and Gale Yee (eds.), *Genesis*, 65–80, Minneapolis: Fortress Press, 2010.

Linafelt, Tod (2010), "Narrative and Poetic Art in the Book of Ruth," *Interpretation*, 64 (2): 117–29.

Livings, Jack (2014), "Tobias Wolff, The Art of Fiction No. 183," *Paris Review* (Fall). Available online: www.theparisreview.org/interviews/5391/the-art-of-fiction-no-183-tobias-wolff.

Lyons, Bonnie K. (1988), "American-Jewish Fiction since 1945," in Lewis Fried (ed.), *Handbook of American-Jewish Literature*, 61–89, New York: Greenwood Press.

Lyons, Bonnie K., Bill Oliver, and Tobias Wolff (1990), "An Interview with Tobias Wolff," *Contemporary Literature*, 31 (1): 1–16.

Malamud, Bernard (1958), *The Magic Barrel*, New York: Farrar Strauss & Giroux.

Max, D. T. (2008), "The Illusionist," review of *Dangerous Laughter* by Steven Millhauser, *New York Times*, February 24. Available online: www.nytimes.com/2008/02/24/books/review/Max-t.html.

May, Charles E. (1994), "The Nature of Knowledge in Short Fiction," in Charles May (ed.), *The New Short Story Theories*, 131–45, Athens, OH: Ohio University Press.

May, Charles E. (2009), "Twenty-five Random Facts about the Short Story," *Reading the Short Story*. Available online: http://may-on-the-short-story.blogspot.com/2009/02/twenty-five-random-facts-about-short.html.

McEwan, Ian (2009), "On John Updike," *New York Review of Books*, March 12. Available online: www.nybooks.com/articles/2009/03/12/on-john-updike/printpage=true.

McTavish, John (2016), *Myth and Gospel in the Fiction of John Updike*, Eugene, OR: Cascade.

Melville, Herman (1983), *White-Jacket, or the World in a Man-O-War, Moby Dick or the Whale*, New York: Library of America.

Meyer, Adam (2004), "Putting the 'Jewish' Back in 'Jewish American Fiction': A Look at Jewish American Fiction from 1977 to 2002 and an Allegorical Reading of Nathan Englander's 'The Gilgul of Park Avenue'," *Shofar*, 22 (1): 104–20.

Millhauser, Steven (1983), "The Fascination of the Miniature," *Grand Street*, 2 (4): 128–35.

Millhauser, Steven (2008), 'The Ambition of the Short Story', *New York Times*, October 5. Available online: www.nytimes.com/2008/10/05/books/review/Millhauser-t.html?_r=0.

Millhauser, Steven (2008), *Dangerous Laughter*, New York: Vintage Contemporaries.

Millhauser, Steven (2012) "A Voice in the Night," *New Yorker*, December 10. Available online: www.newyorker.com/magazine/2012/12/10/a-voice-in-the-night.

Nguyen, Quyen (2014), "An Interview with Tobias Wolff," *Boston Review*. Available online: http://bostonreview.net/books-ideas/quyen-nguyen-tobias-wolff-interview.

Nickel, Matthew C. (2013), *Hemingway's Dark Night: Catholic Influences and Intertextualities in the Work of Ernest Hemingway*, Wickford, RI: New Street Publications.

Noll, Mark A. (1982), "The Image of the United States as a Biblical Nation, 1776–1865," in Nathan O. Hatch and Mark Noll (eds.), *The Bible in America: Essays in Cultural History*, 42–49. New York: Oxford.

Noll, Mark A. (1998), "The Bible and Slavery," in Randall M. Miller (ed.), *Religion and the American Civil War*, 43–73, New York and Oxford: Oxford University Press.

Norton, David (2011), *A History of the English Bible as Literature*, Cambridge: Cambridge University Press.

Oates, Joyce Carol, ed. (1992), *The Oxford Book of American Short Stories*, Oxford and New York: Oxford University Press.

O'Connor, Flannery (1974), *Mystery and Manners: Occasional Prose Selected and Edited by Sally and Robert Fitzgerald*, New York: Farrar, Straus & Giroux.

O'Connor, Flannery (1979), *The Habit of Being: Letters Edited and with an Introduction by Sally Fitzgerald*, New York: Farrar, Straus & Giroux.

O'Connor, Flannery (2001), *The Complete Stories of Flannery O'Connor*, New York: Farrar, Straus & Giroux.

O'Connor, Frank (2004), *The Lonely Voice: A Study of the Short Story*, Hoboken, NJ: Melville House Publishing.

Omer-Sherman, Raanen (2004), "Orthodox Community and Individuality," *Religion and Literature*, 36 (2): 75–97.

Omer-Sherman, Raanen (2004), "Tradition and Desire," *MELUS*, 29 (2): 265–89.

Owens, Louis (2007), "The American Joads," in Harold Bloom (ed.), *Bloom's Modern Critical Interpretations: The Grapes of Wrath*, 67–76, New York: Chelsea House.

Paine, Thomas (1894), "Appendix to Common Sense," in Moncure Daniel Conway (ed.), *The Writings of Thomas Paine*, vol. 1: 1774–1779, New York: G. P. Putnam's Sons.

Paley, Grace (2007), *The Collected Stories: Grace Paley*, New York: Farrar Strauss and Giroux.

Path, James, ed. (1994), *Conversations with John Updike*, Jackson: University Press of Mississippi.

Paz, Octavio (1961), *Labyrinth of Solitude: Life and Thought in Mexico*, translated by Lysander Kemp, New York: Grove Press.

Perry, L. Tom (2012), "The Tradition of Light and Testimony," *Ensign*, https://www.lds.org/ensign/2012/12/the-tradition-of-light-and-testimony?lang=eng.

Phy, Allene Stuart (1985), "The Bible as Literature for American Children," in Allene S. Phy (ed.), *The Bible and American Popular Culture*, 165–91, Philadelphia: Fortress Press.

Pinsker, Sanford (1975), "Bernard Malamud's Ironic Heroes," in Leslie Field and Joyce Field (eds.), *Bernard Malamud*, 45–71, New York: New York University Press.

Plimpton, George (1958), "Ernest Hemingway, The Art of Fiction No. 21," interview, *Paris Review* 18 (Spring). Available online: www.theparisreview.org/interviews/4825/the-art-of-fiction-no-21-ernest-hemingway.

Poe, Edgar Allen (1994), "Poe on Short Fiction," in Charles May (ed.), *The New Short Story Theories*, 59–72, Athens, OH: Ohio University Press.

Preziosi, Dominic (2015), "Writing into Uncertainty," *Commonweal*. Available online: www.commonwealmagazine.org/interview-kirstin-valdez-quade.

Prickett, Stephen (1996), *Origins of Narrative: The Romantic Appropriation of the Bible*, Cambridge: Cambridge University Press.

Prose, Francine (2010), "What Makes a Short Story," in Tom Bailey (ed.), *On Writing Short Stories*, 3–12, New York: Oxford University.

Quatro, Jamie (2009), "God Texts the Ten Commandments," *Timothy McSweeney's Internet Tendency*. Available online: www.mcsweeneys.net/articles/god-texts-the-ten-commandments.

Quatro, Jamie (2012), "A Plain Kiss (Letters to Allison, 2006)," in *Forty Stories: New Writing from Harper Perennials*, New York: Harper Collins. Available online: //glose.com/book/forty-stories/35-a-plain-kiss-letters-to-allison-2-6-by-jamie-quatro#7089.

Quatro, Jamie (2014), *I Want to Show You More*, New York; Grove Press.

Quatro, Jamie (2015), "Asking Directions," *New Oxford Review*. Available online: www.oxfordamerican.org/magazine/item/592-asking-for-directions.

Quatro, Jamie (2016), "The Pleasure of Suddenness," interview with Brian Blanchfield, *New Oxford American*. Available online: www.oxfordamerican.org/item/891-the-pleasure-of-suddenness.

Raphael, Lev (2006), *Secret Anniversaries of the Heart: New and Selected Stories*, New York: Leapfrog.

Ray, Laura Krugman (1978), "Dickens and 'The Magic Barrel'," *Studies in American Jewish Literature*, 4: 35–40.

Reynolds, Richard (1973), "The Magic Barrel: Pinye Salzman's Kaddish," *Studies in Short Fiction*, 10 (1): 100–02.

Rhoads, Asa (1803), *The New Instructor: Being the Second Part of the American Spelling-Book Designed for the Use of Our Common Schools*, Stanford: Daniel Lawrence.

Ripatrazone, Nick (2013), "Interview of Jamie Quatro," *The Fine Delight: Book and Interview Series: Contemporary Catholic Literature*. Available online: http://catholiclit.blogspot.com/2013/09/jamie-quatro.html.

Robertson, David (2009), "Fish and the Book of Tobit in Malamud's 'The Magic Barrel'," *Studies in American Jewish Literature*, 28: 73–81.

Rodgers, Daniel T. (2014), *The Work Ethic in Industrial America 1850–1920*, Chicago: University of Chicago Press.

Rosenmeier, Jesper (1974), "'With my owne eyes': William Bradford's *of Plymouth Plantation*," in Sacvan Bercovitch (ed.), *The American Puritan Imagination*, 77–104, Cambridge: Cambridge University Press.

Roth, Philip (1981), *Goodbye, Columbus*, New York: Bantam.

Saltzman, Arthur M. (1996), "In the Millhauser Archives," *Critique*, 37 (2): 149–60.

Saunders, George (2000), *Pastoralia*, New York: Riverhead Books.

Scofield, Martin, ed. (2006), *Cambridge Introduction to the American Short Story*, Cambridge: Cambridge and New York.

Setzer, Claudia and David A. Shefferman, eds. (2011), *The Bible and American Culture*, Abingdon and New York: Routledge.

Shavit, Yaacov, Mordechai Eran, and Chaya Naor (2007), *The Hebrew Bible Reborn: From Holy Scripture to the Book of Books: A History of Biblical Culture and the Battles over the Bible in Modern Judaism*, Berlin: DeGruyter.

Shakespeare, William (1954), *As You Like It*, New Haven: Yale University Press.

Shechner, Mark (2015), *Conversion of the Jews and Other Essays*, New York: St. Martin's Press.

Shepard, Jim (2003), "Steven Millhauser," *Bomb*, 83 (Spring): 76–80.

Sheres, Ita (1978), "The Alienated Sufferer: Malamud's Novels from the Perspective of Old Testament and Jewish Mystical Thought," *Studies in American Jewish Literature*, 4 (1): 68–76.

Sidor, Daphne (2015), "Review of *Night at the Fiestas*, by Kirstin Valdez Quade," *Lambda Literary*, July 5. Available online: www. lambdaliterary.org/reviews/07/05/night-at-the-fiestas-by-kirstin-valdez-quade/.

Sloan, Gary (1995), "Malamud's Unmagic Barrel," *Studies in Short Fiction*, 32 (1): 51–57.

Stahlberg, Lesleigh Cushing (2008), *Sustaining Fictions: Intertextuality, Midrash, Translation, and the Literary Afterlife of the Bible*, New York: T&T Clark.

Stewart, Randall (1958), *American Literature and Christian Doctrine*, Baton Rouge: Louisiana State University Press.

Stephens, Randall (2012), "American Literature and the King James Bible: An Interview with Robert Alter," *Religion in American History*, March. Available online: http://usreligion.blogspot.com/2012/03/american-literature-and-king-james.html.

Stout, Harry (1982), "Word and Order in Colonial New England," in Nathan O. Hatch and Mark Noll (eds.), *The Bible in America: Essays in Cultural History*, New York: Oxford.

Street, Nicholas (1971), "The American States Acting over the Part of the Children of Israel in the Wilderness and Thereby Impeding Their Entrance into Canaan's Rest," in Conrad Cherry (ed.), *God's New Israel: Religious Interpretations of America's Destiny*, 67–81, Englewood Cliffs, NJ: Prentice Hall.

Tackach, James (2007), "The Biblical Foundation of James Baldwin's 'Sonny's Blues,'" *Renascence: Essays on Values in Literature*, 59 (2): 109–18.

Trilling, Lionel (1979), *Prefaces to the Experience of Literature*, New York: Harcourt, Brace, & Jovanovich

Updike, John, ed. (1984), *Best American Short Stories*, Boston: Houghton Mifflin.

Updike, John (1989), *Self-Consciousness: Memoirs*, New York: Random House.

Updike, John (1990), "The Gospel according to Matthew," in Alfred Corn (ed.), *Incarnation: Contemporary Writers on the New Testament*, 1–11, New York: Viking.

Updike, John (1991), *Odd Jobs: Essays and Criticism*, New York: Alfred A. Knopf.

Updike, John (2008), *Due Considerations: Essays and Criticism*, New York: Random House.

Updike, John (2013), *Updike: Collected Early Stories*, edited by Christopher Carduff, New York: Library of America.

Updike, John (2014), *More Matter: Essays and Criticism*, New York: Random House.

Wolfe, Gregory (2013), "Cultural Anorexia: Doubting the Decline of Faith in Fiction," First Things, December. Available online: www.firstthings.com/web-exclusives/2013/12/cultural-anorexia-doubting-the-decline-of-faith-in-fiction.

Wolff, Geoffrey (2009), "Heavy Lifting," in Andrew Blauner (ed.), *Brothers: 26 Stories of Love and Rivalry*, 125–40, San Francisco, CA: Jossey-Bass.

Wolff, Tobias (1983), *Matters of Life and Death: New American Stories*, Green Harbor, MA: Wampeter Press.

Wolff, Tobias (2000), "Foreword," in Tom Bailey (ed.), *On Writing Short Stories*, xi–xii, New York and Oxford: Oxford University Press.

Wolff, Tobias (2008), *Our Story Begins: New and Selected Stories*, New York: Alfred A. Knopf.

Wolff, Tobias (2009), "A Brother's Story," in Andrew Blauner (ed.), *Brothers: 26 Stories of Love and Rivalry*, 141–48, San Francisco, CA: Jossey-Bass.

Wolff, Tobias (2015), "Long Road Home: Thoughts on the Prodigal Son," in Andrew Blauner (ed.), *The Good Book: Writers Reflect on Favorite Bible Passages*, 210–14, New York: Simon & Schuster.

Wood, James (2013), "Broken Vows: Jamie Quatro's Stories," *New Yorker*, March 11. Available online: www.newyorker.com/magazine/2013/03/11/broken-vows.

Wood, Ralph C. (1982), "The Modest and Charitable Humanism of John Cheever," *Religion-Online*. Available online: www.religion-online.org/showarticle.asp?title=1353.

Wood, Ralph C. (2004), *Flannery O'Connor and the Christ-Haunted South*, Grand Rapids, MI: William B. Eerdmans.

Wright, Melanie (2003), *Moses in America: The Cultural Uses of Biblical Narrative*, Oxford: Oxford University Press.

Yeats, W. B. (1964), *The Collected Poems of W. B. Yeats*, New York: Macmillan.

Young, James E. (1999), "Men in Black," review of *For the Relief of Unbearable Urges* by Nathan Englander, April 25. Available online: *New York Times*, http://www.nytimes.com/1999/04/25/books/men-in-black.html?_r=0.

Index

Index of Biblical Books and Verses

CPSIA information can be obtained
at www.ICGtesting.com
Printed in the USA
LVOW07*1913021117
554763LV00010B/127/P